The Way of the House Husband

KOUSUKE OONO

4

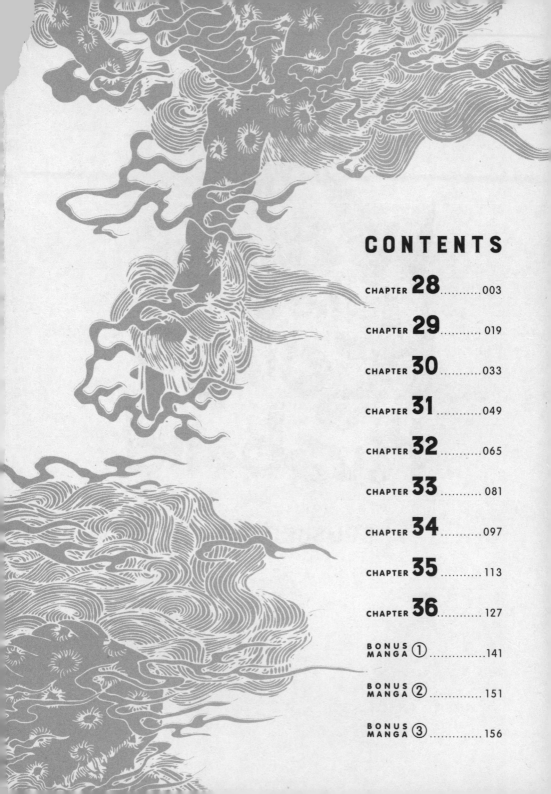

CONTENTS

CHAPTER 28

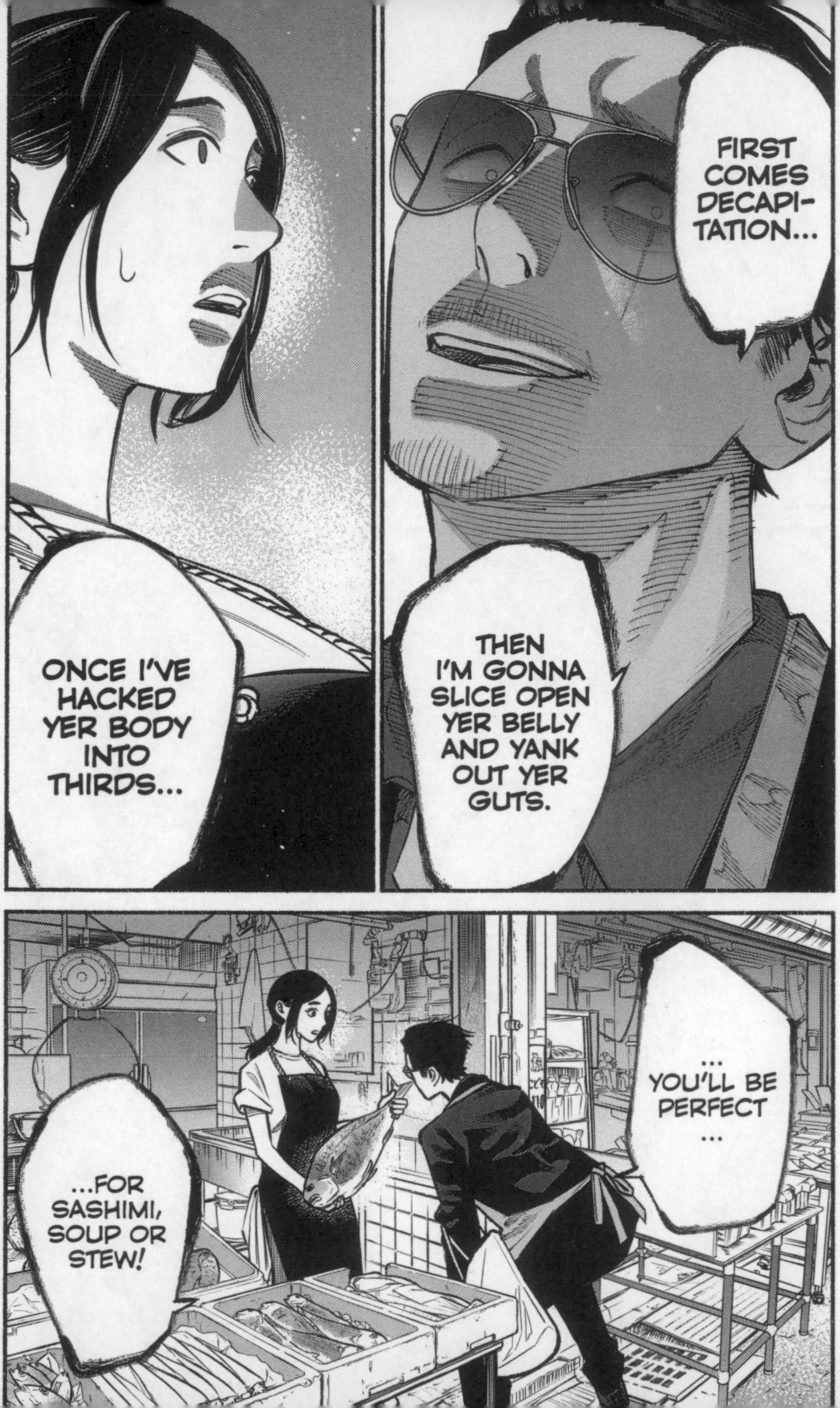
FIRST COMES DECAPI-TATION...
THEN I'M GONNA SLICE OPEN YER BELLY AND YANK OUT YER GUTS.
ONCE I'VE HACKED YER BODY INTO THIRDS...
... YOU'LL BE PERFECT ...
...FOR SASHIMI, SOUP OR STEW!

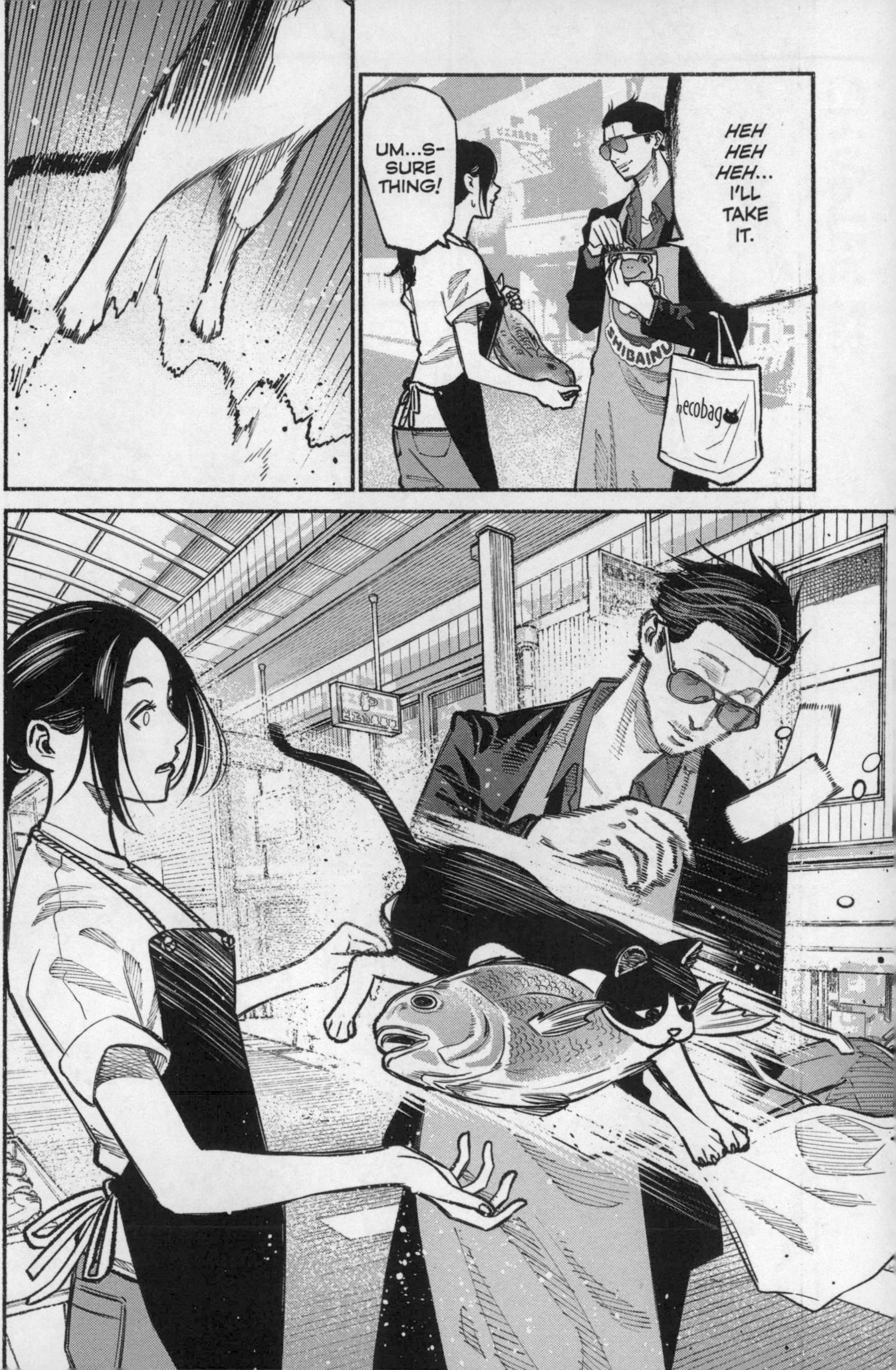
HEH HEH HEH... I'LL TAKE IT.
UM...S-SURE THING!
SHIBAINU
necobag

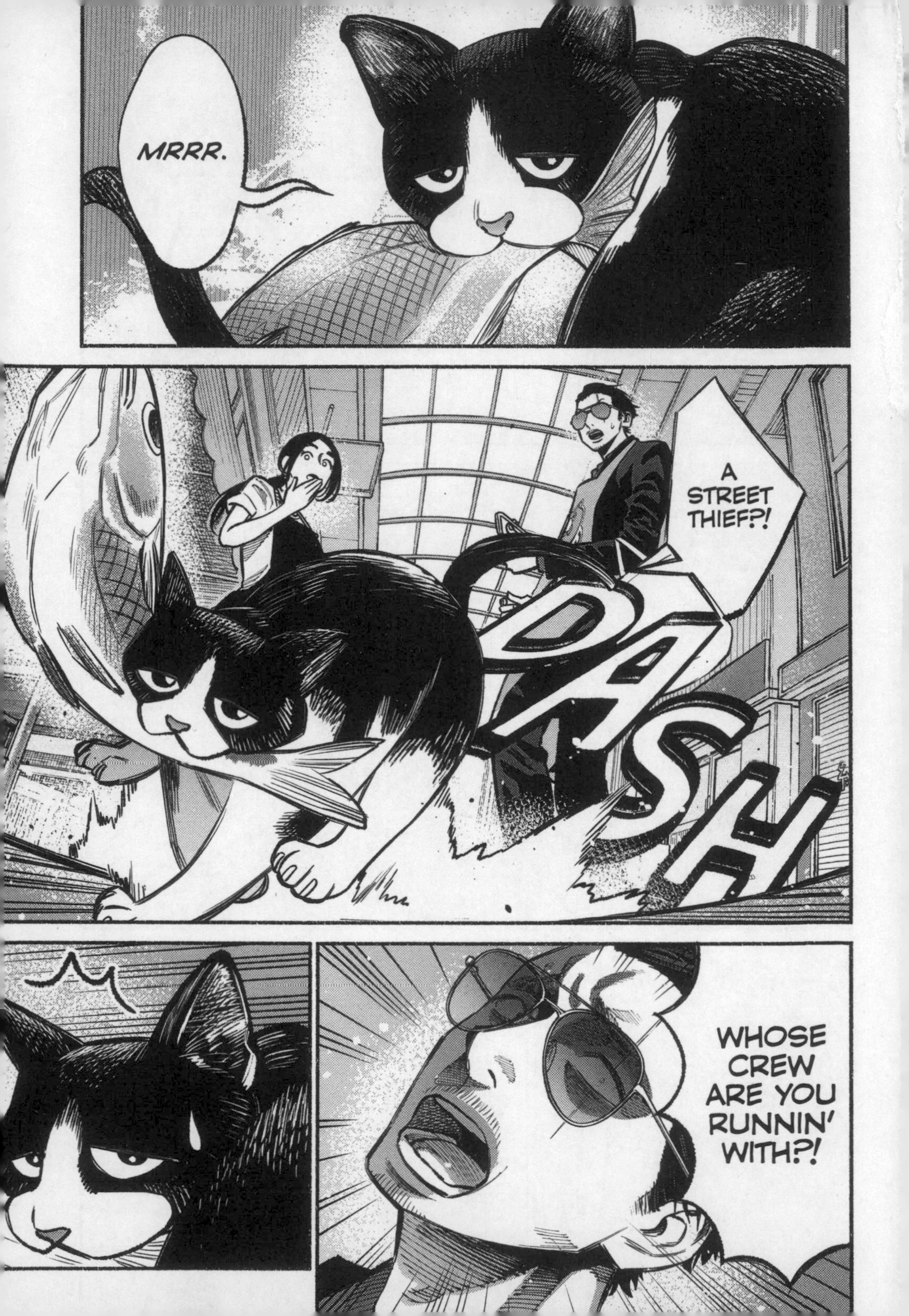
MRRR.
A STREET THIEF?!
DASH
WHOSE CREW ARE YOU RUNNIN' WITH?!

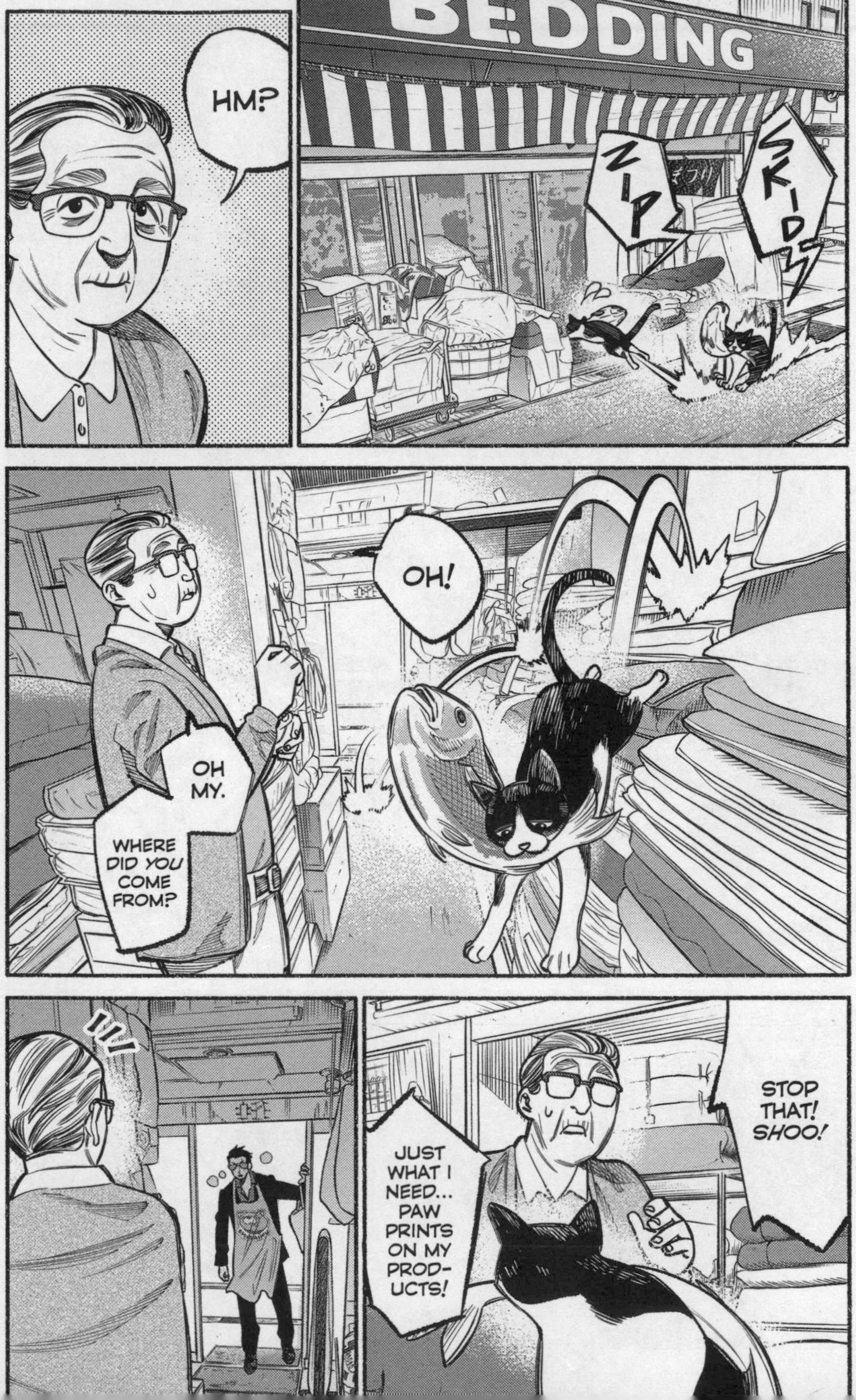
BEDDING
ZIP
SKID
HM?
OH!
OH MY.
WHERE DID YOU COME FROM?
STOP THAT! SHOO!
JUST WHAT I NEED... PAW PRINTS ON MY PROD-UCTS!

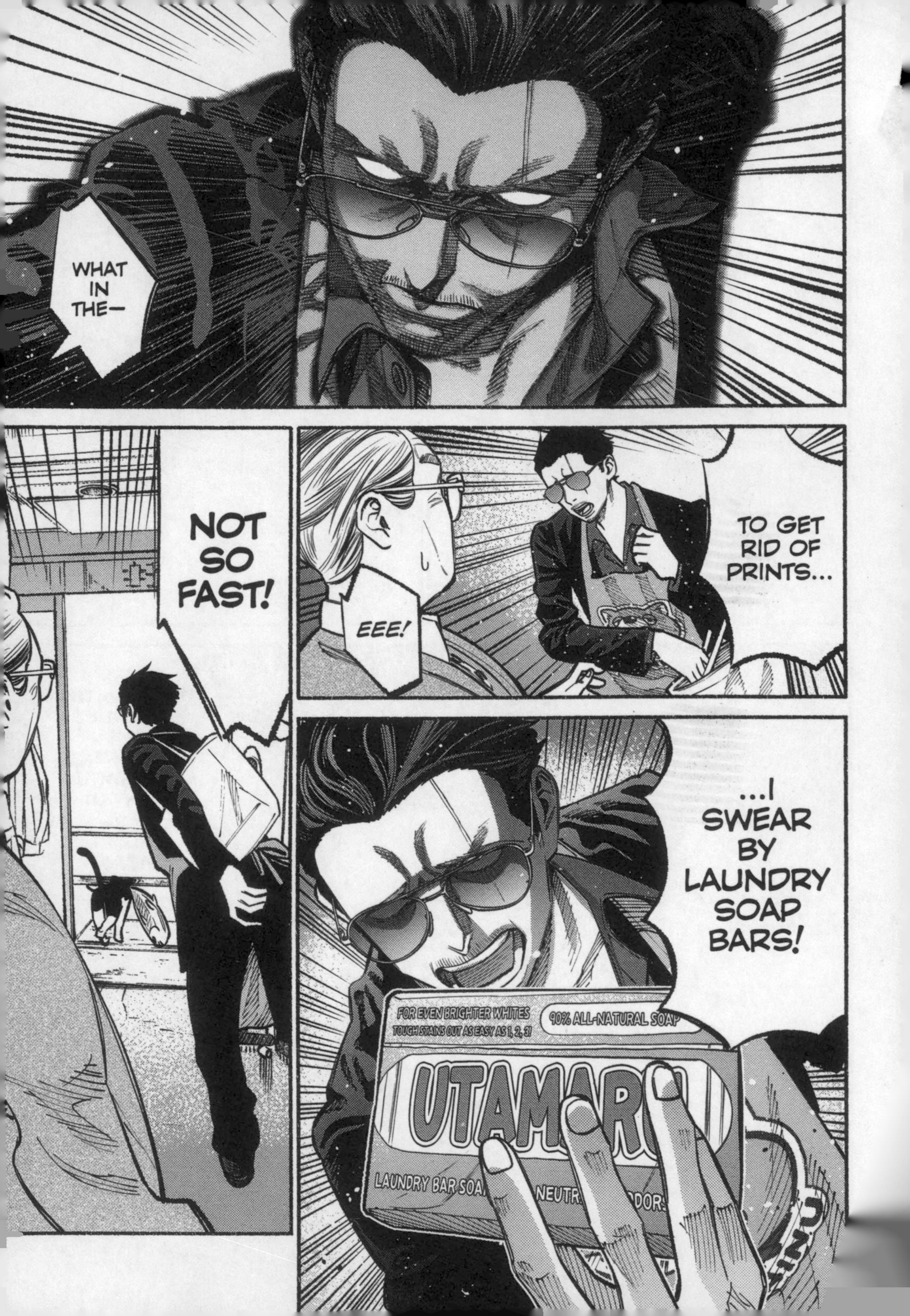
WHAT IN THE—
TO GET RID OF PRINTS...
EEE!
...I SWEAR BY LAUNDRY SOAP BARS!
FOR EVEN BRIGHTER WHITES
TOUGH STAINS OUT AS EASY AS 1, 2, 3!
90% ALL-NATURAL SOAP
NOT SO FAST!

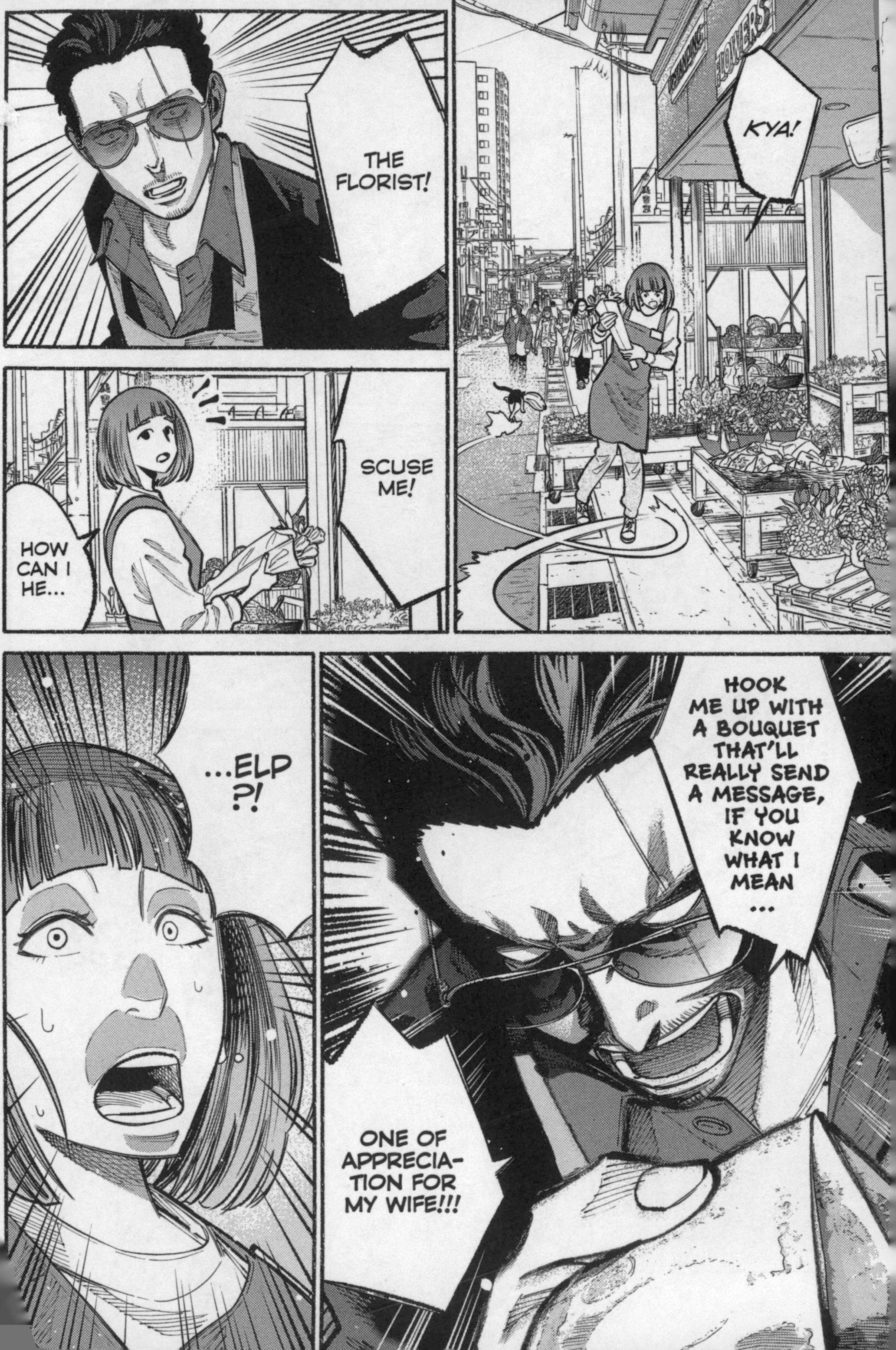
KYA!
THE FLORIST!
SCUSE ME!
HOW CAN I HE...
HOOK ME UP WITH A BOUQUET THAT'LL REALLY SEND A MESSAGE, IF YOU KNOW WHAT I MEAN ...
ONE OF APPRECIATION FOR MY WIFE!!!
...ELP ?!

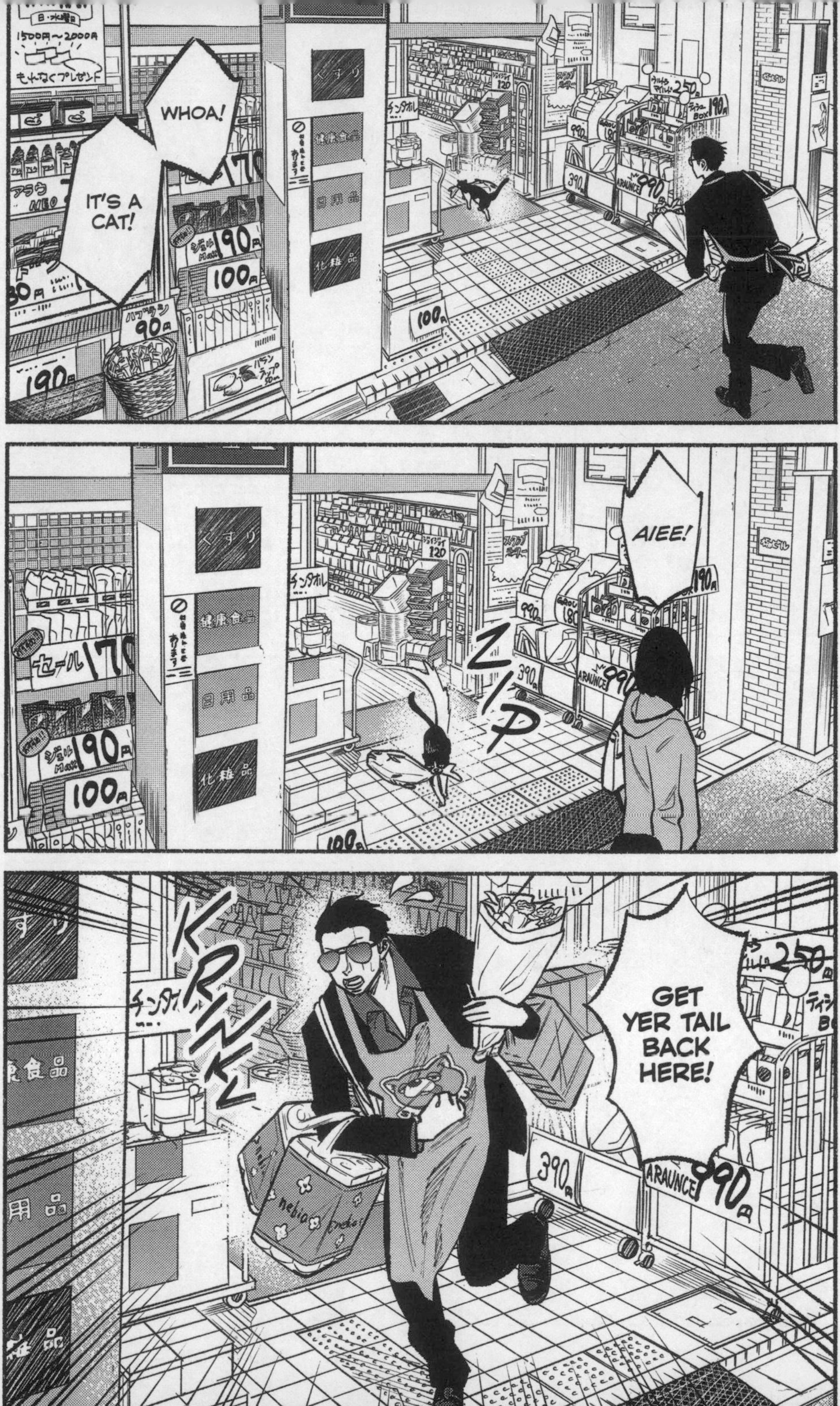
WHOA!
IT'S A CAT!
AIEE!
ZIP
GET YER TAIL BACK HERE!
KRNK

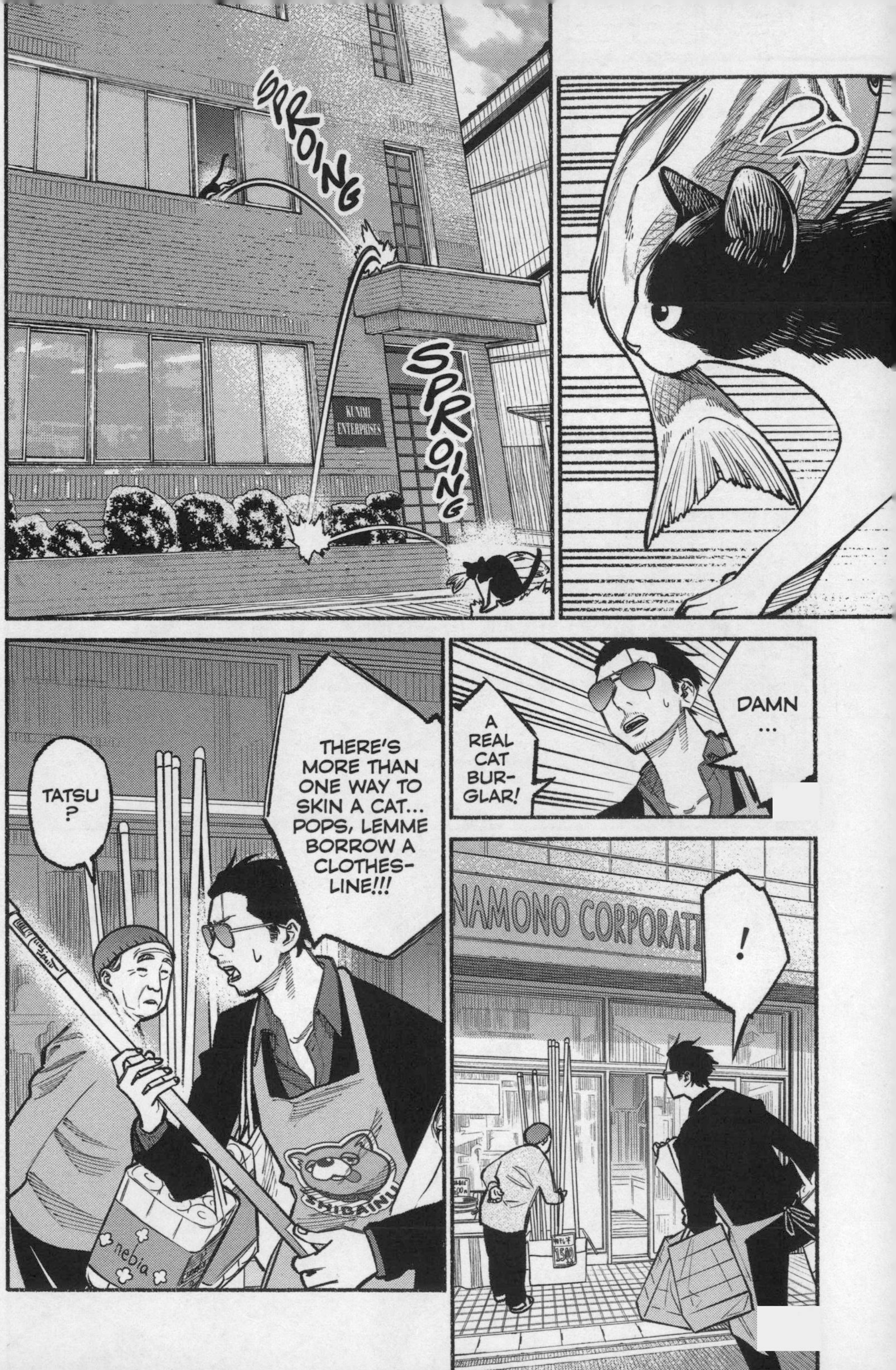
SPROING
SPROING
KUNIMI ENTERPRISES
DAMN ...
A REAL CAT BURGLAR!
!
NAMONO CORPORATI
THERE'S MORE THAN ONE WAY TO SKIN A CAT... POPS, LEMME BORROW A CLOTHESLINE!!!
TATSU?
SHIBAINU
nebia

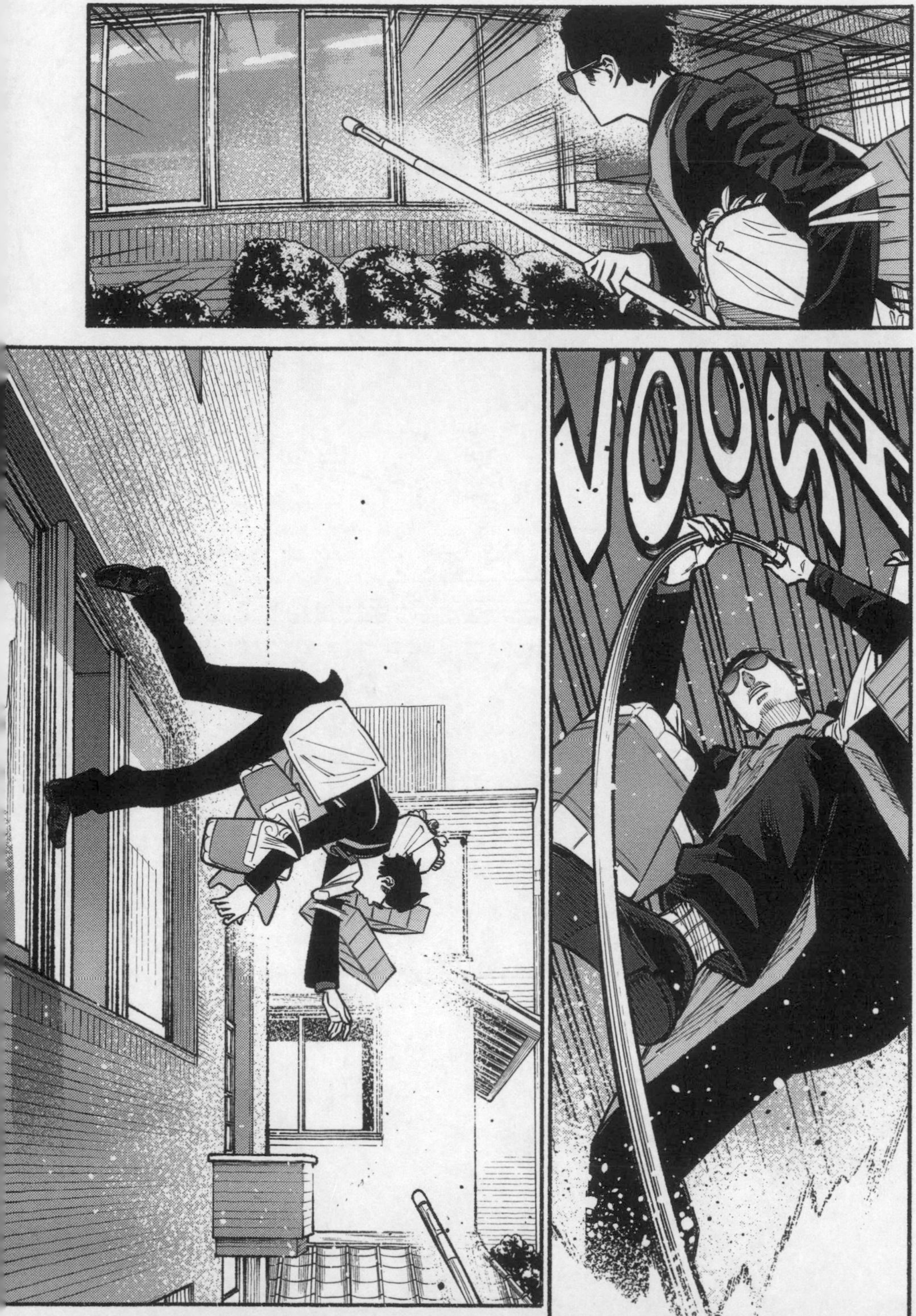
VOOSH

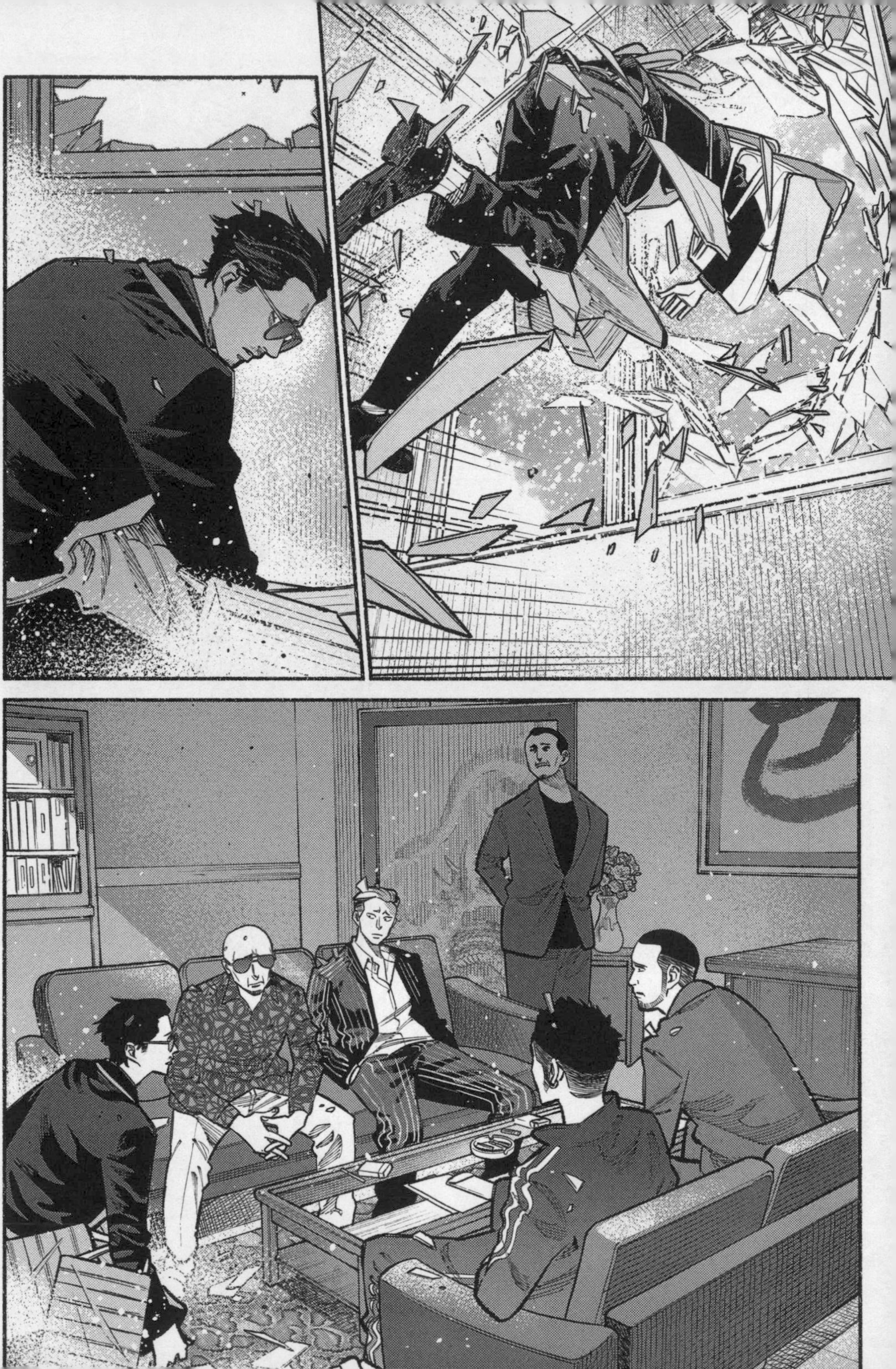

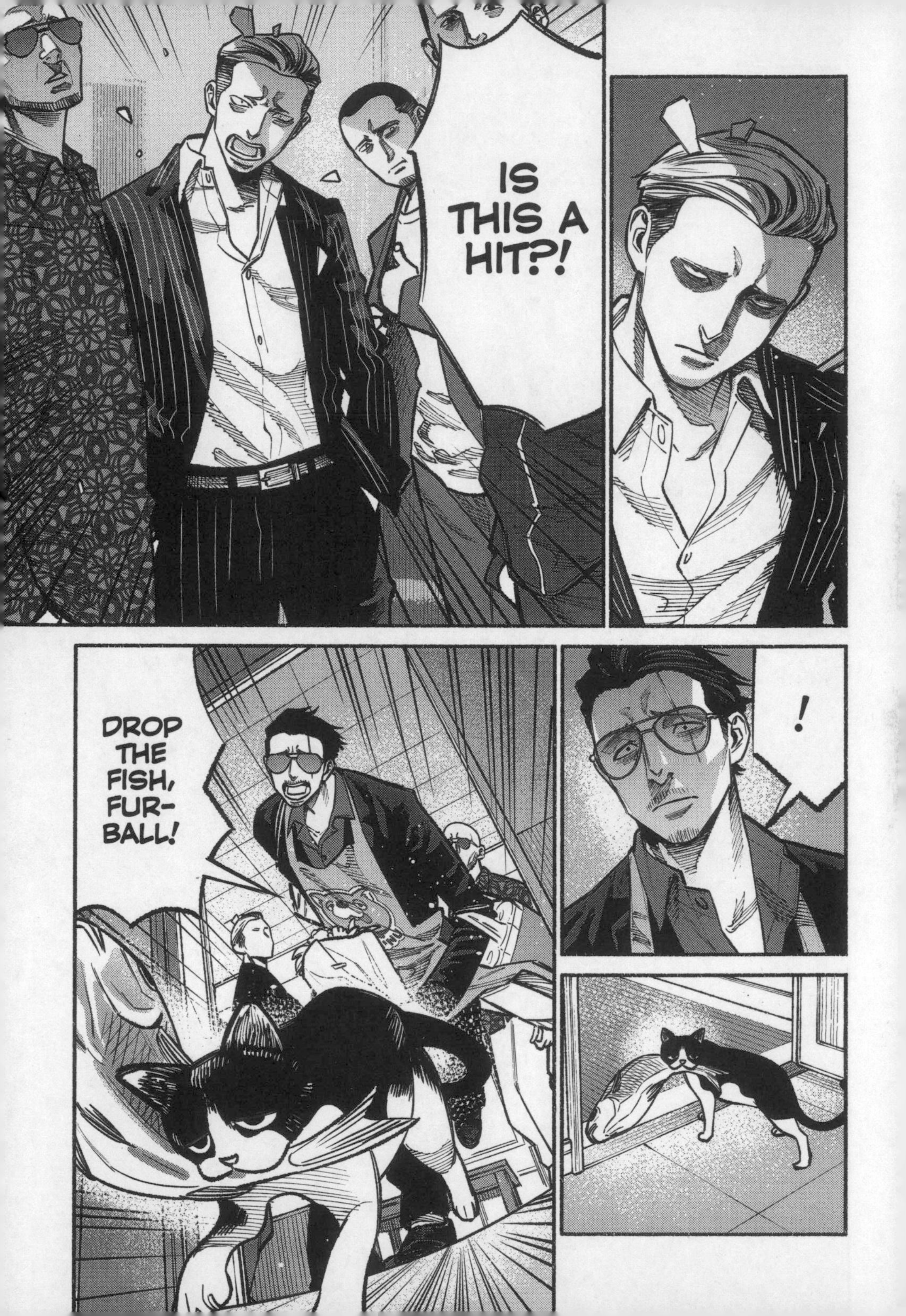
IS THIS A HIT?!
!
DROP THE FISH, FUR-BALL!

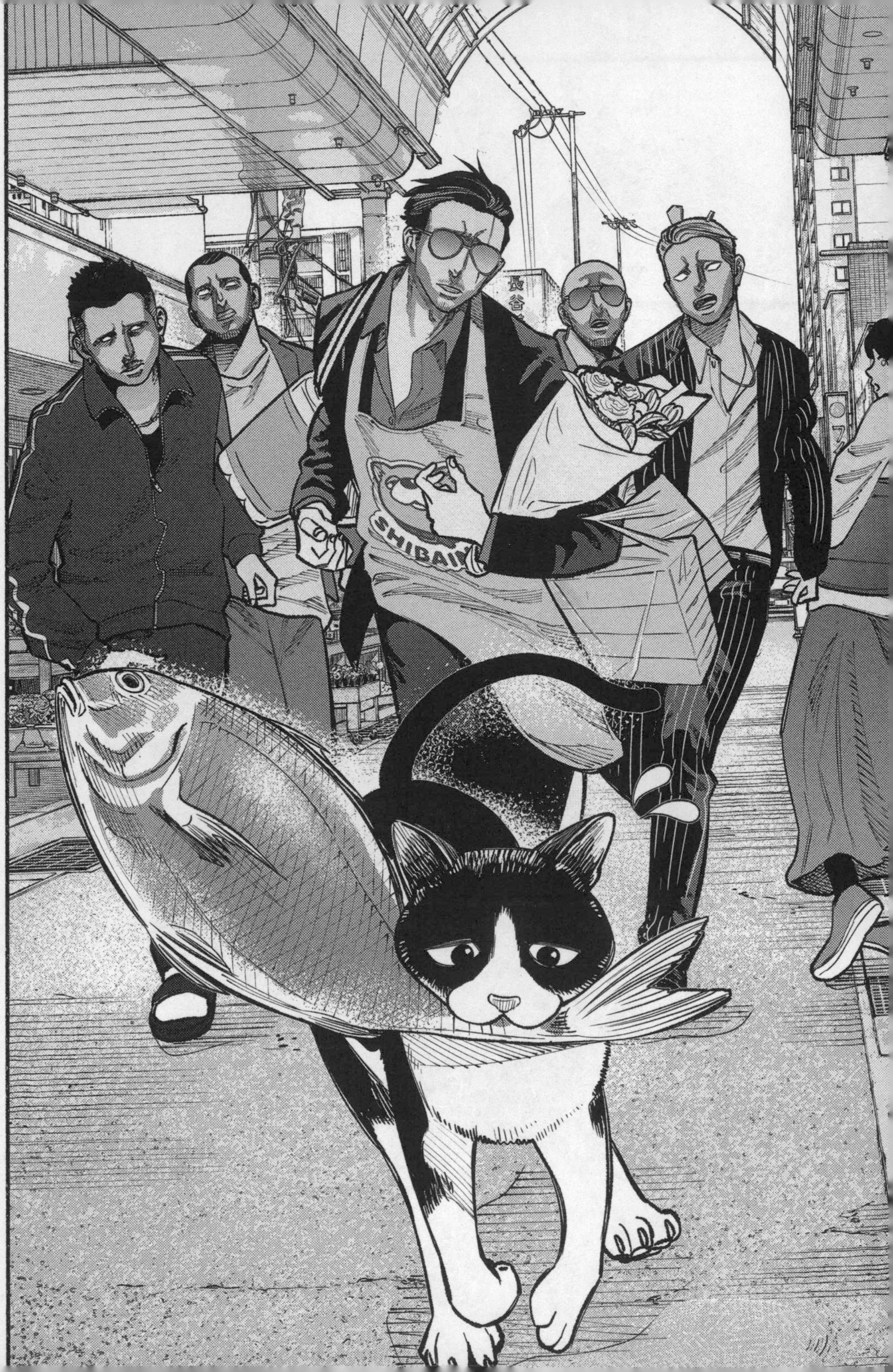

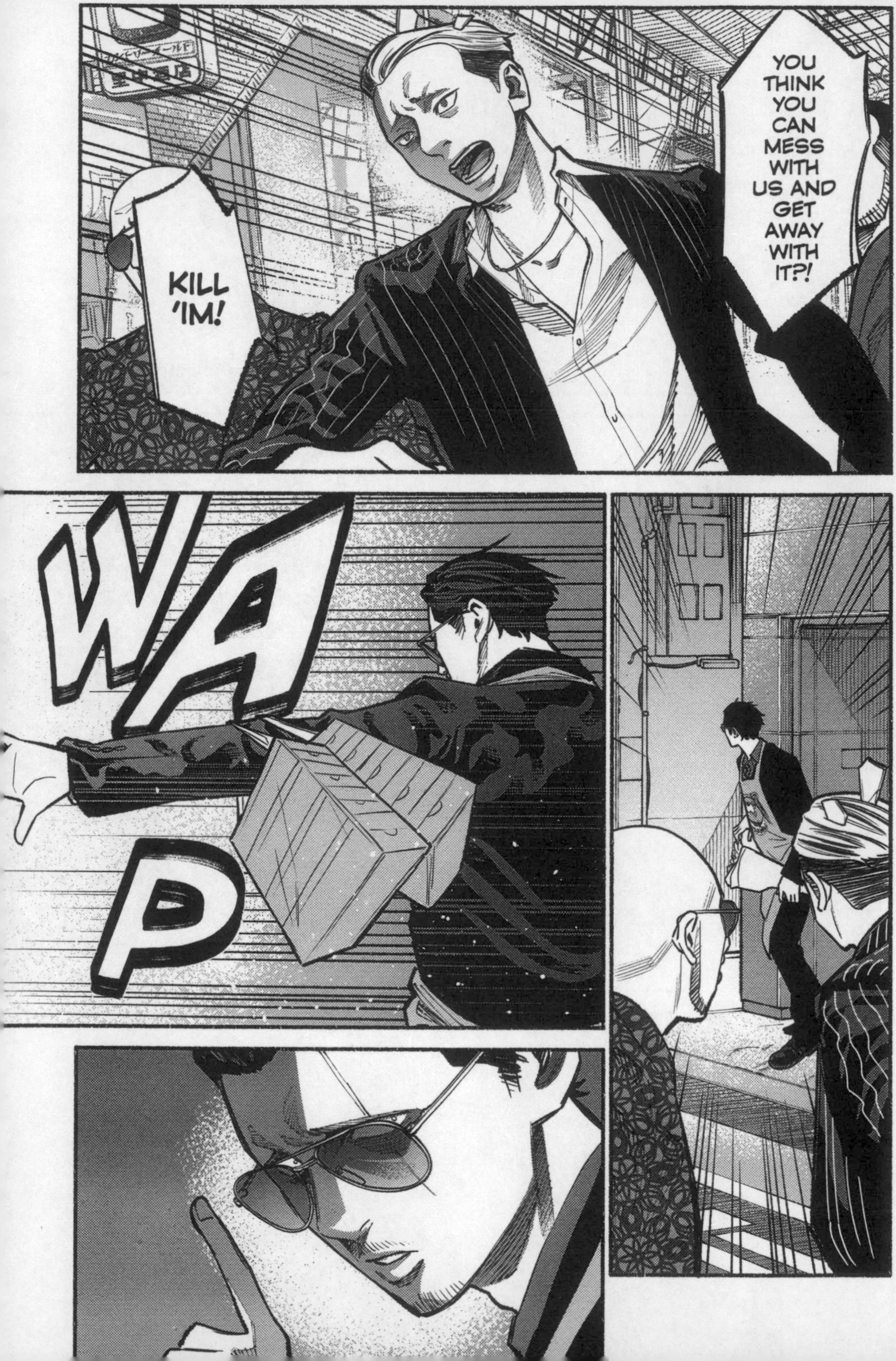
YOU THINK YOU CAN MESS WITH US AND GET AWAY WITH IT?!
KILL 'IM!
WAP

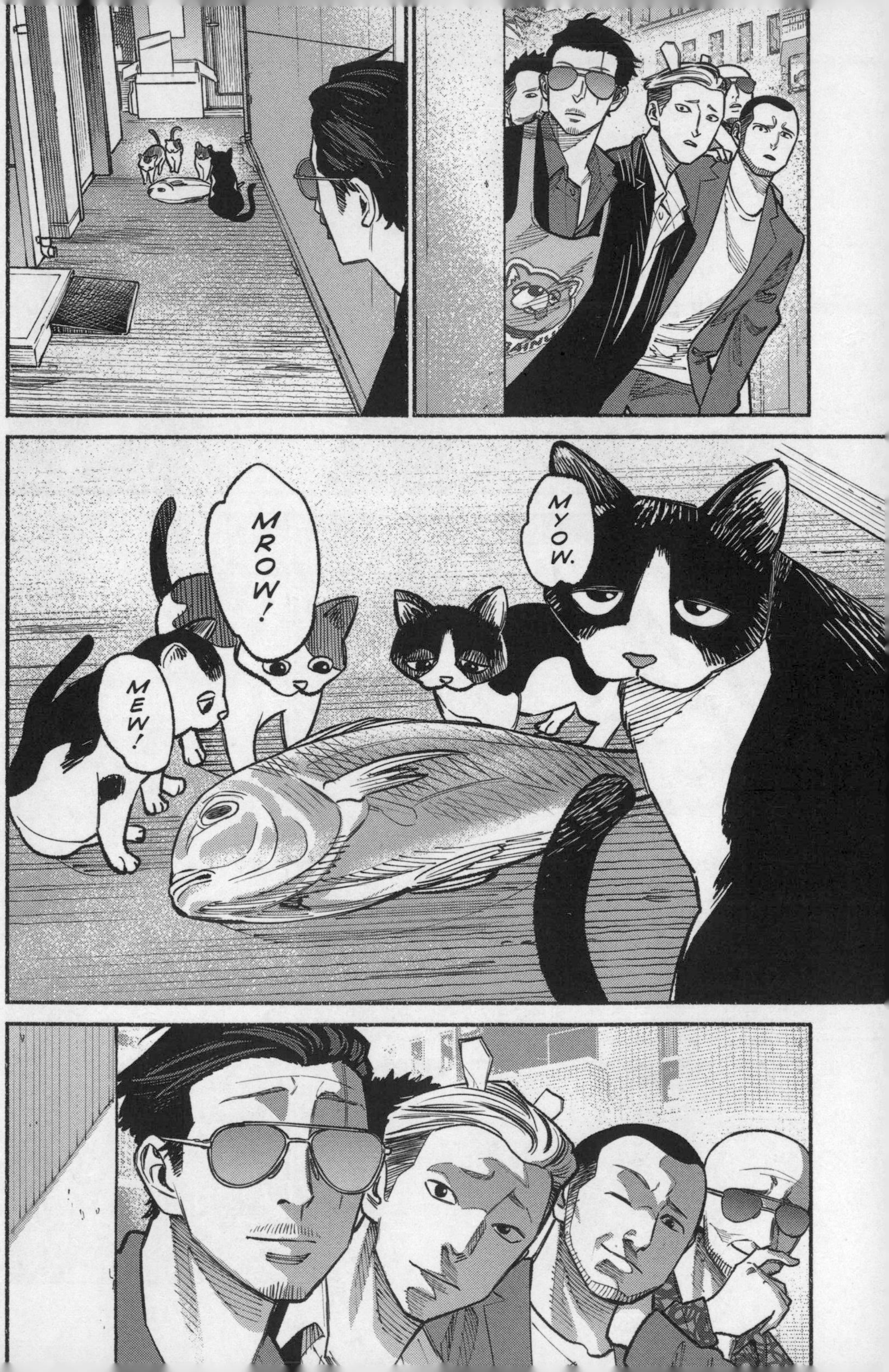
MYOW.
MROW!
MEW!

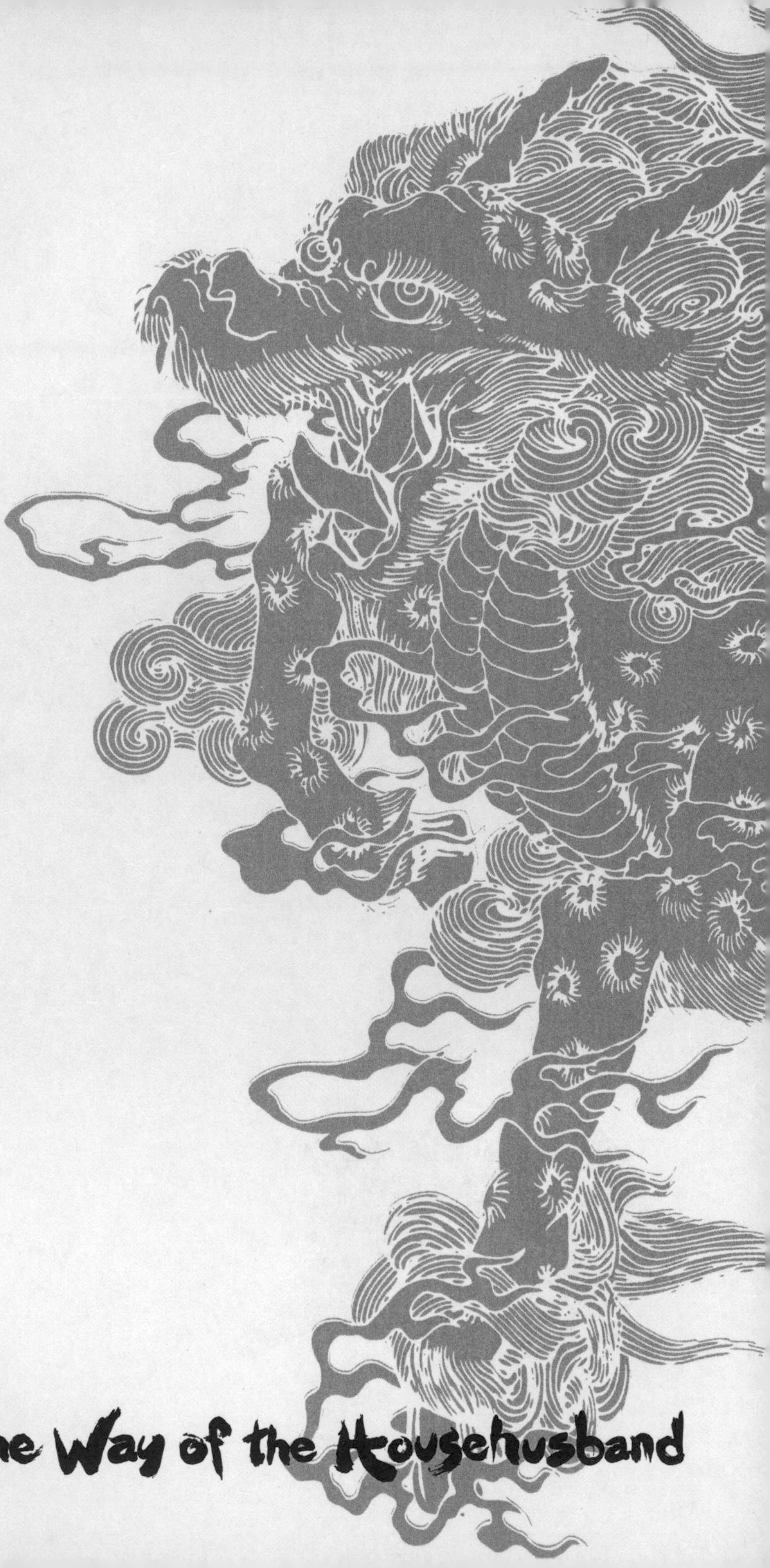

The Way of the Househusband

CHAPTER 29

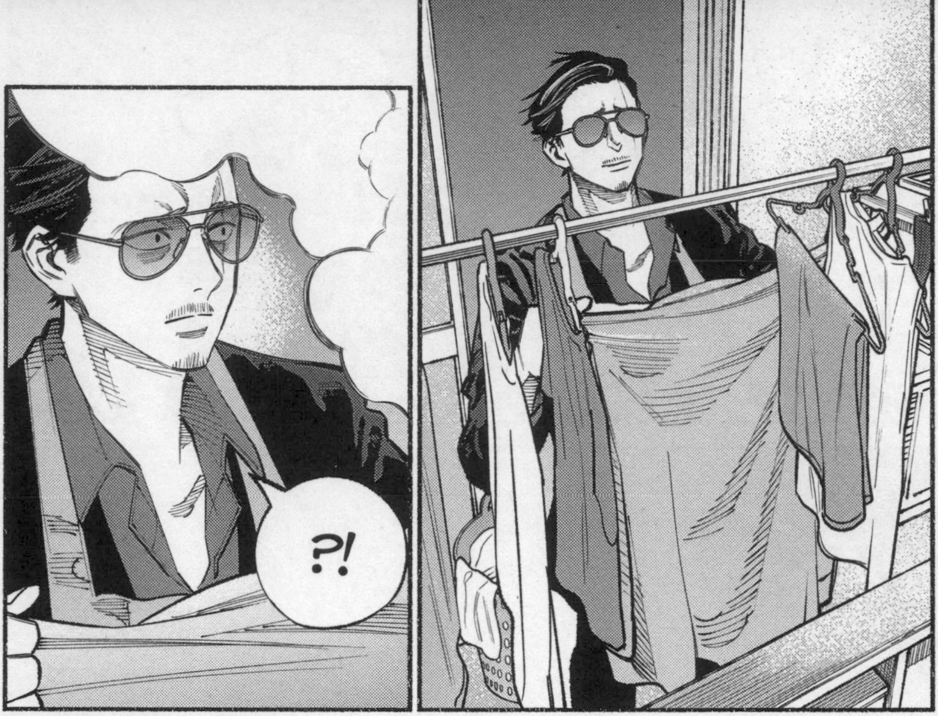
?!

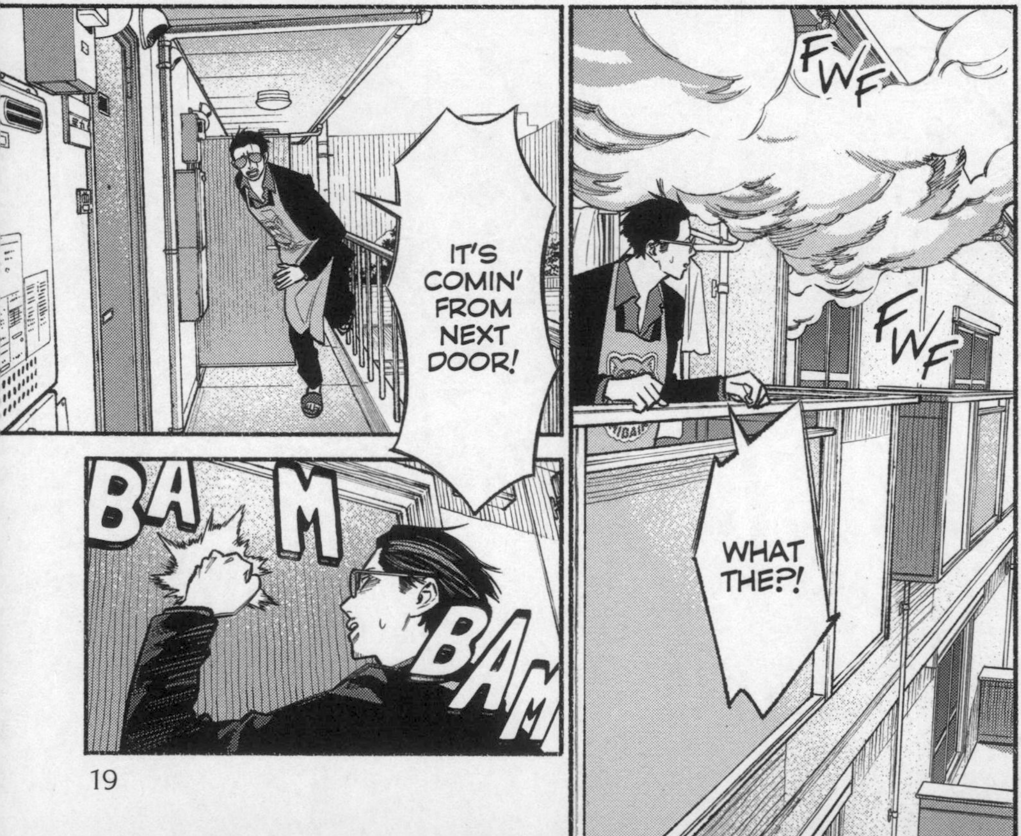
FWF
FWF
WHAT THE?!
IT'S COMIN' FROM NEXT DOOR!
BAM
BAM

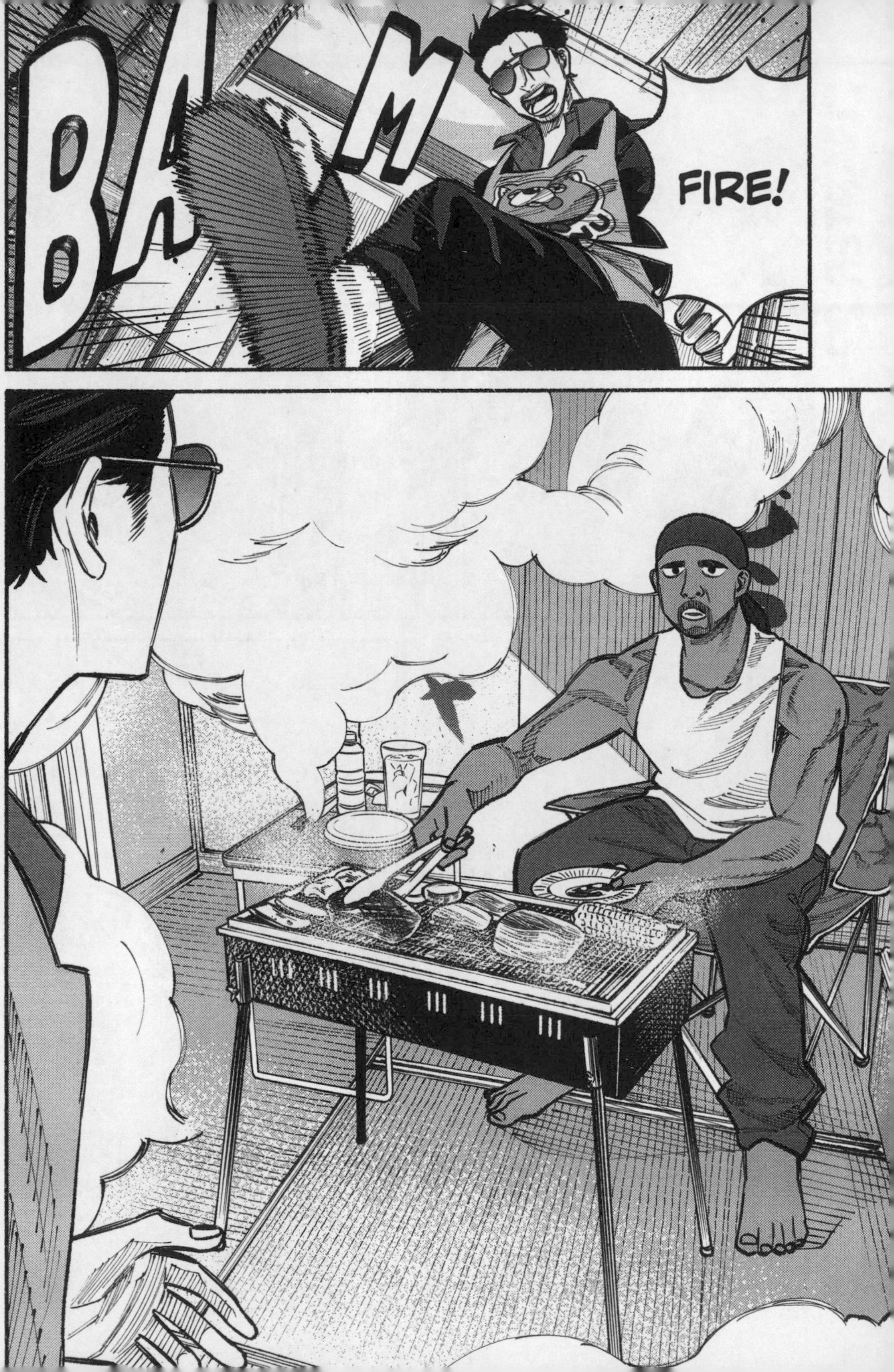
FIRE!
BAM

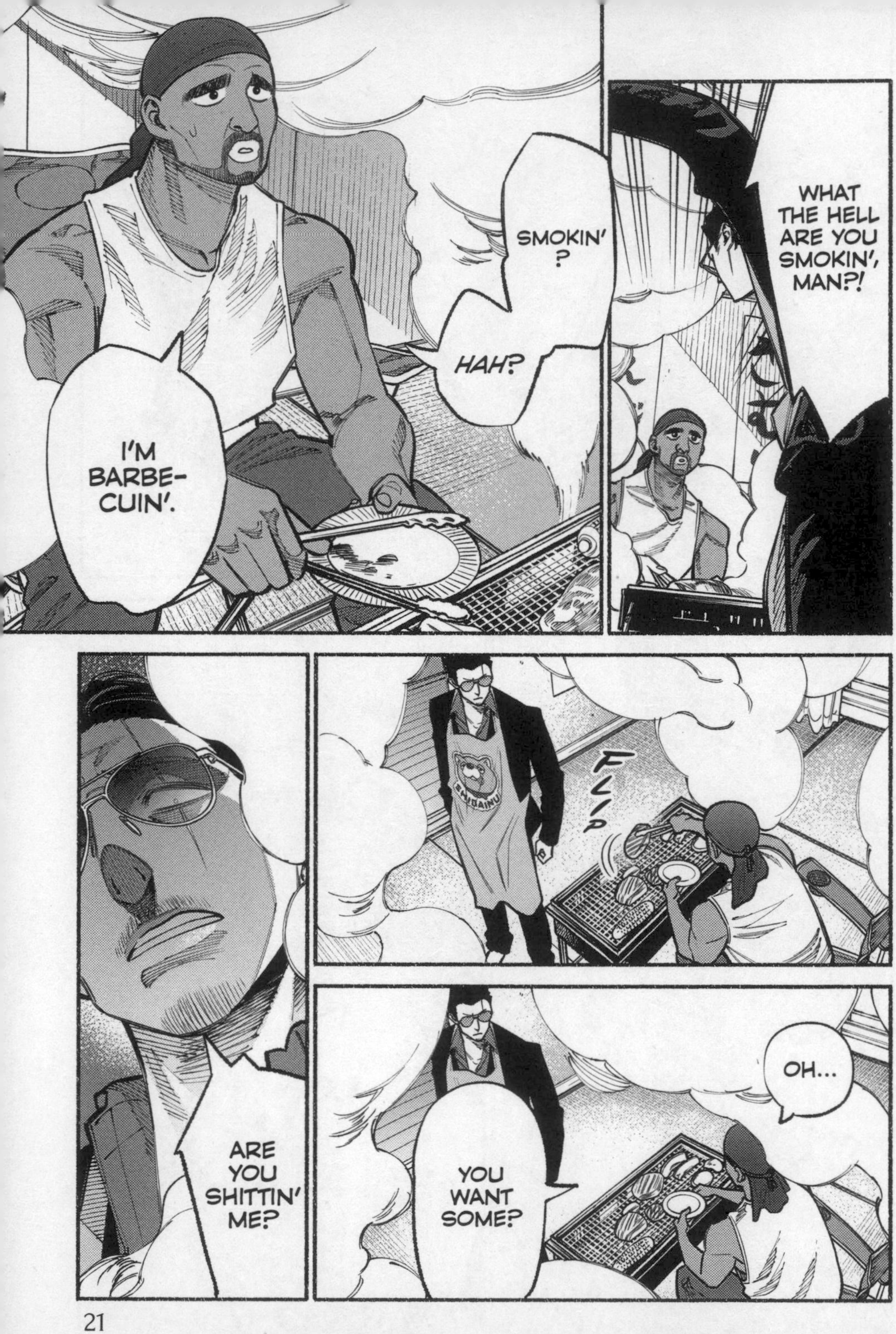
WHAT THE HELL ARE YOU SMOKIN', MAN?!
SMOKIN'?
HAH?
I'M BARBE-CUIN'.
FLIP
OH...
YOU WANT SOME?
ARE YOU SHITTIN' ME?

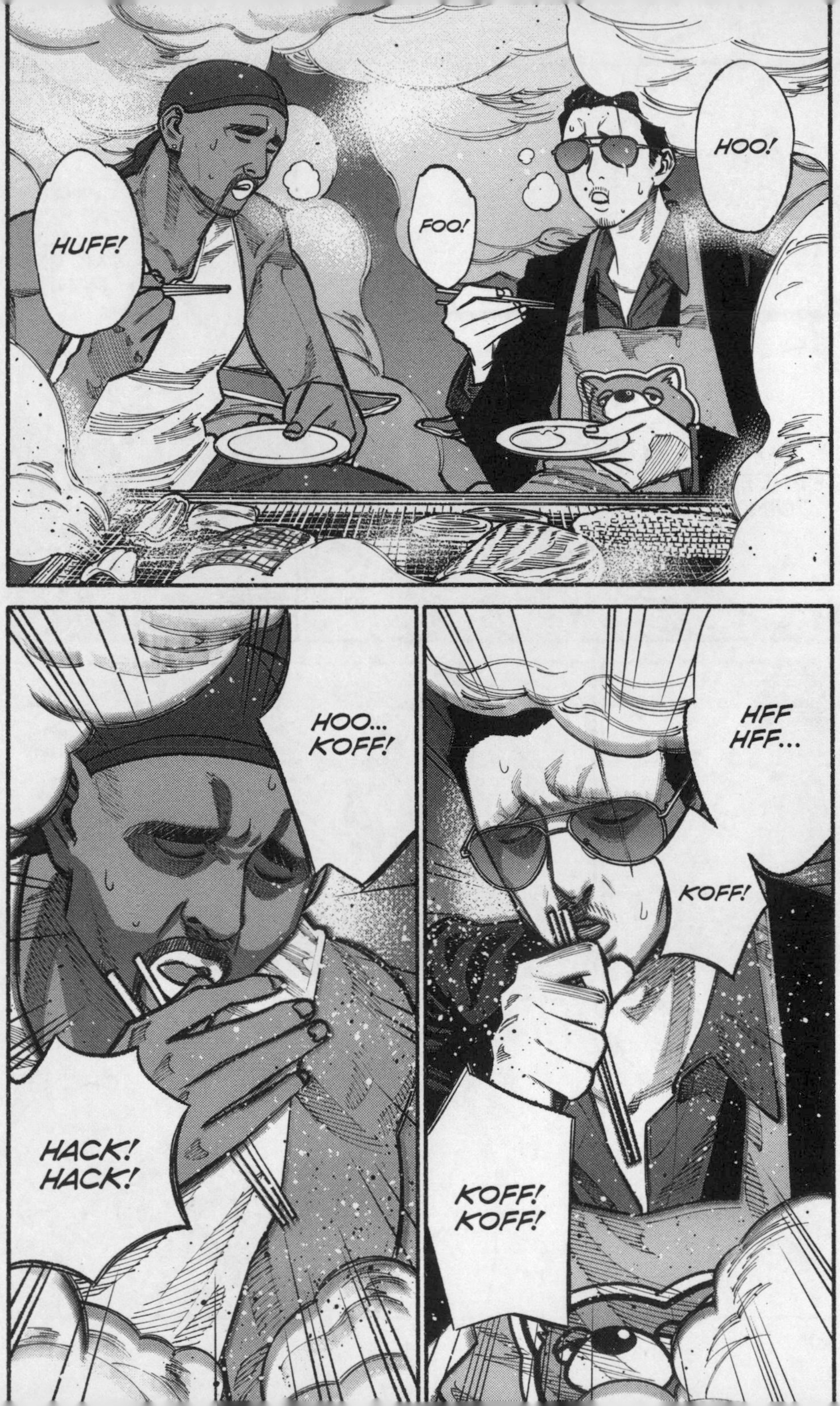
HOO!
FOO!
HUFF!
HFF HFF...
KOFF!
KOFF! KOFF!
HOO... KOFF!
HACK! HACK!

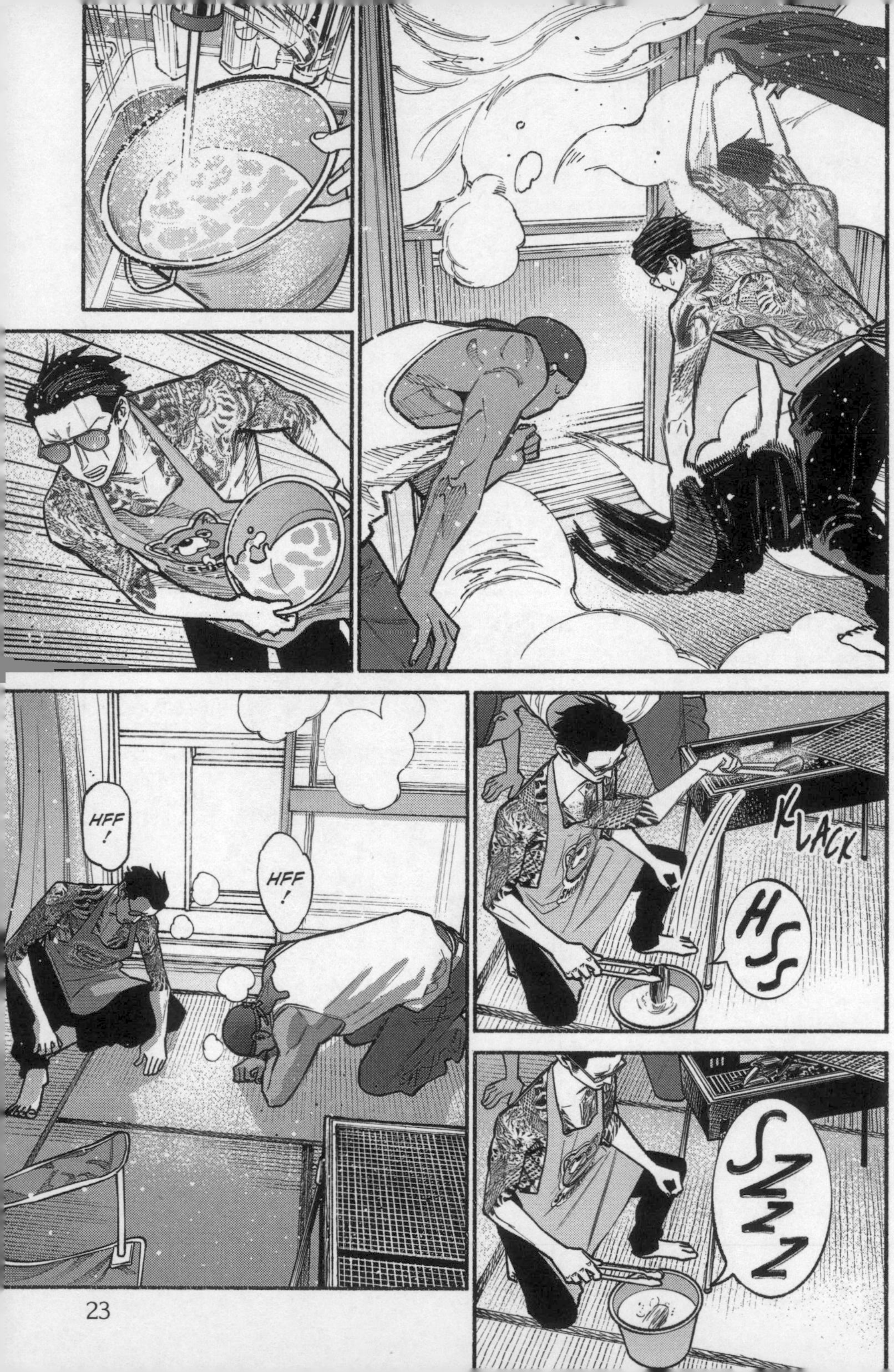
KLACK
HSS
SZZZ
HFF!
HFF!

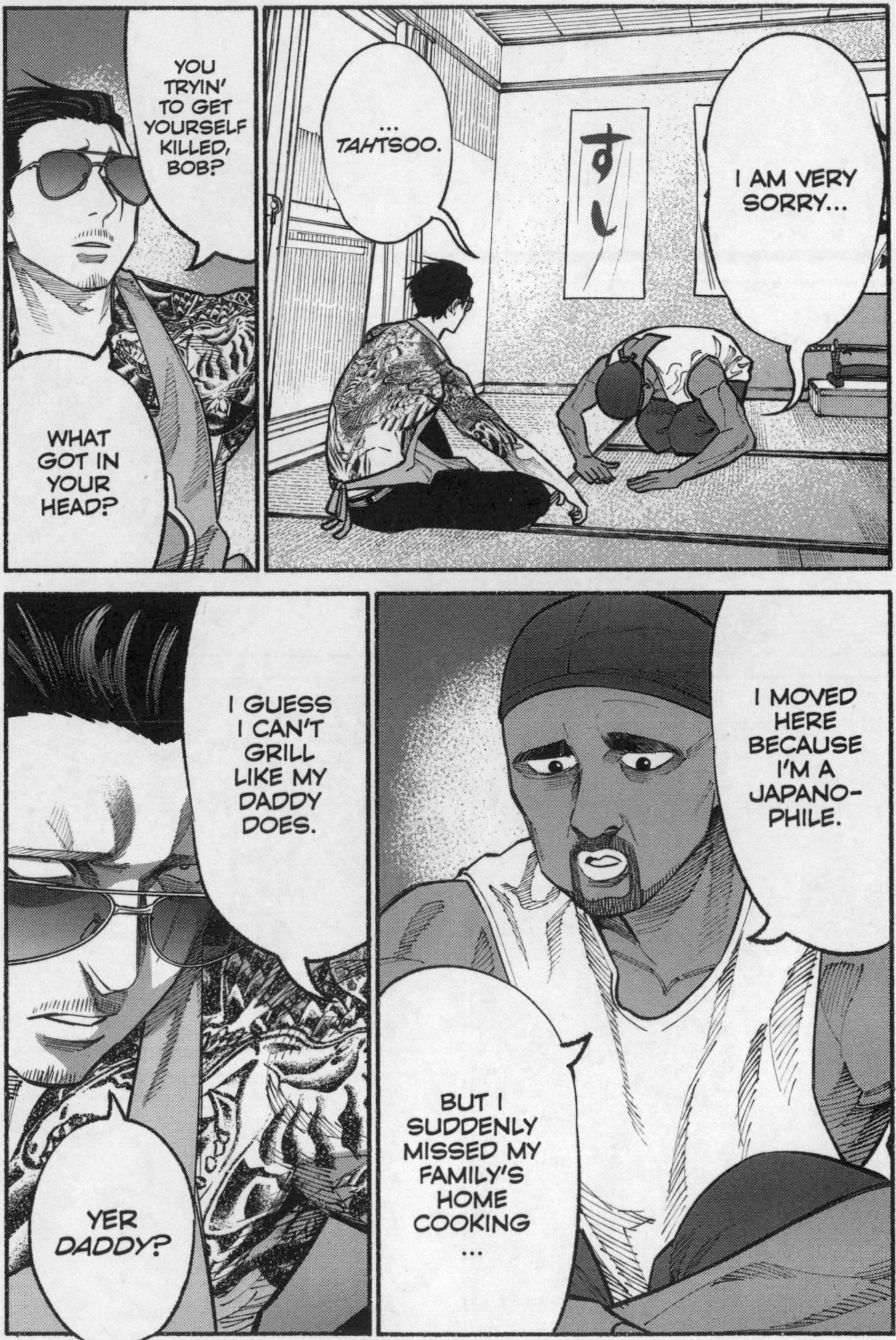
I AM VERY SORRY...
すし
... TAHTSOO.
YOU TRYIN' TO GET YOURSELF KILLED, BOB?
WHAT GOT IN YOUR HEAD?
I MOVED HERE BECAUSE I'M A JAPANO-PHILE.
BUT I SUDDENLY MISSED MY FAMILY'S HOME COOKING ...
I GUESS I CAN'T GRILL LIKE MY DADDY DOES.
YER DADDY?

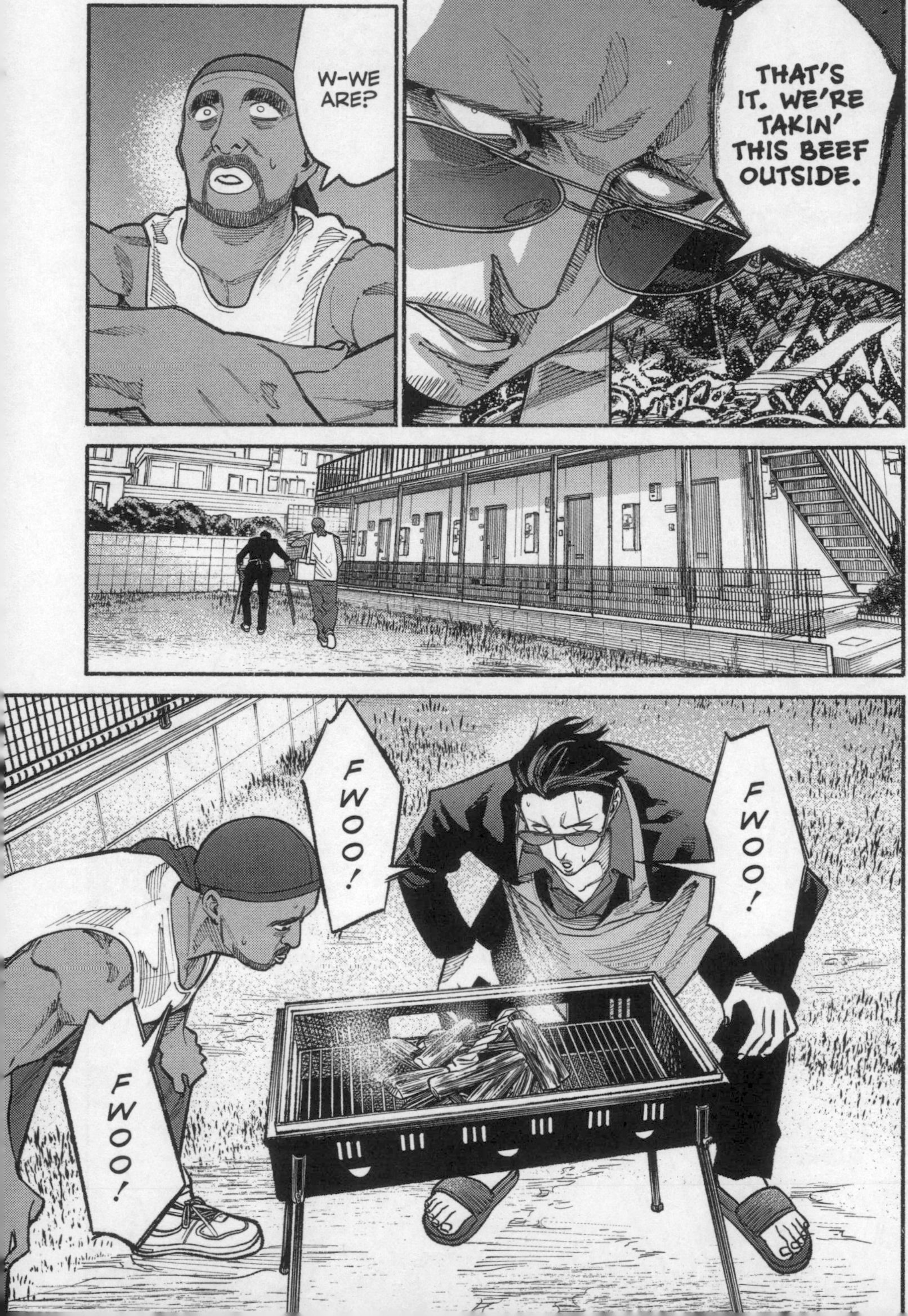
THAT'S IT. WE'RE TAKIN' THIS BEEF OUTSIDE.
W-WE ARE?
FWOO!
FWOO!
FWOO!

YOU GOT THE GOODS?

A WHOLE COOLER'S WORTH. I WENT TO DOSTCO.

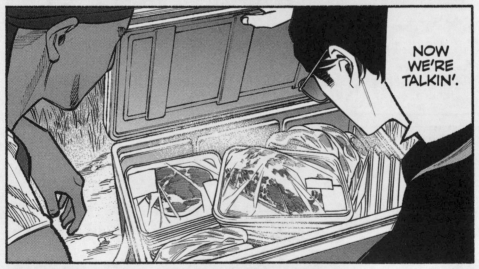

NOW WE'RE TALKIN'.

I'M GONNA SHOW YOU HOW THE JAPANESE ...

... HANDLE A BEEF.

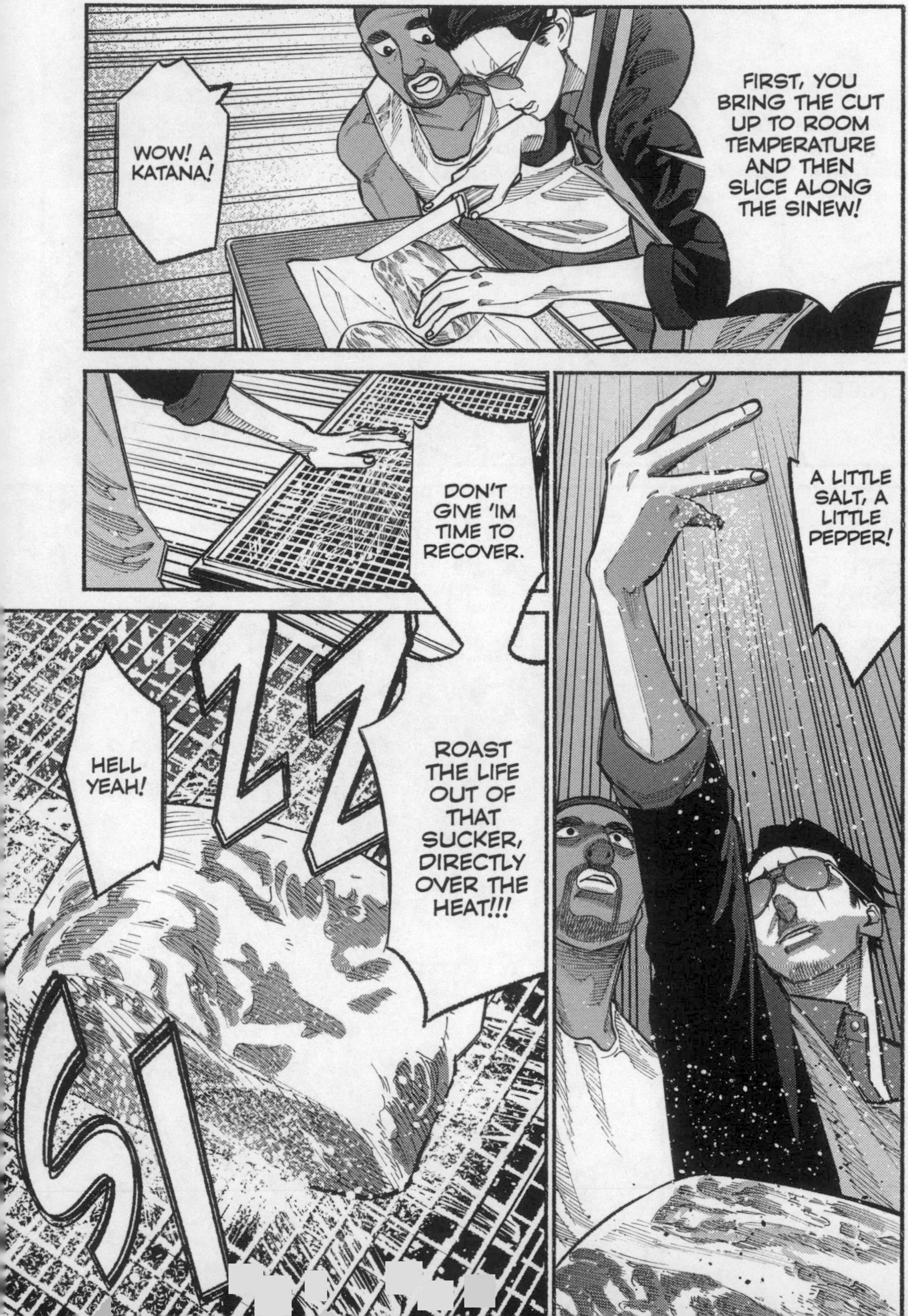
FIRST, YOU BRING THE CUT UP TO ROOM TEMPERATURE AND THEN SLICE ALONG THE SINEW!
WOW! A KATANA!
A LITTLE SALT, A LITTLE PEPPER!
DON'T GIVE 'IM TIME TO RECOVER.
ROAST THE LIFE OUT OF THAT SUCKER, DIRECTLY OVER THE HEAT!!!
HELL YEAH!
SIZZ

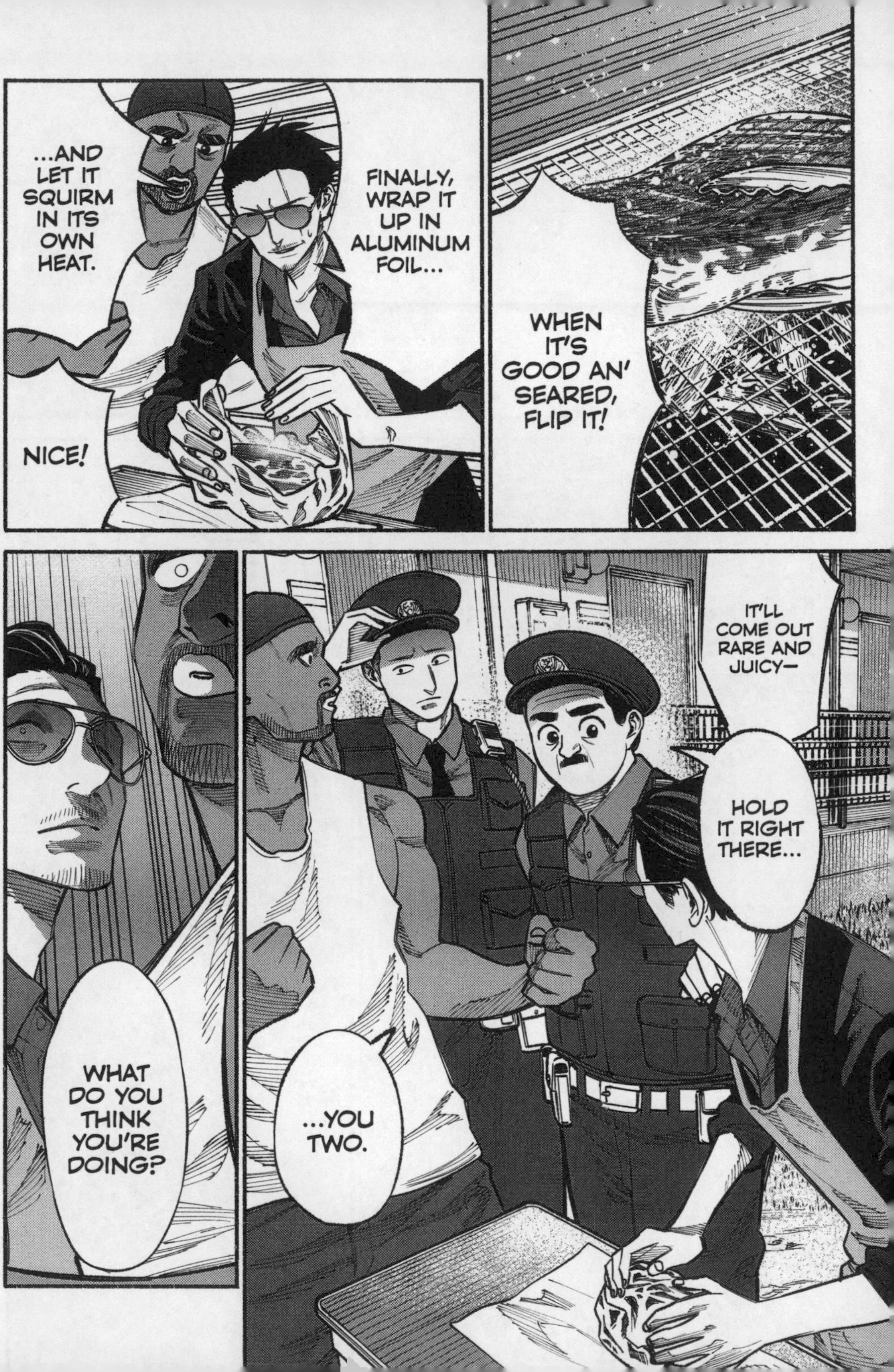
WHEN IT'S GOOD AN' SEARED, FLIP IT!
FINALLY, WRAP IT UP IN ALUMINUM FOIL...
...AND LET IT SQUIRM IN ITS OWN HEAT.
NICE!
IT'LL COME OUT RARE AND JUICY—
HOLD IT RIGHT THERE...
...YOU TWO.
WHAT DO YOU THINK YOU'RE DOING?

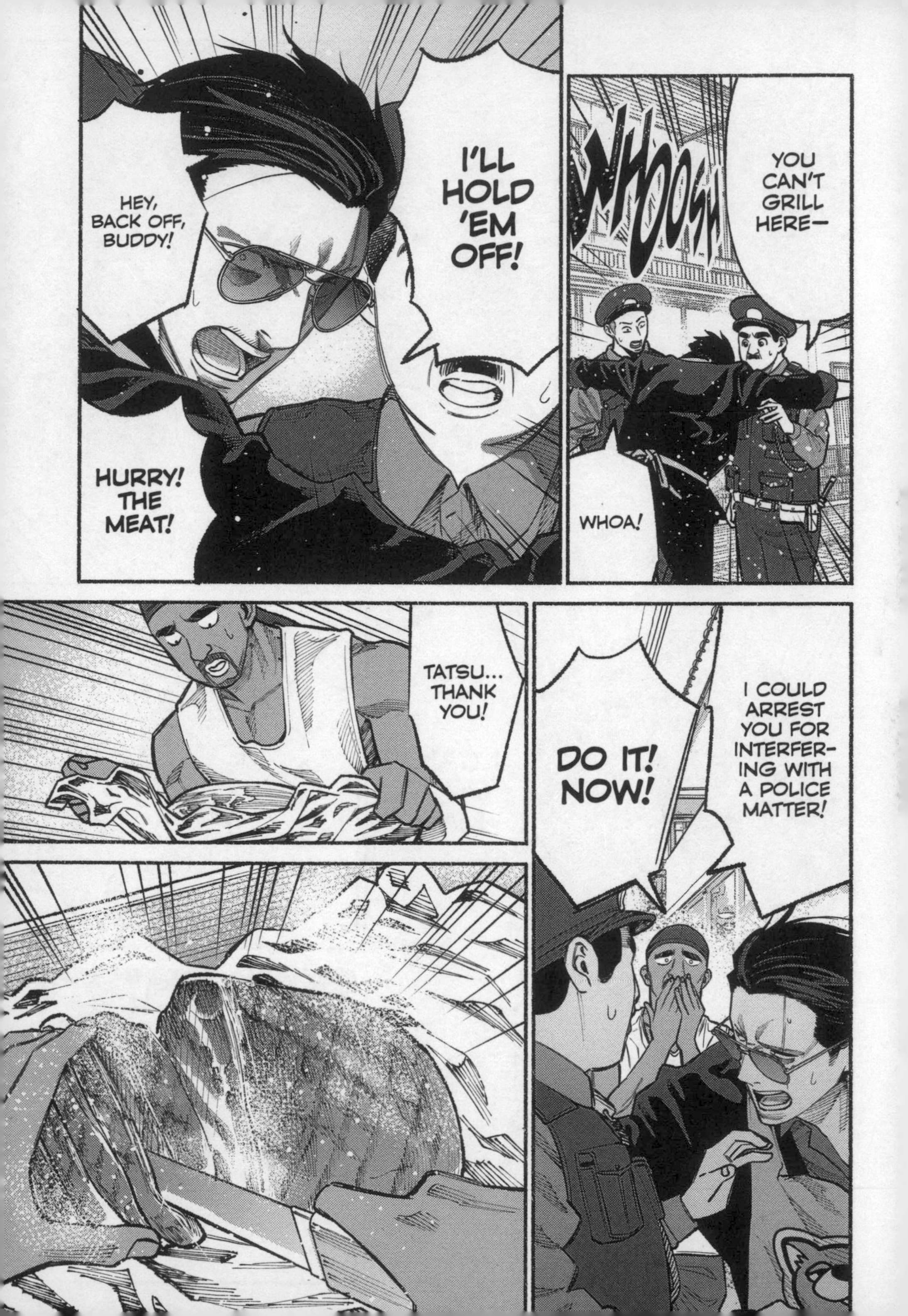
YOU CAN'T GRILL HERE—
WHOOSH
WHOA!
I'LL HOLD 'EM OFF!
HEY, BACK OFF, BUDDY!
HURRY! THE MEAT!
I COULD ARREST YOU FOR INTERFER-ING WITH A POLICE MATTER!
DO IT! NOW!
TATSU... THANK YOU!

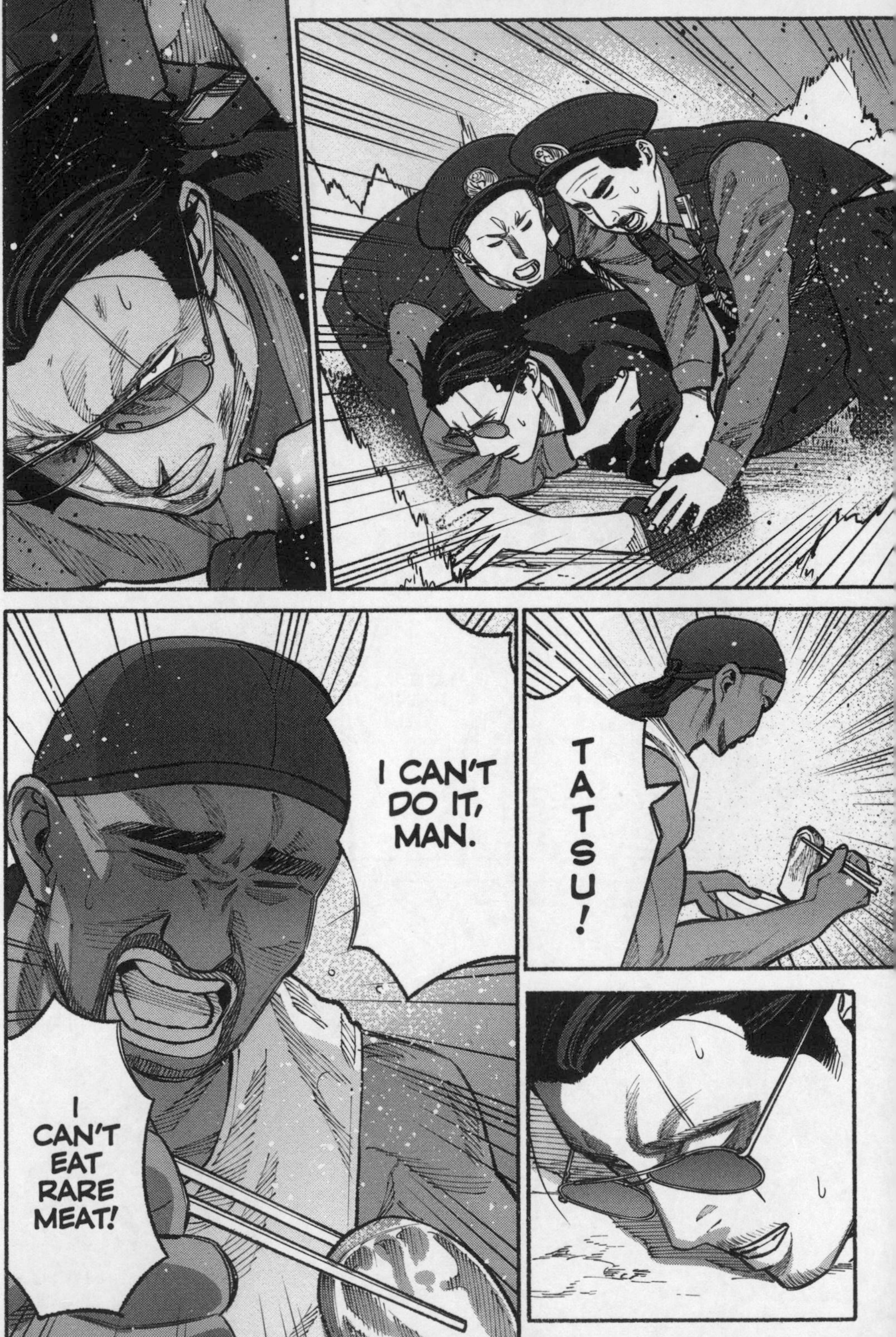
TATSU!
I CAN'T DO IT, MAN.
I CAN'T EAT RARE MEAT!

*SUSHI

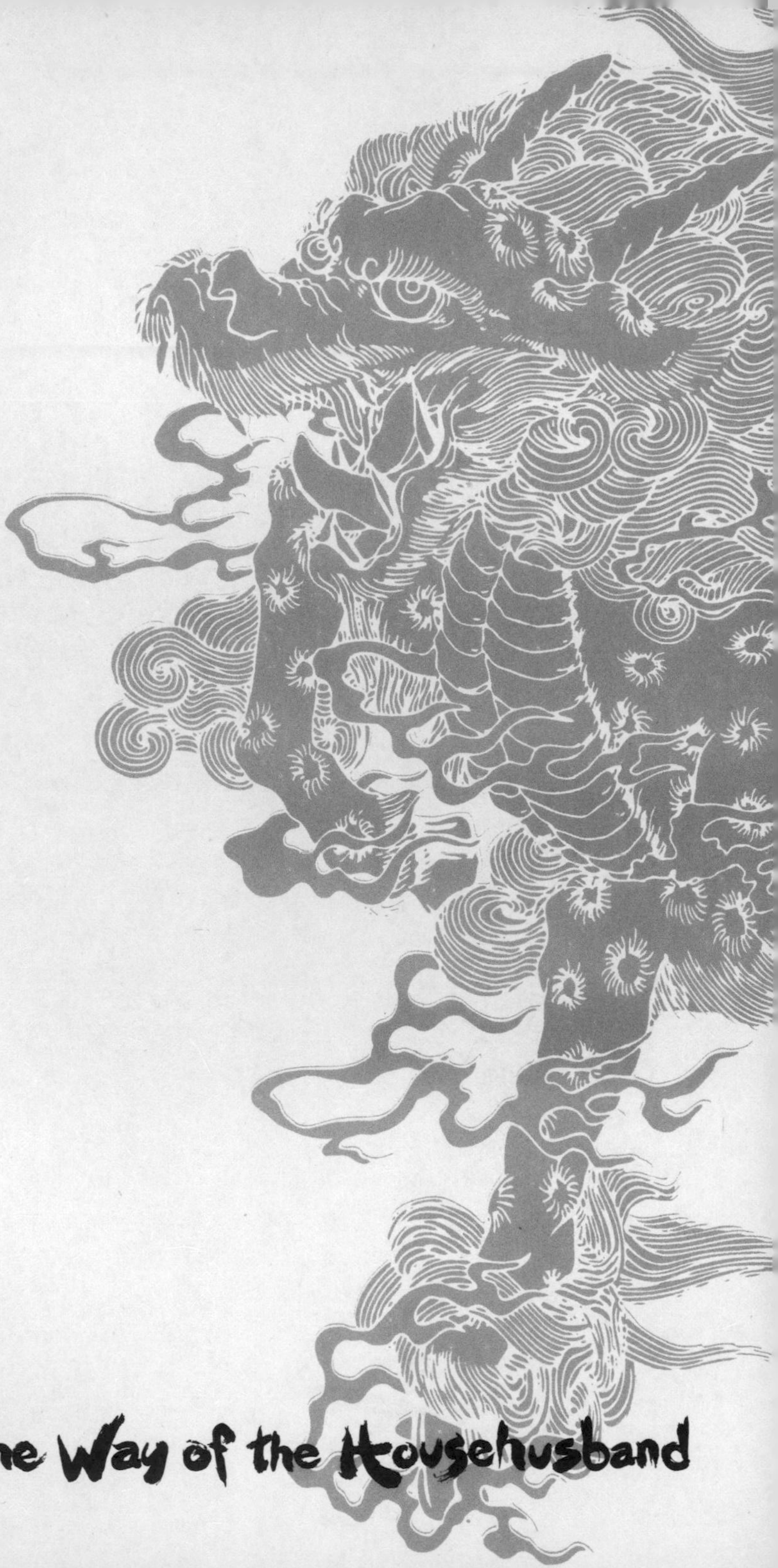

The Way of the Househusband

CHAPTER 30

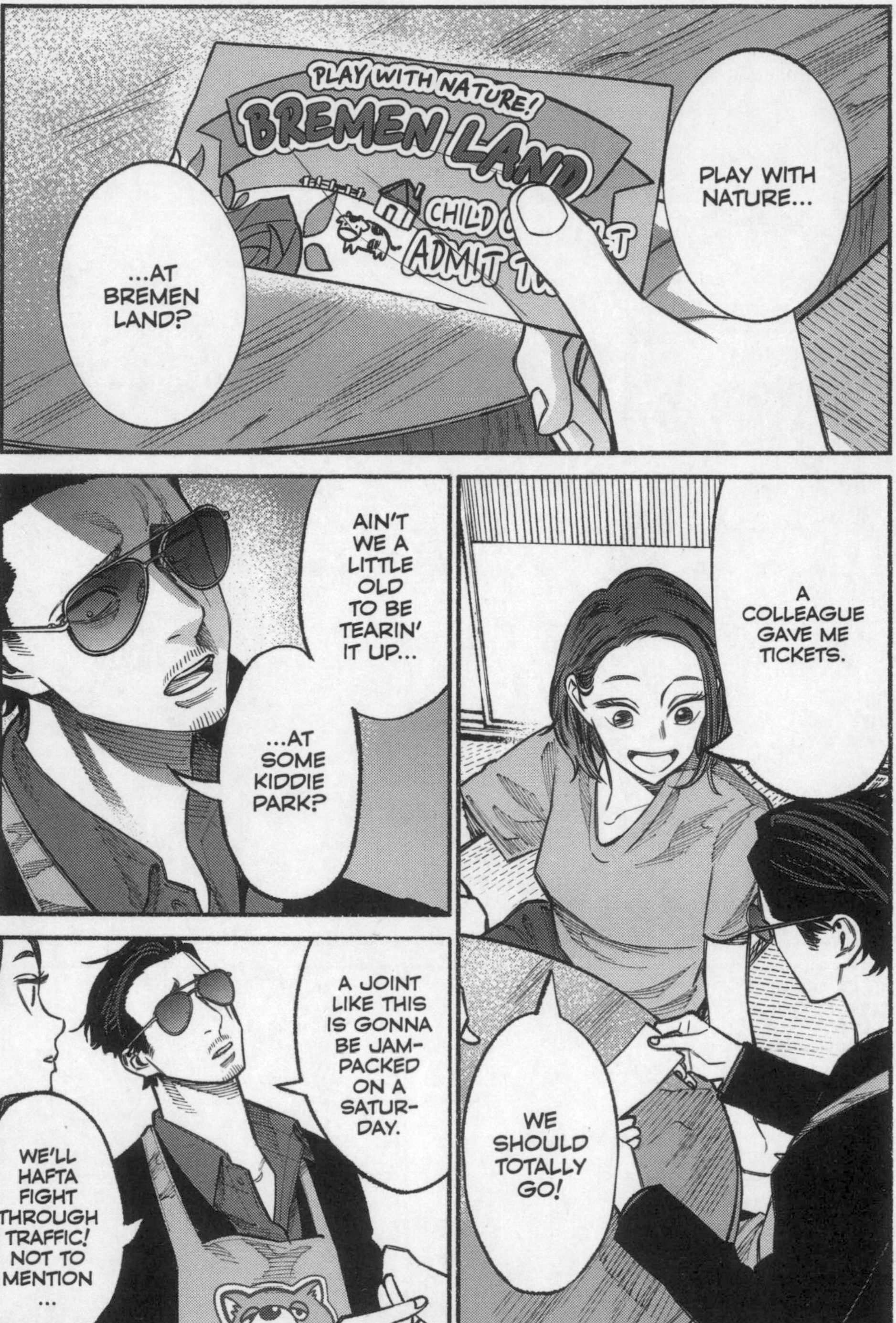
PLAY WITH NATURE!
BREMEN LAND
PLAY WITH NATURE...
...AT BREMEN LAND?
A COLLEAGUE GAVE ME TICKETS.
AIN'T WE A LITTLE OLD TO BE TEARIN' IT UP...
...AT SOME KIDDIE PARK?
WE SHOULD TOTALLY GO!
A JOINT LIKE THIS IS GONNA BE JAM-PACKED ON A SATUR-DAY.
WE'LL HAFTA FIGHT THROUGH TRAFFIC! NOT TO MENTION ...

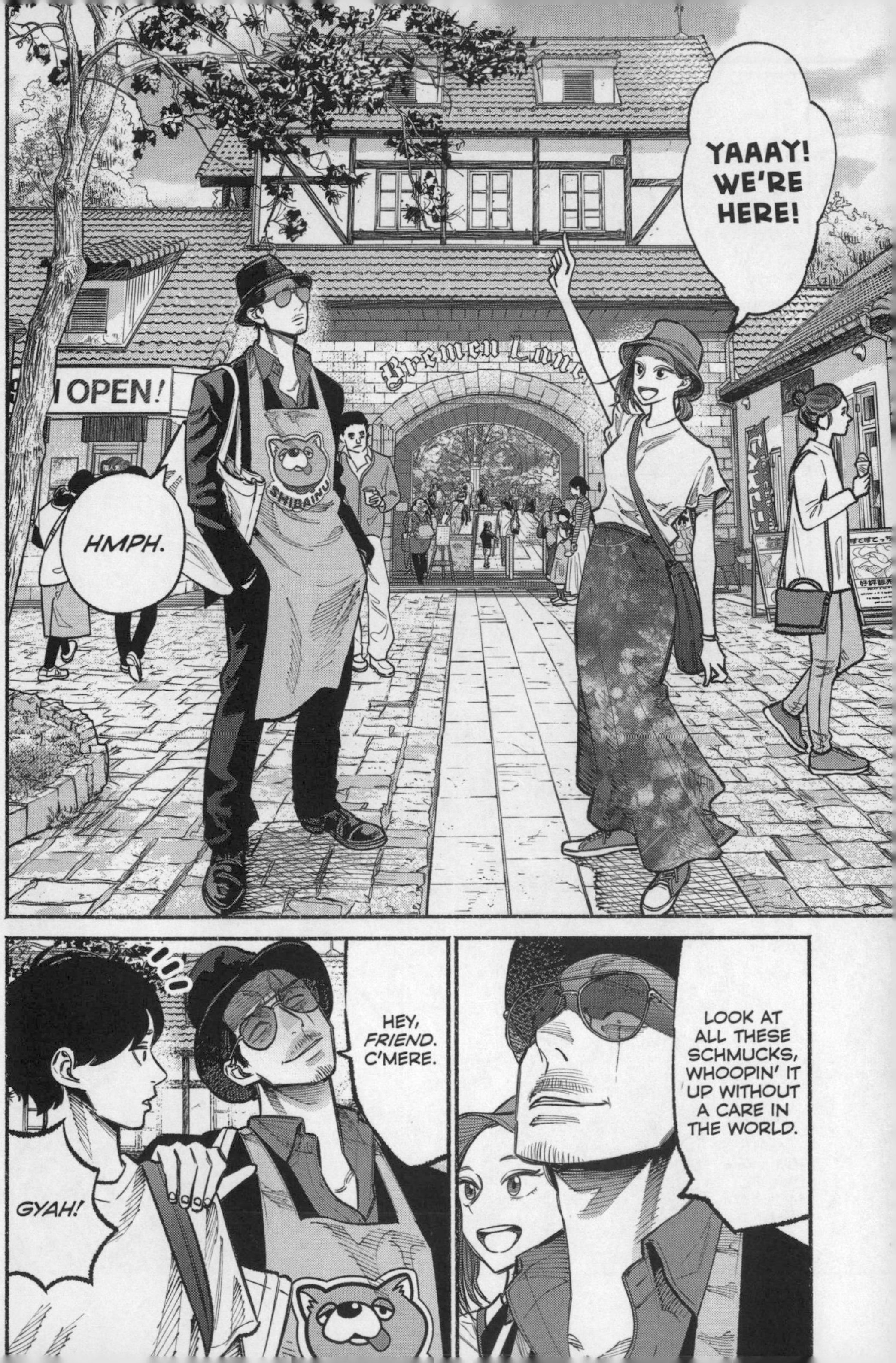
YAAAY! WE'RE HERE!
Bremen Lane
OPEN!
SHIBAINU
HMPH.
LOOK AT ALL THESE SCHMUCKS, WHOOPIN' IT UP WITHOUT A CARE IN THE WORLD.
HEY, FRIEND. C'MERE.
GYAH!

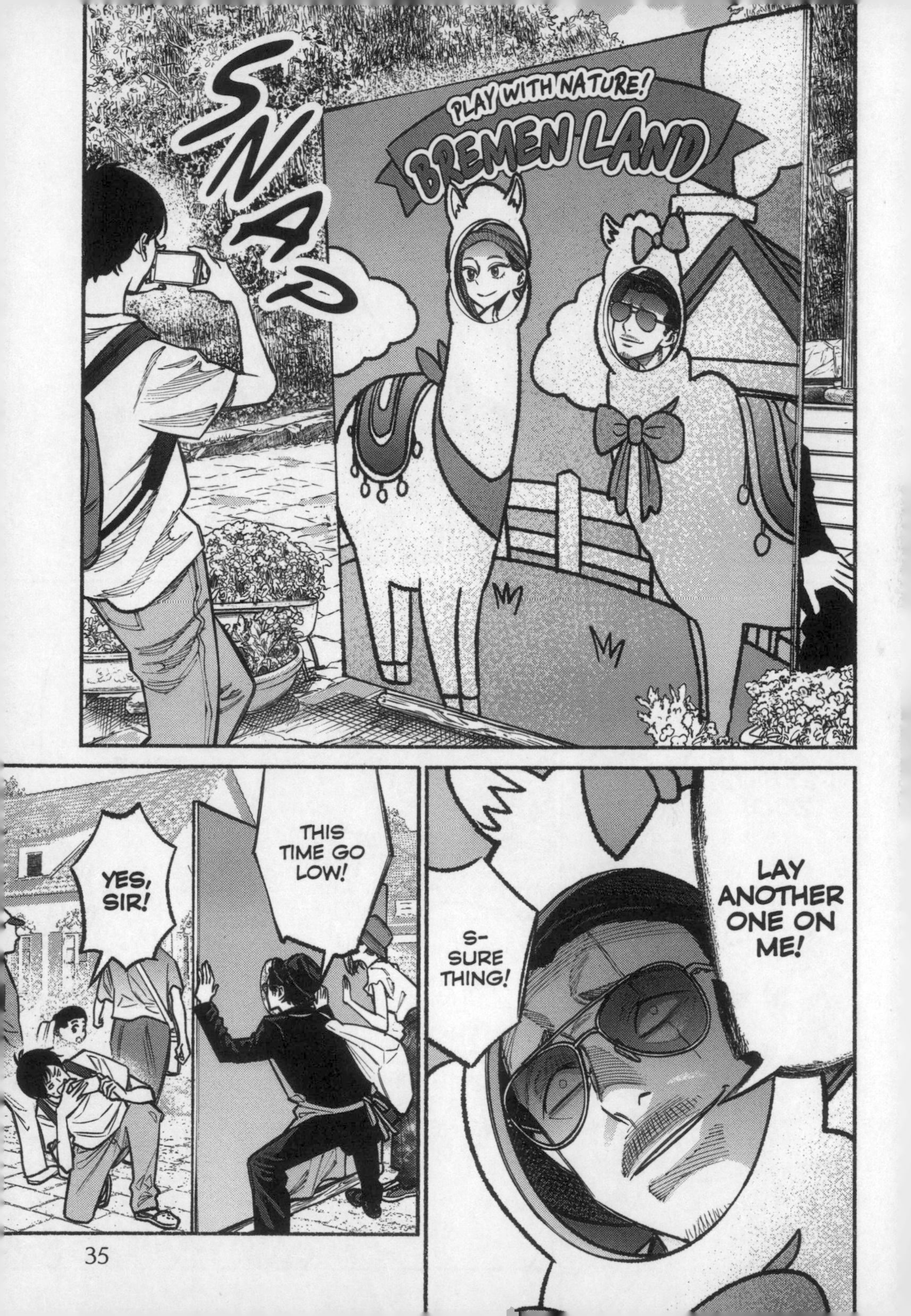
PLAY WITH NATURE!
BREMEN LAND
SNAP
LAY ANOTHER ONE ON ME!
S-SURE THING!
THIS TIME GO LOW!
YES, SIR!

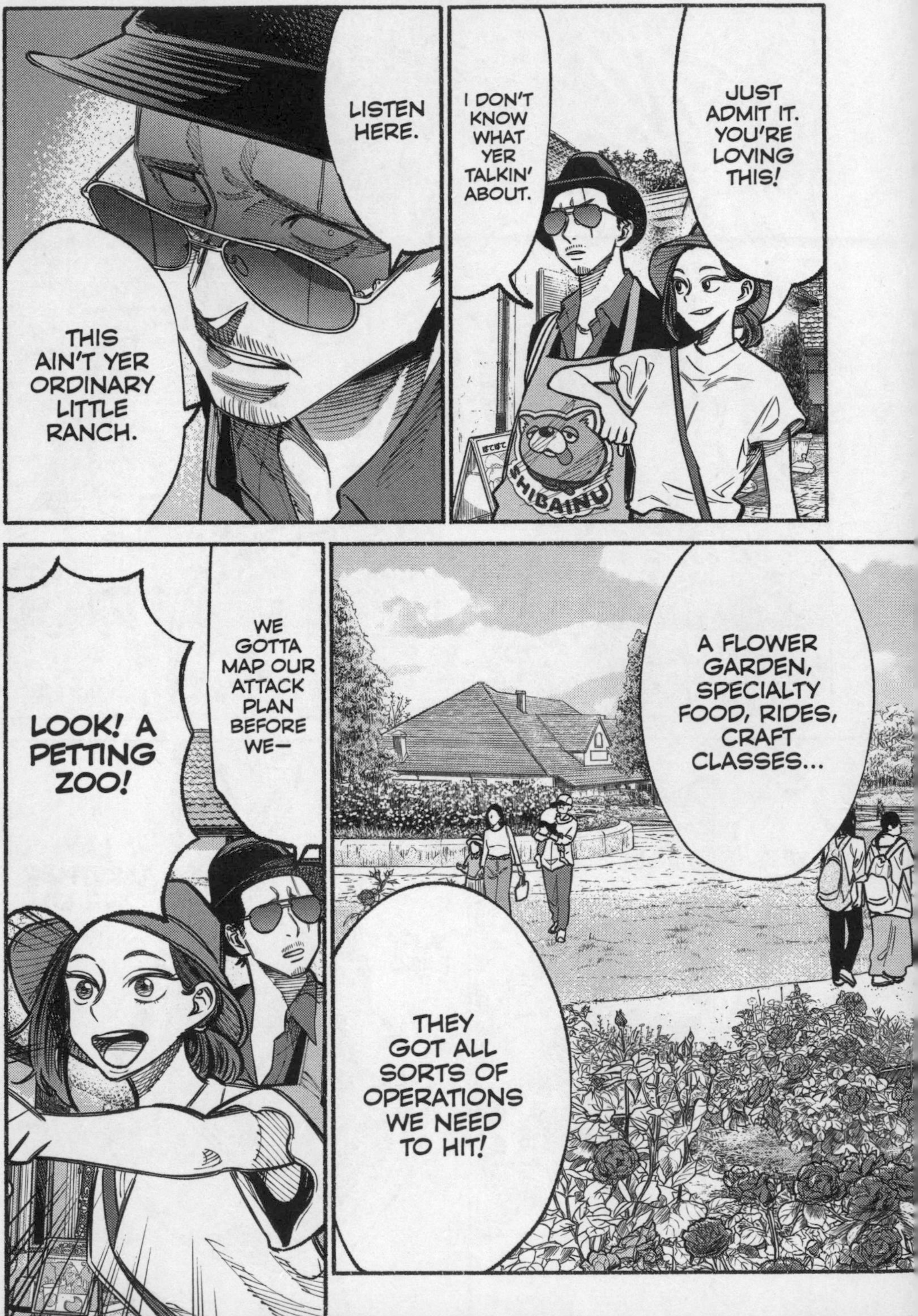
JUST ADMIT IT. YOU'RE LOVING THIS!
I DON'T KNOW WHAT YER TALKIN' ABOUT.
SHIBAINU
LISTEN HERE.
THIS AIN'T YER ORDINARY LITTLE RANCH.
A FLOWER GARDEN, SPECIALTY FOOD, RIDES, CRAFT CLASSES...
THEY GOT ALL SORTS OF OPERATIONS WE NEED TO HIT!
WE GOTTA MAP OUR ATTACK PLAN BEFORE WE—
LOOK! A PETTING ZOO!

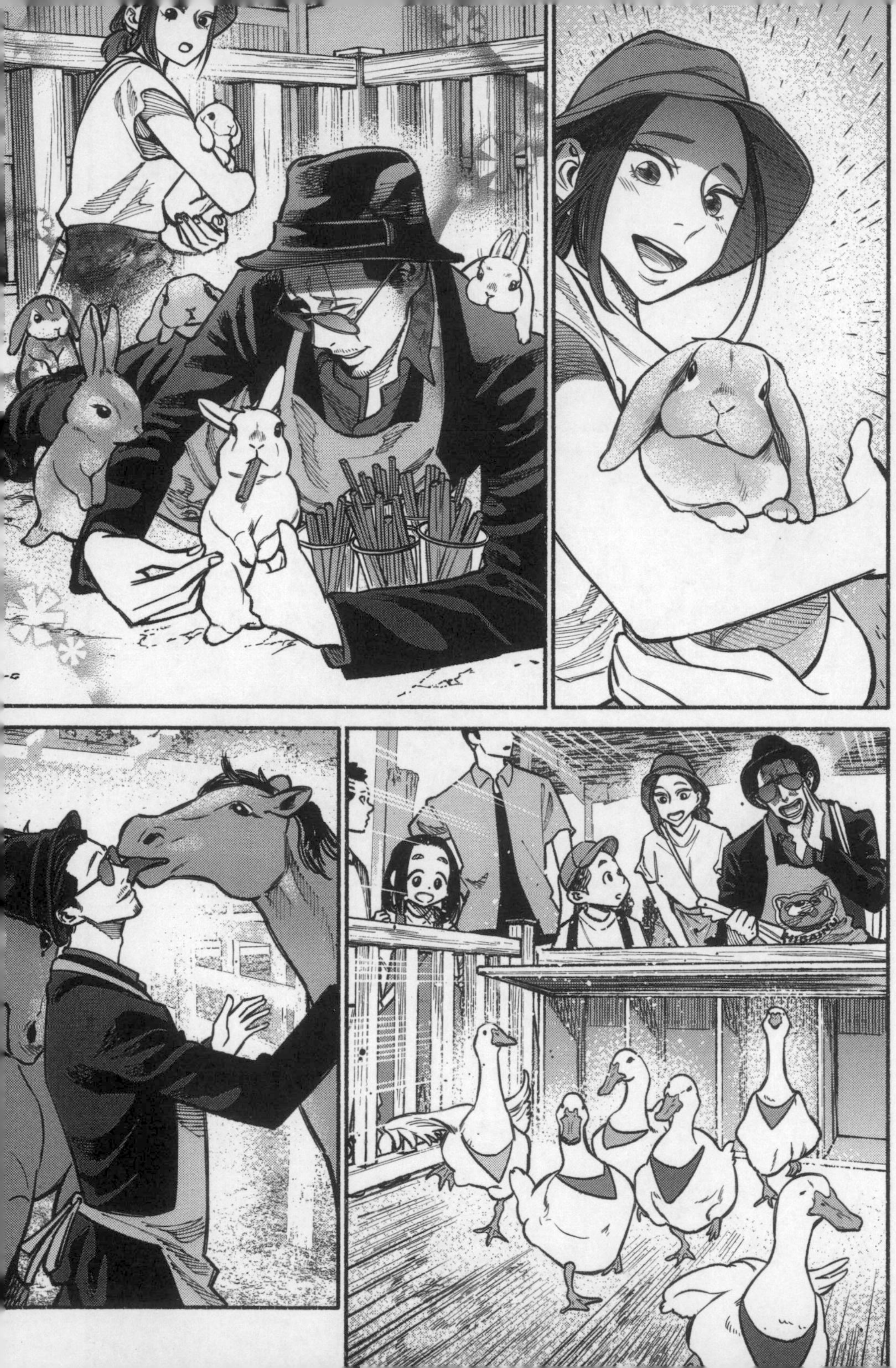

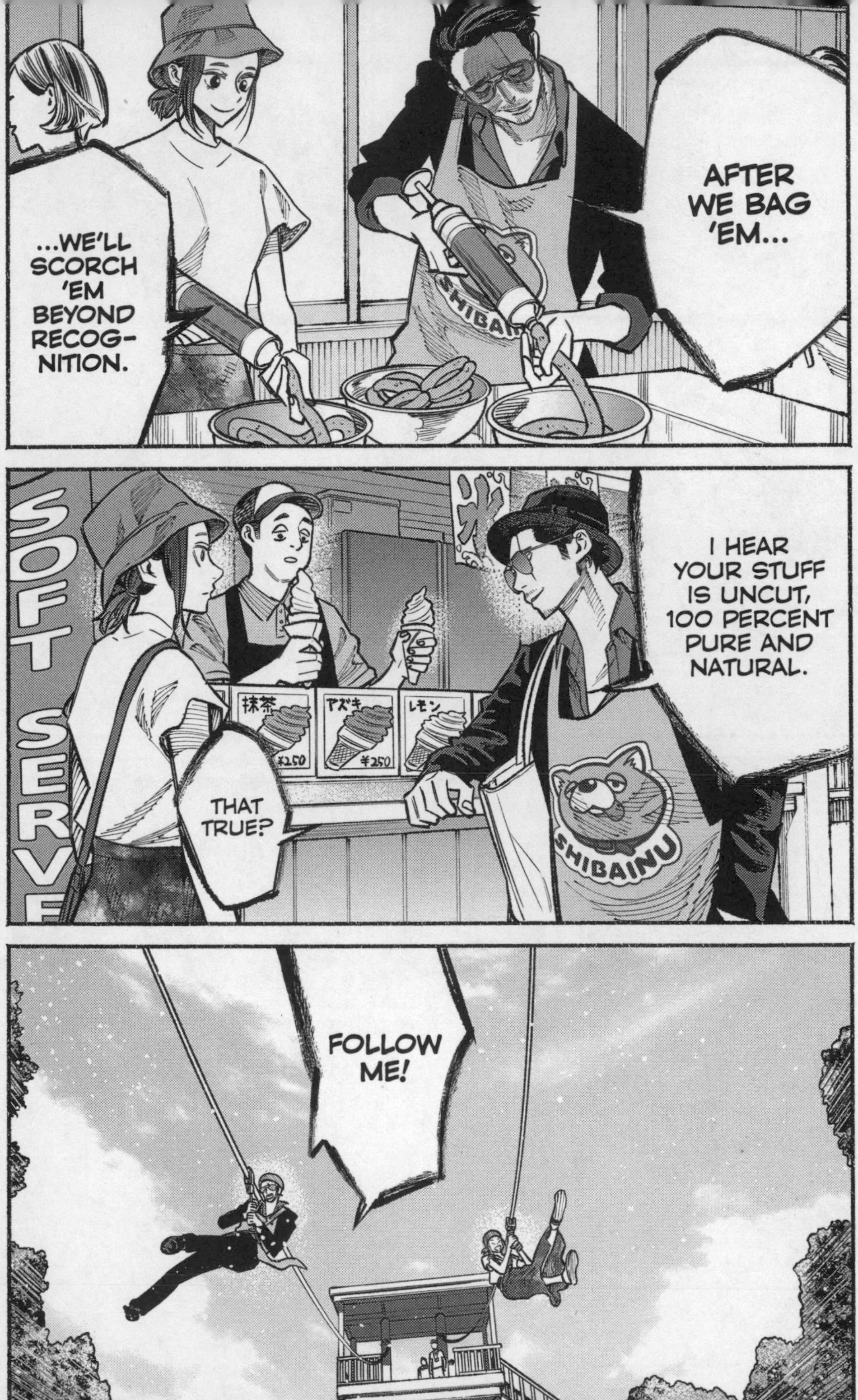
AFTER WE BAG 'EM...
...WE'LL SCORCH 'EM BEYOND RECOG- NITION.
SHIBAINU
I HEAR YOUR STUFF IS UNCUT, 100 PERCENT PURE AND NATURAL.
THAT TRUE?
抹茶
アズキ
レモン
¥250
SHIBAINU
FOLLOW ME!

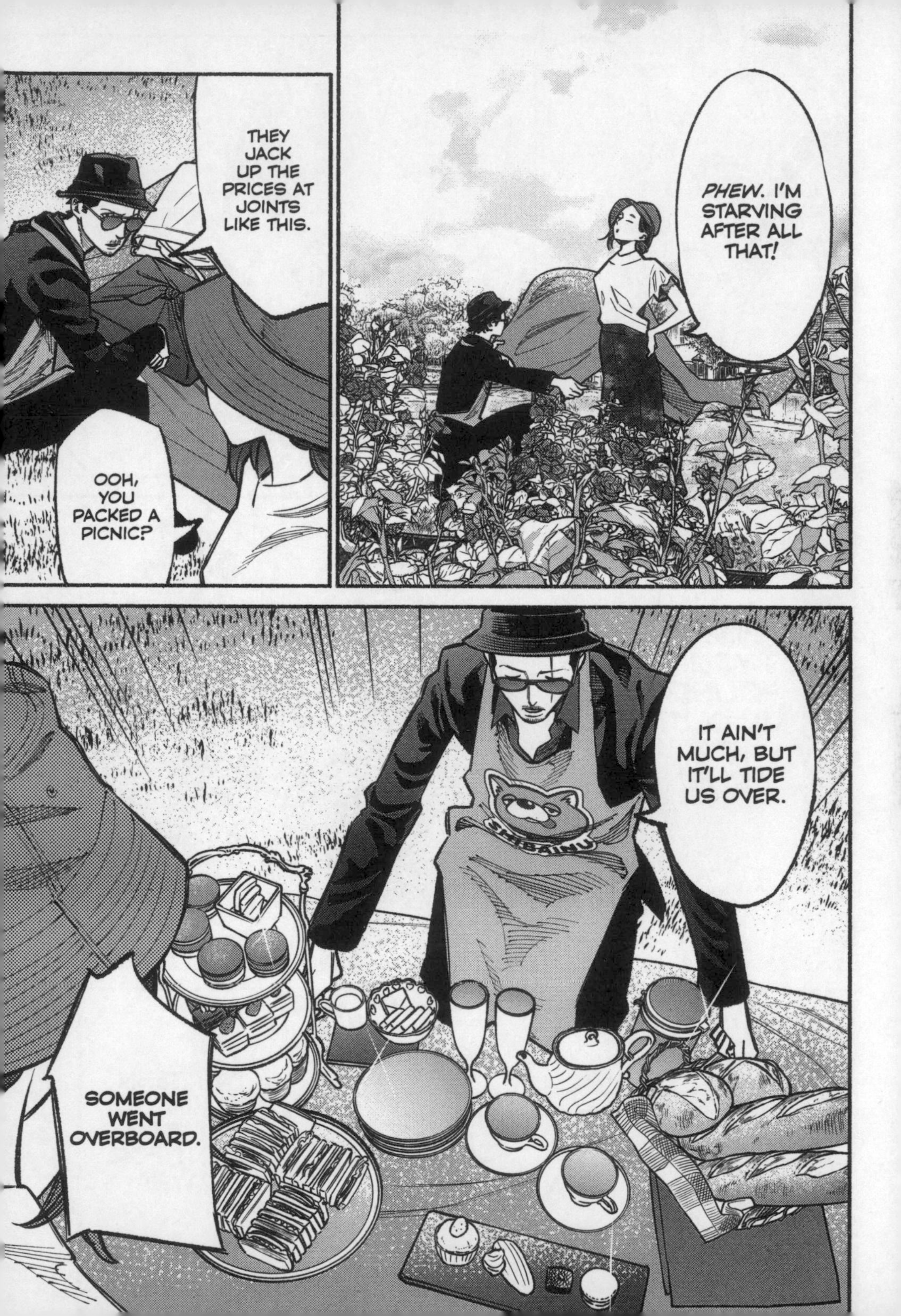
PHEW. I'M STARVING AFTER ALL THAT!
THEY JACK UP THE PRICES AT JOINTS LIKE THIS.
OOH, YOU PACKED A PICNIC?
IT AIN'T MUCH, BUT IT'LL TIDE US OVER.
SOMEONE WENT OVERBOARD.

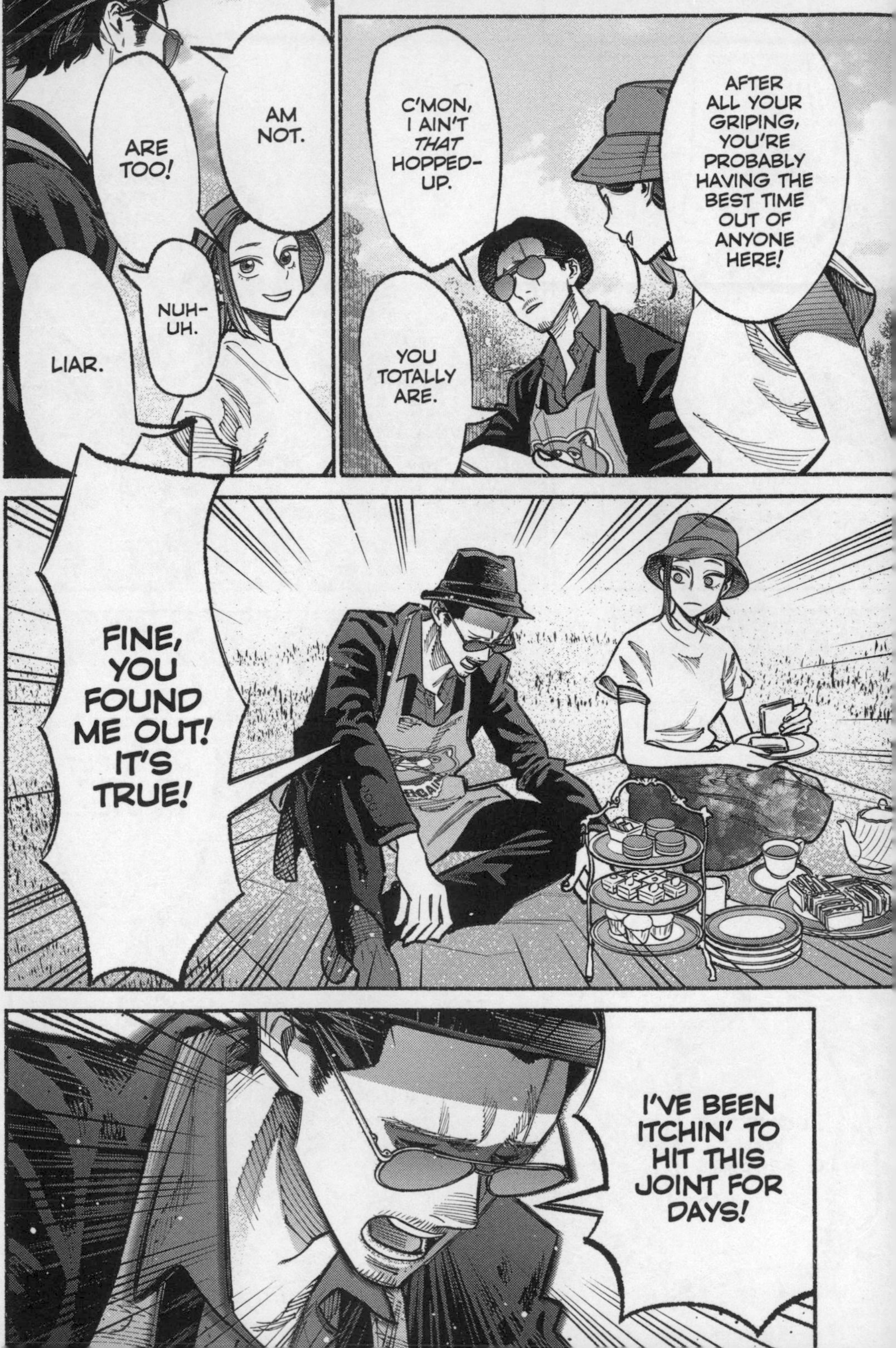
AFTER ALL YOUR GRIPING, YOU'RE PROBABLY HAVING THE BEST TIME OUT OF ANYONE HERE!
C'MON, I AIN'T *THAT* HOPPED-UP.
YOU TOTALLY ARE.
AM NOT.
ARE TOO!
NUH-UH.
LIAR.
FINE, YOU FOUND ME OUT! IT'S TRUE!
I'VE BEEN ITCHIN' TO HIT THIS JOINT FOR DAYS!

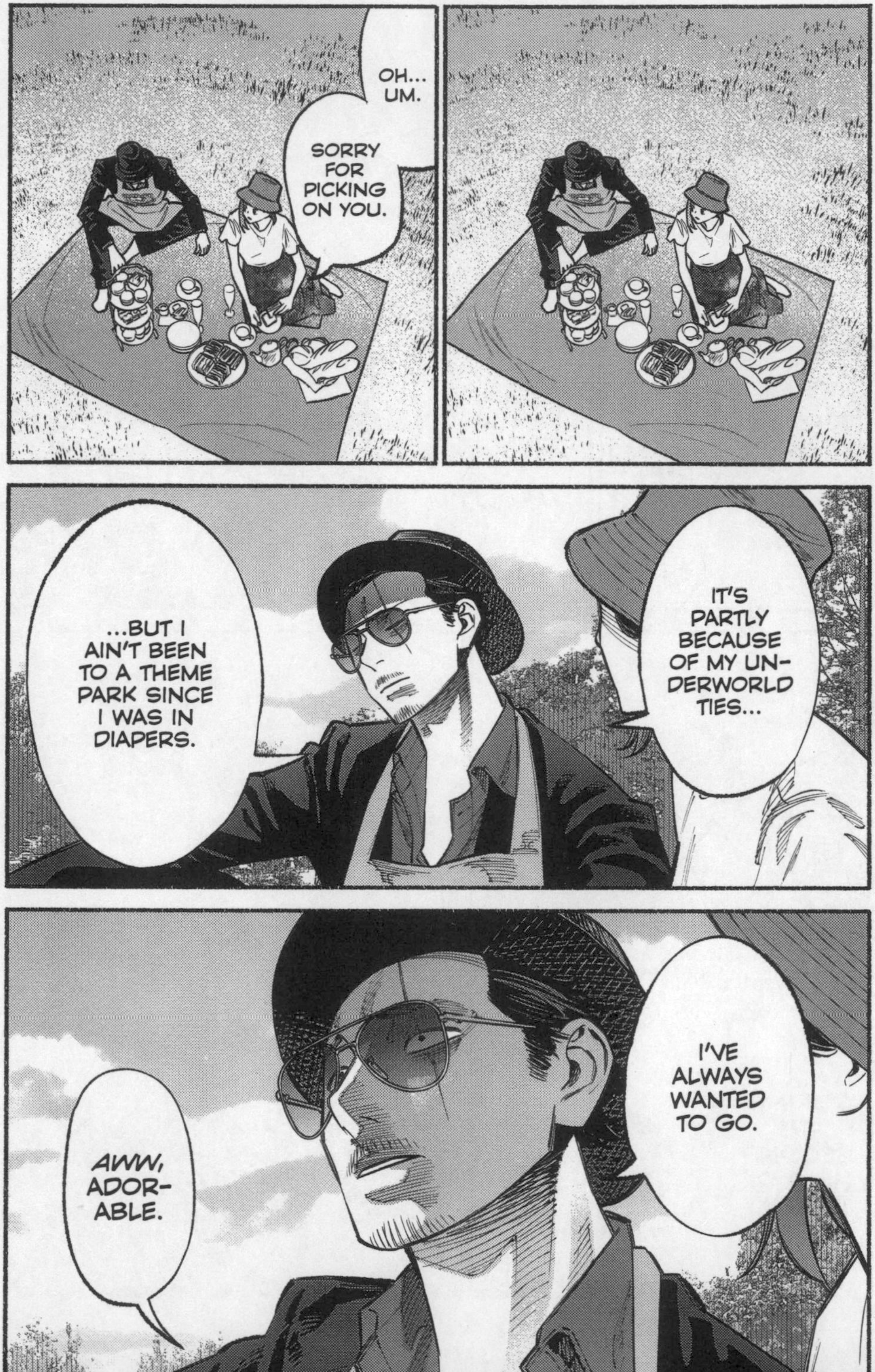
OH... UM.
SORRY FOR PICKING ON YOU.
IT'S PARTLY BECAUSE OF MY UNDERWORLD TIES...
...BUT I AIN'T BEEN TO A THEME PARK SINCE I WAS IN DIAPERS.
I'VE ALWAYS WANTED TO GO.
AWW, ADORABLE.

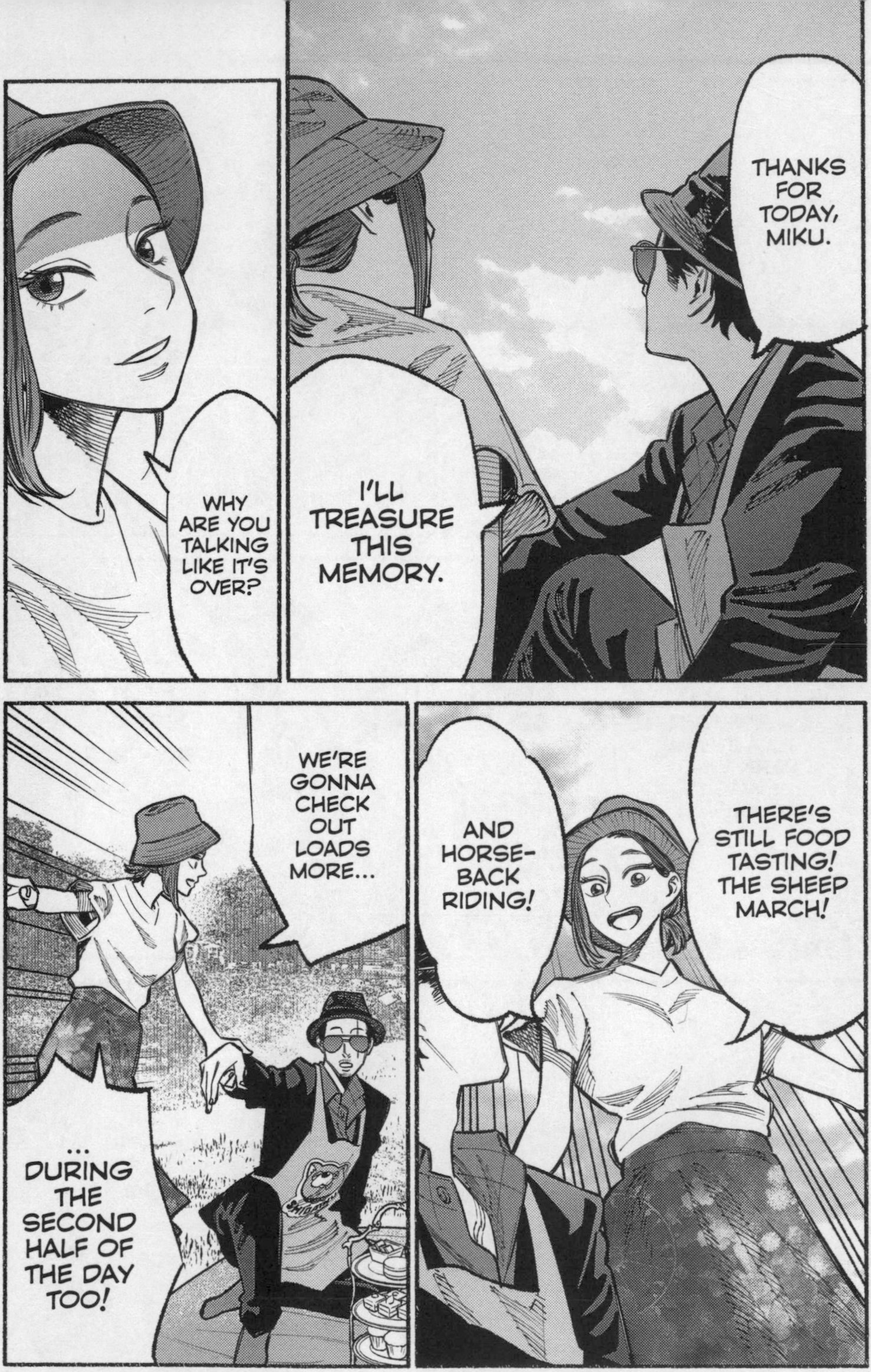
THANKS FOR TODAY, MIKU.
I'LL TREASURE THIS MEMORY.
WHY ARE YOU TALKING LIKE IT'S OVER?
THERE'S STILL FOOD TASTING! THE SHEEP MARCH!
AND HORSE-BACK RIDING!
WE'RE GONNA CHECK OUT LOADS MORE...
...DURING THE SECOND HALF OF THE DAY TOO!

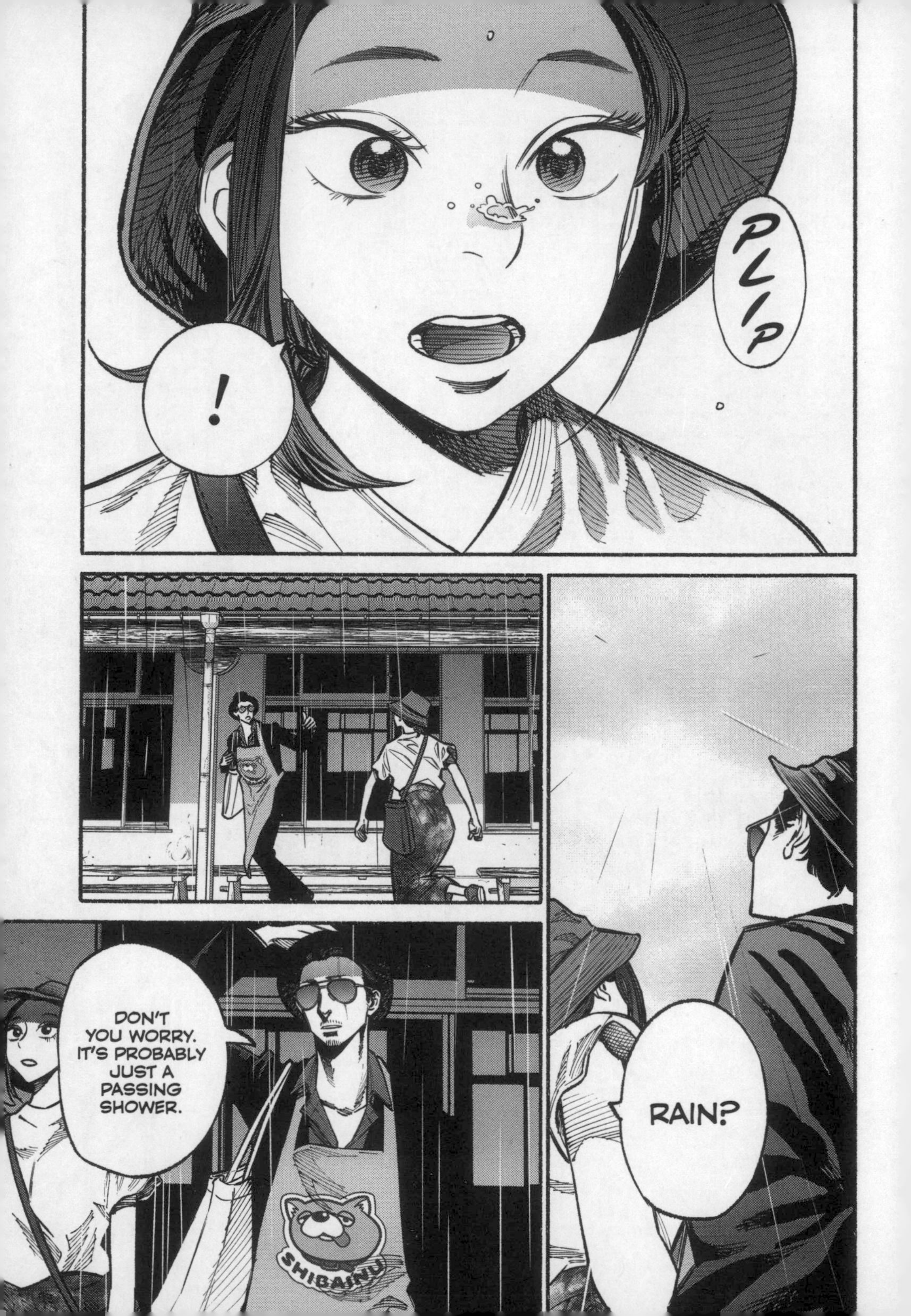
PLIP
!
RAIN?
DON'T YOU WORRY. IT'S PROBABLY JUST A PASSING SHOWER.
SHIBAINU

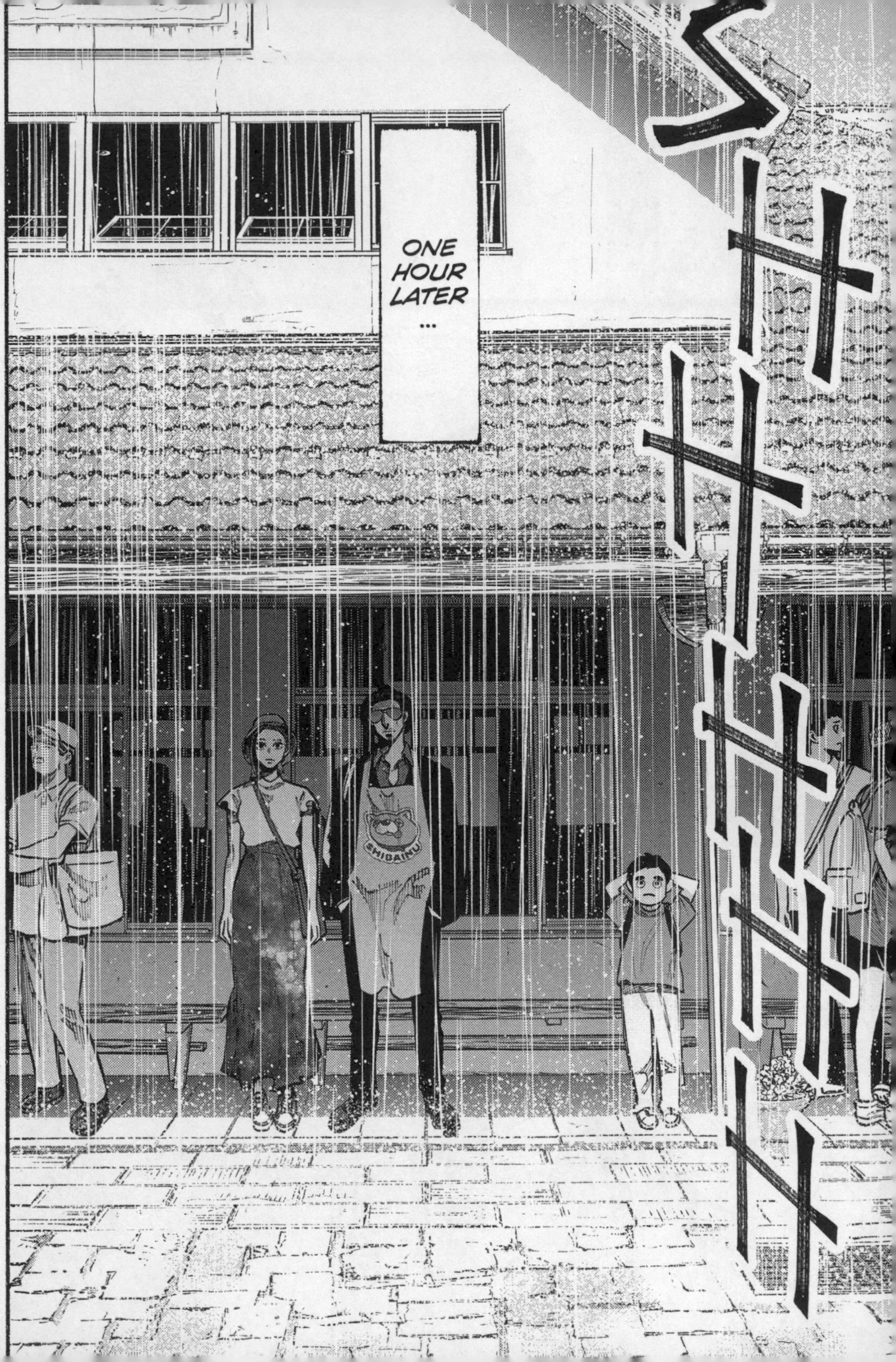
ONE HOUR LATER ...

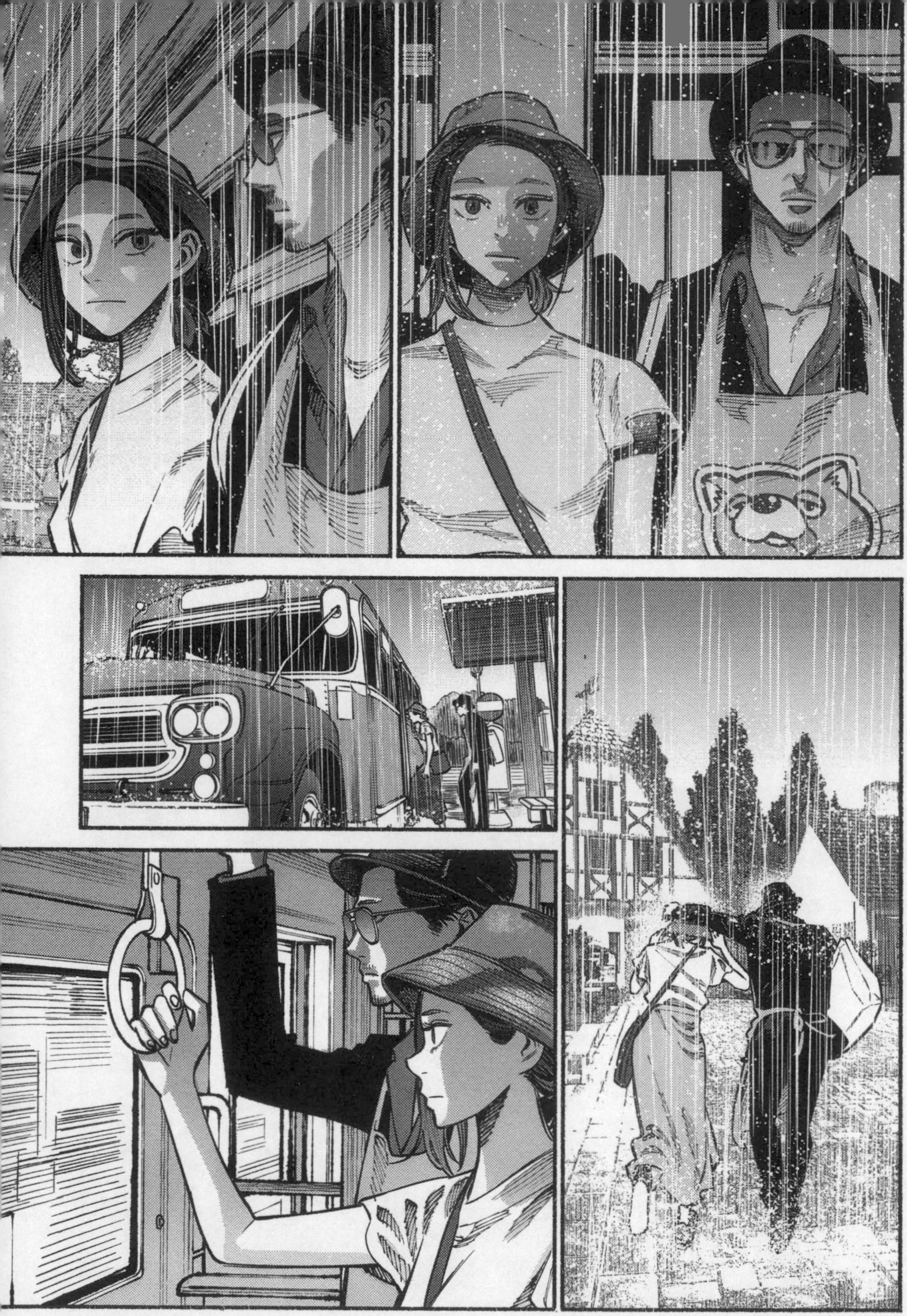

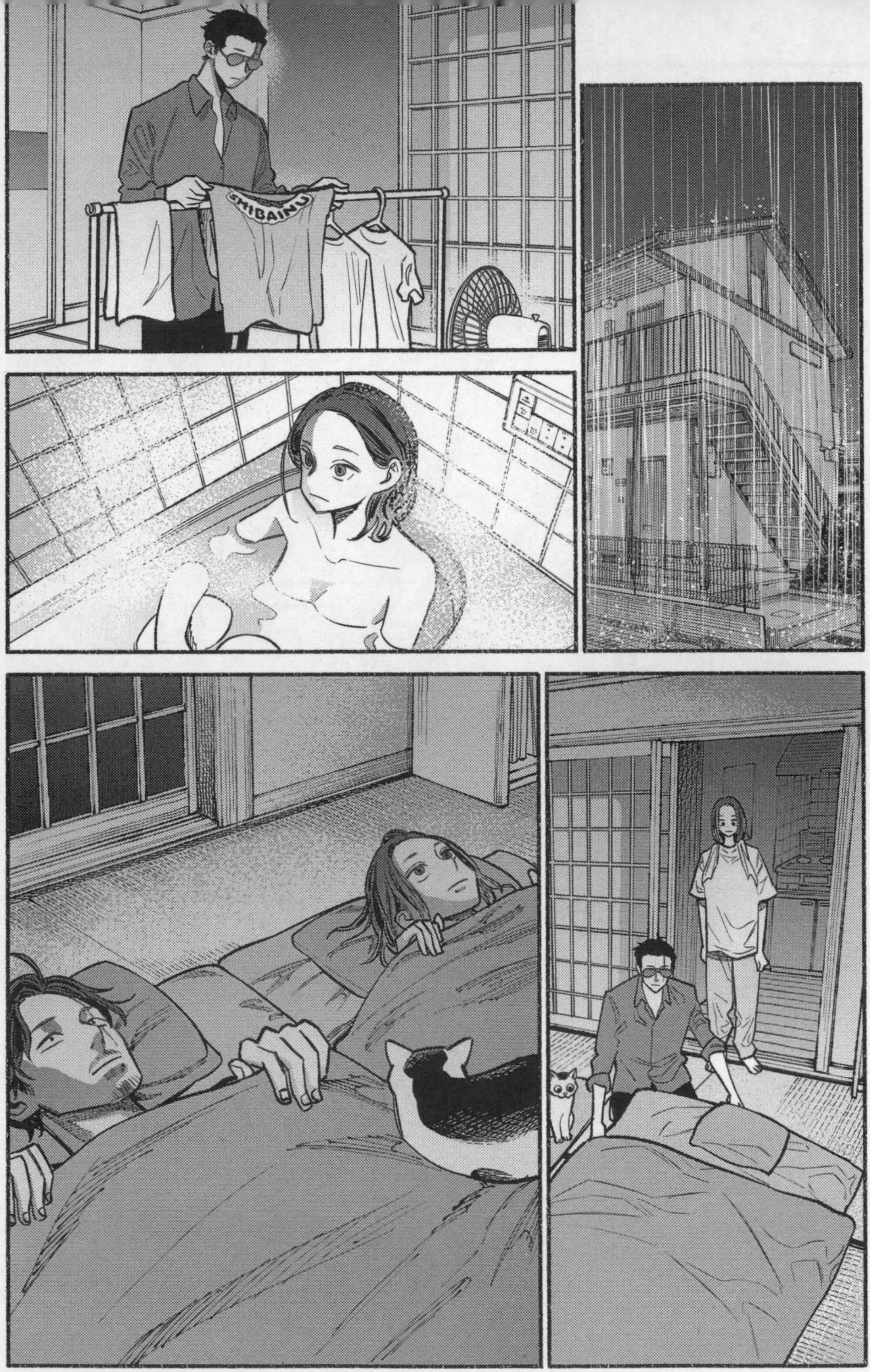
SHIBAINU

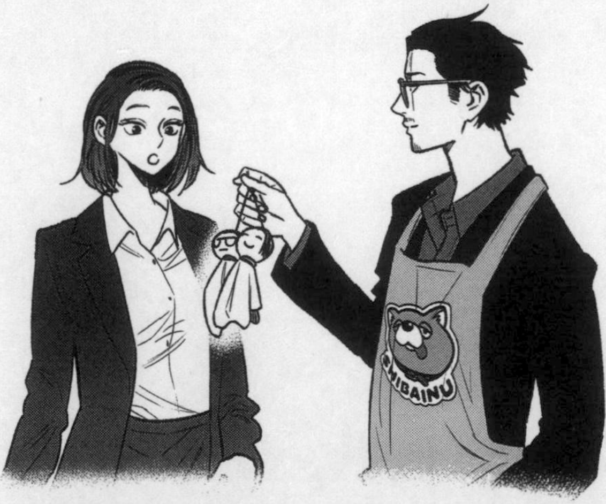
SHIBAINU

*GOOD-WEATHER CHARMS

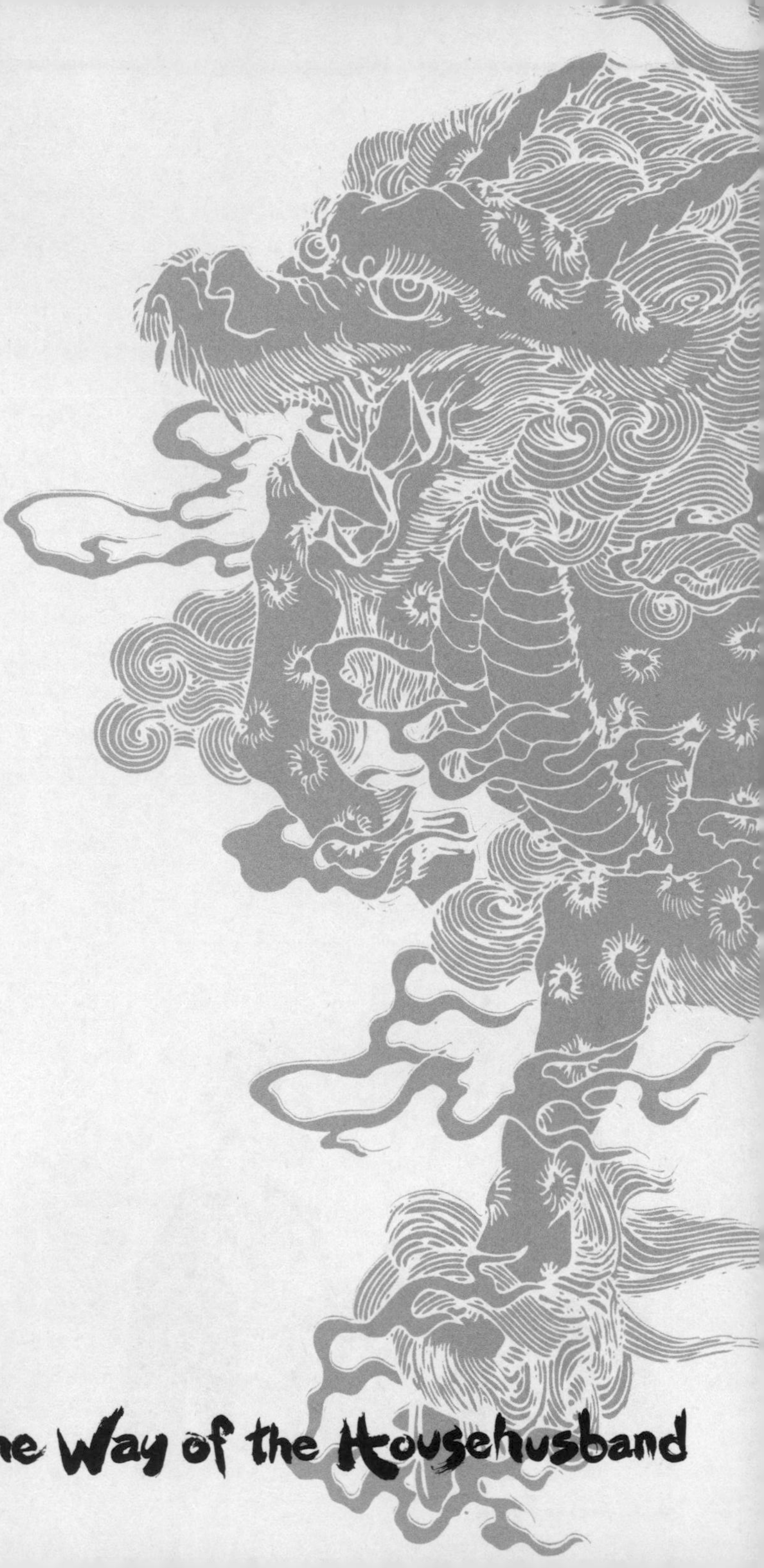

The Way of the Househusband

CHAPTER 31

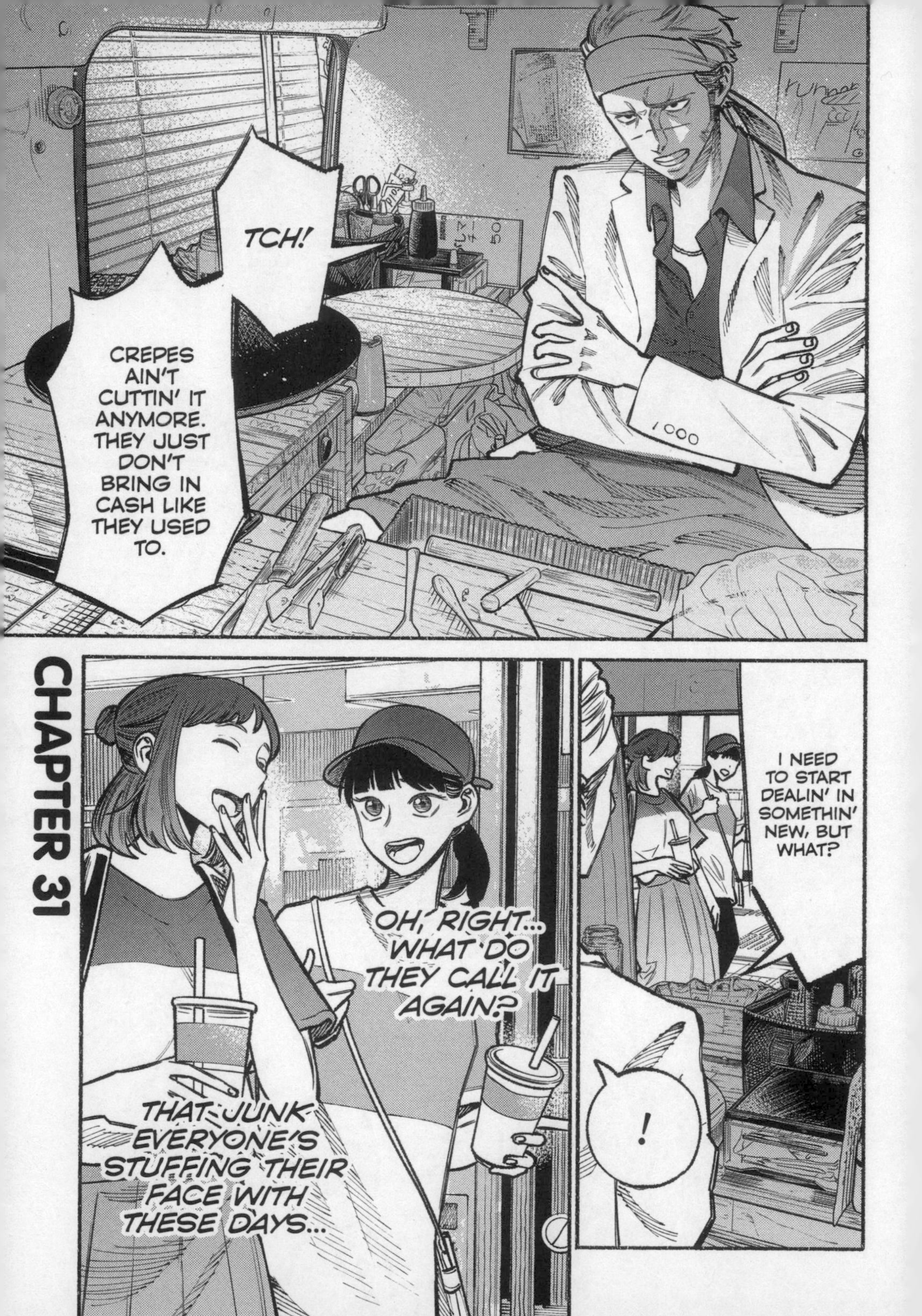
TCH!
CREPES AIN'T CUTTIN' IT ANYMORE. THEY JUST DON'T BRING IN CASH LIKE THEY USED TO.
I NEED TO START DEALIN' IN SOMETHIN' NEW, BUT WHAT?
!
OH, RIGHT... WHAT DO THEY CALL IT AGAIN?
THAT JUNK EVERYONE'S STUFFING THEIR FACE WITH THESE DAYS...

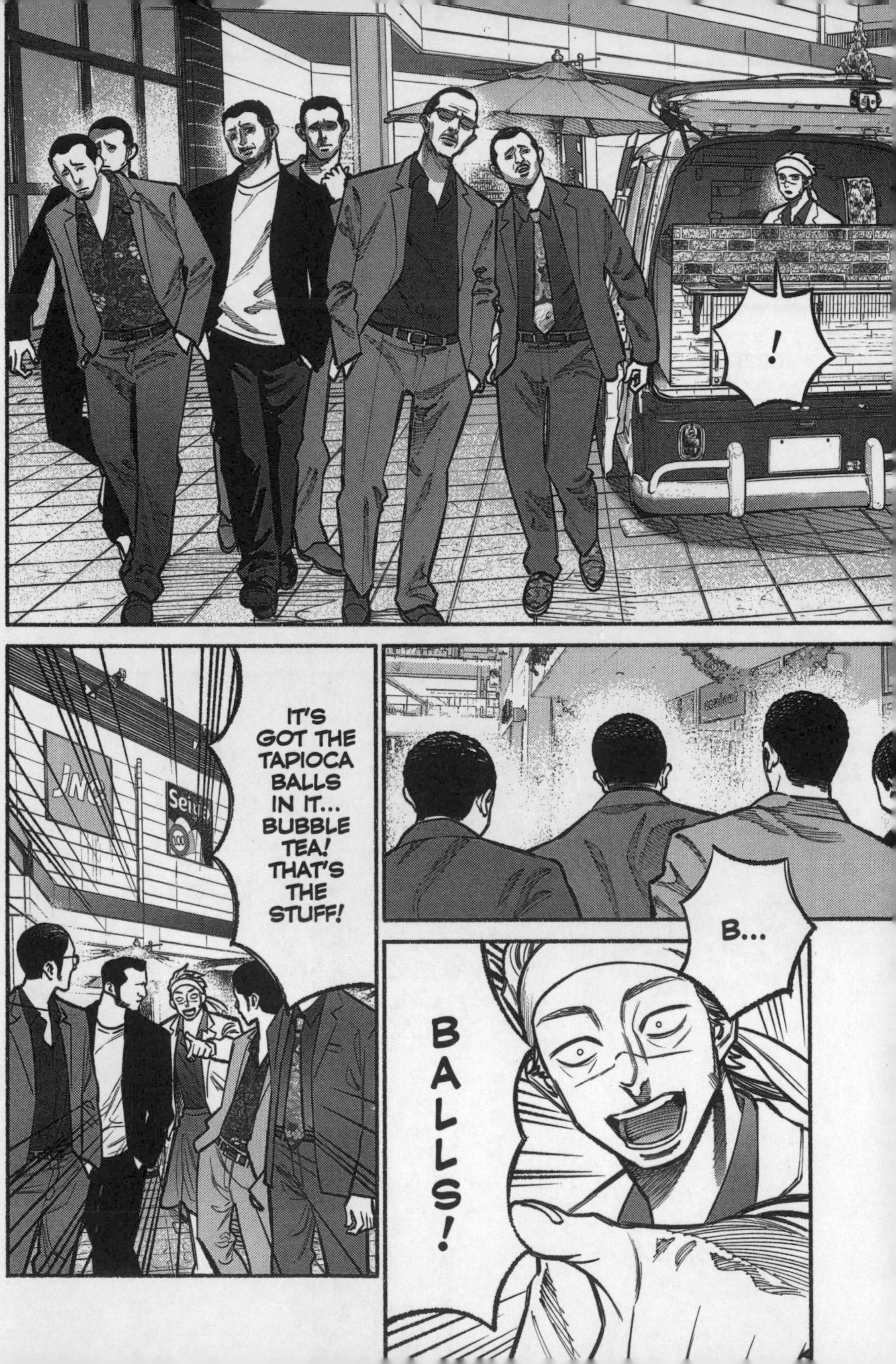
!
B...
BALLS!
IT'S GOT THE TAPIOCA BALLS IN IT... BUBBLE TEA! THAT'S THE STUFF!

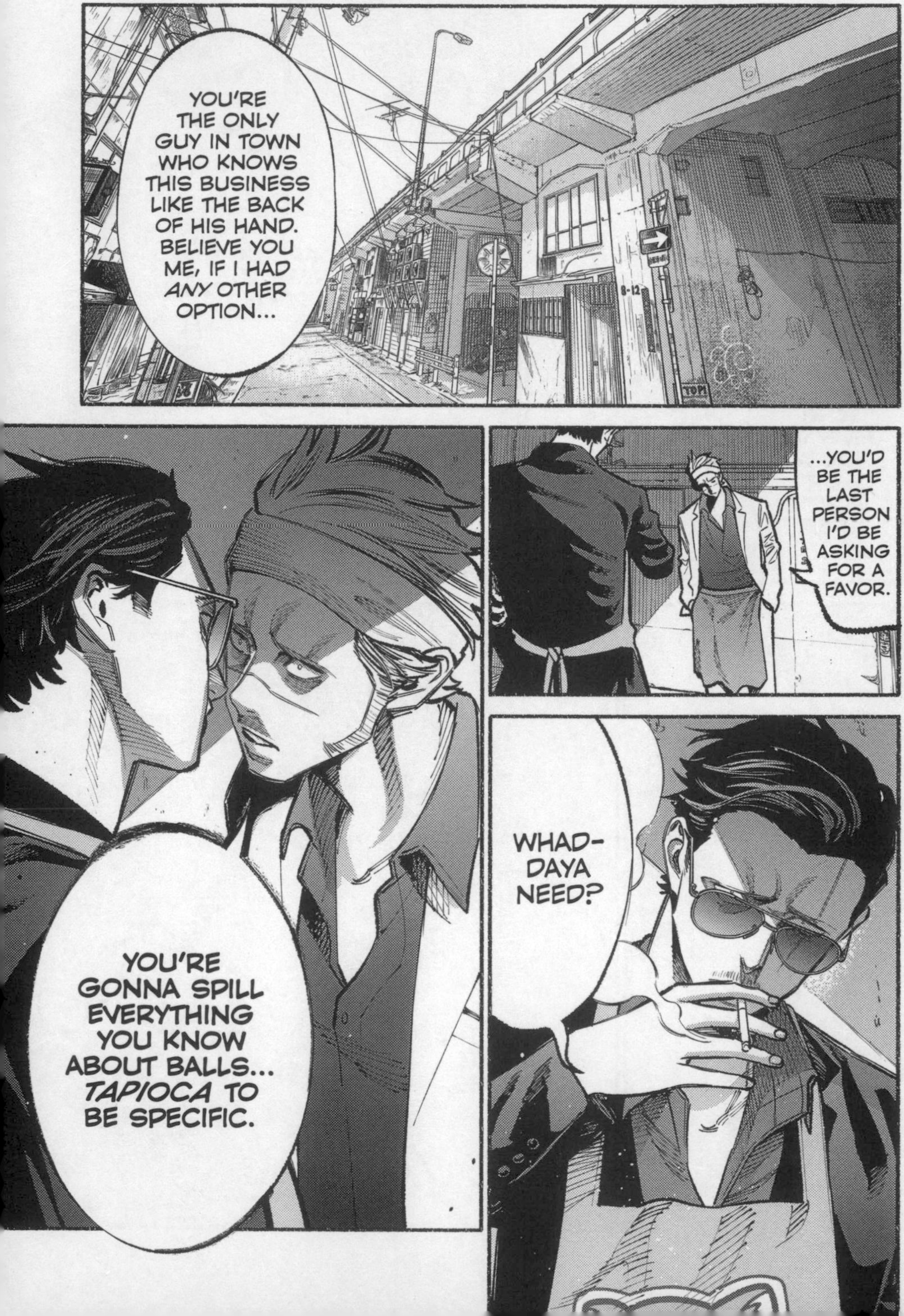
YOU'RE THE ONLY GUY IN TOWN WHO KNOWS THIS BUSINESS LIKE THE BACK OF HIS HAND. BELIEVE YOU ME, IF I HAD *ANY* OTHER OPTION...
...YOU'D BE THE LAST PERSON I'D BE ASKING FOR A FAVOR.
WHAD-DAYA NEED?
YOU'RE GONNA SPILL EVERYTHING YOU KNOW ABOUT BALLS... *TAPIOCA* TO BE SPECIFIC.

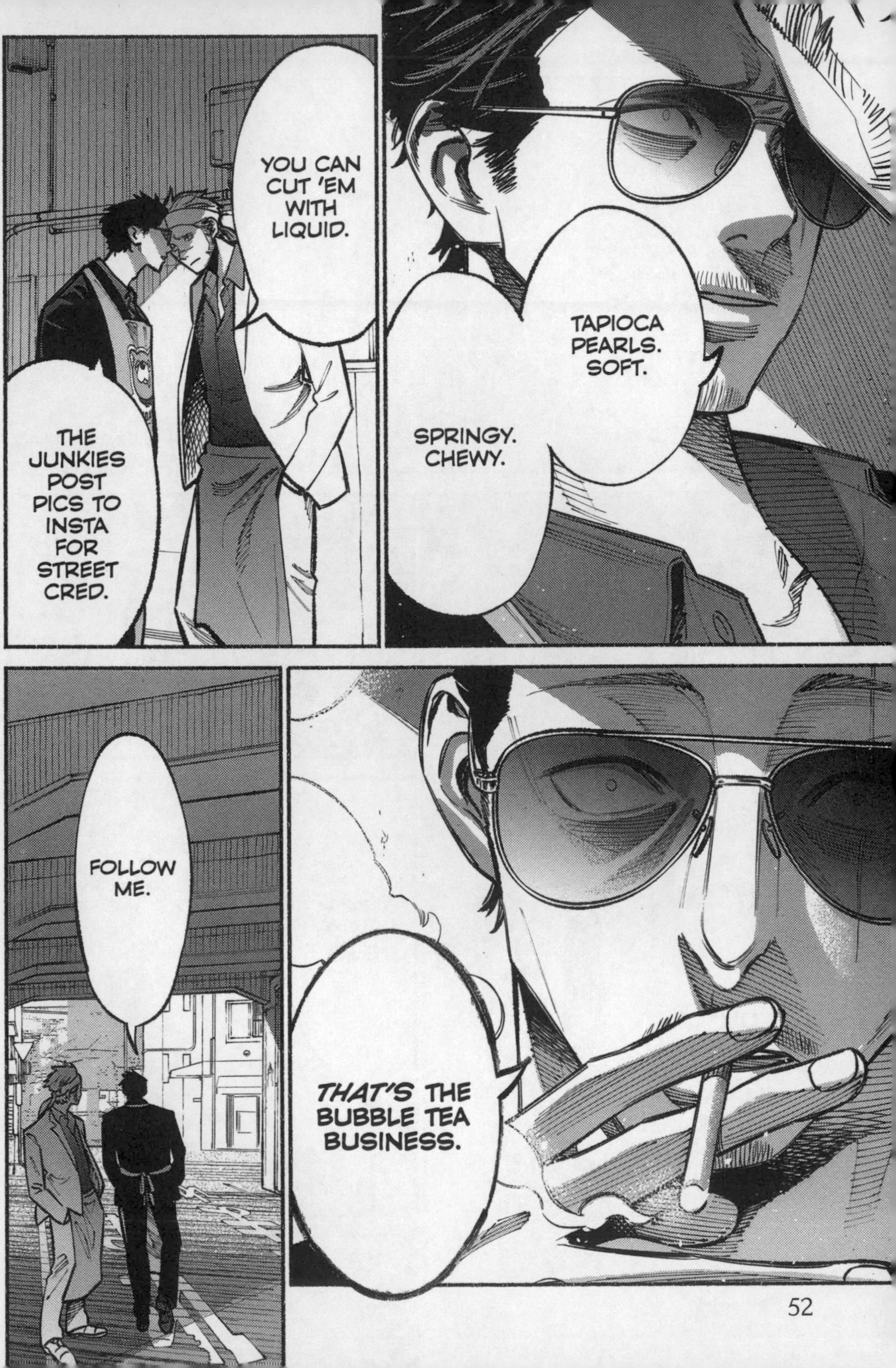
TAPIOCA PEARLS. SOFT.
SPRINGY. CHEWY.
YOU CAN CUT 'EM WITH LIQUID.
THE JUNKIES POST PICS TO INSTA FOR STREET CRED.
THAT'S THE BUBBLE TEA BUSINESS.
FOLLOW ME.

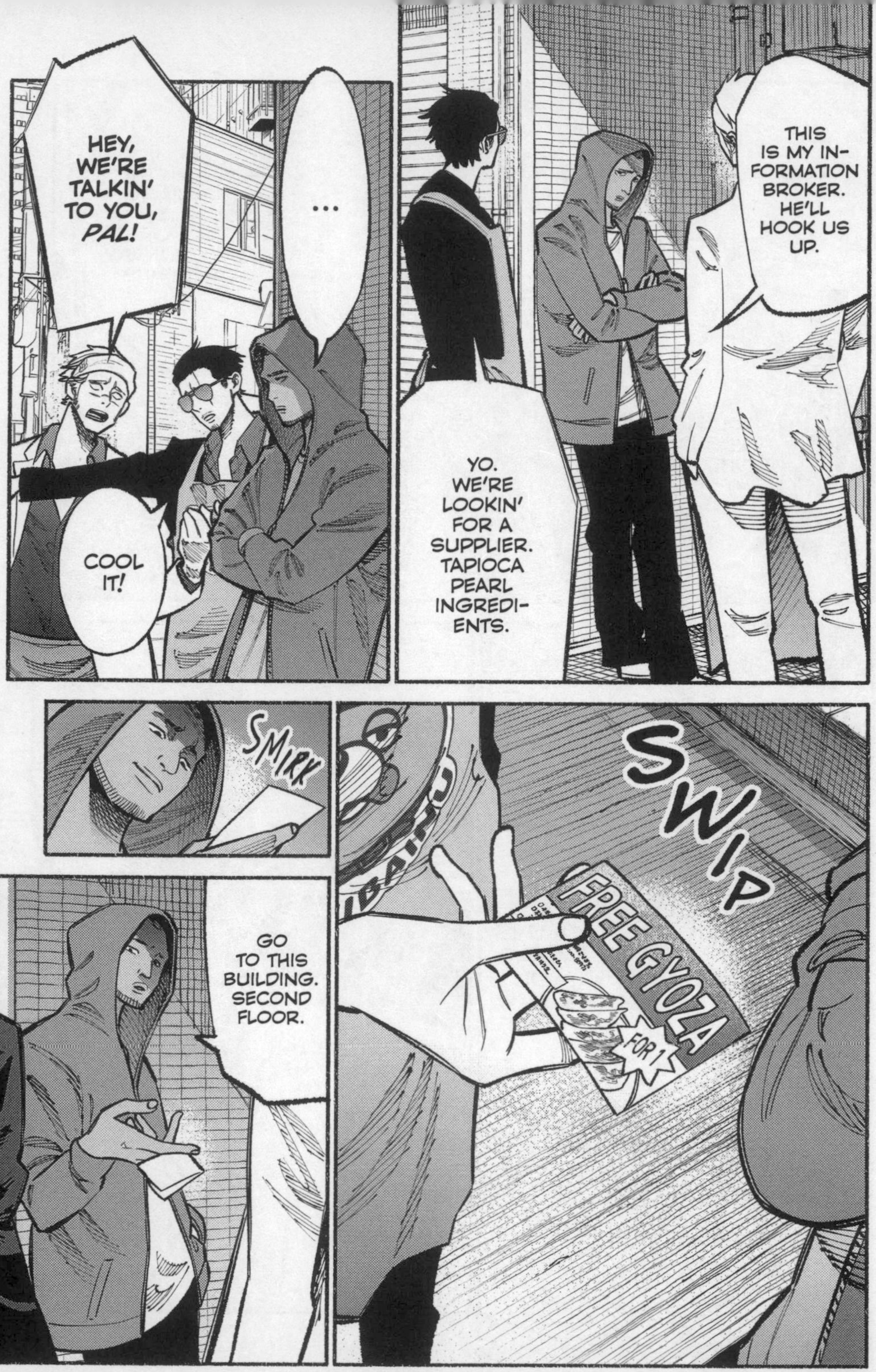
THIS IS MY IN-FORMATION BROKER. HE'LL HOOK US UP.
YO. WE'RE LOOKIN' FOR A SUPPLIER. TAPIOCA PEARL INGREDI-ENTS.
HEY, WE'RE TALKIN' TO YOU, *PAL!*
...
COOL IT!
SWIP
FREE GYOZA
FOR 1
SMIRK
GO TO THIS BUILDING. SECOND FLOOR.

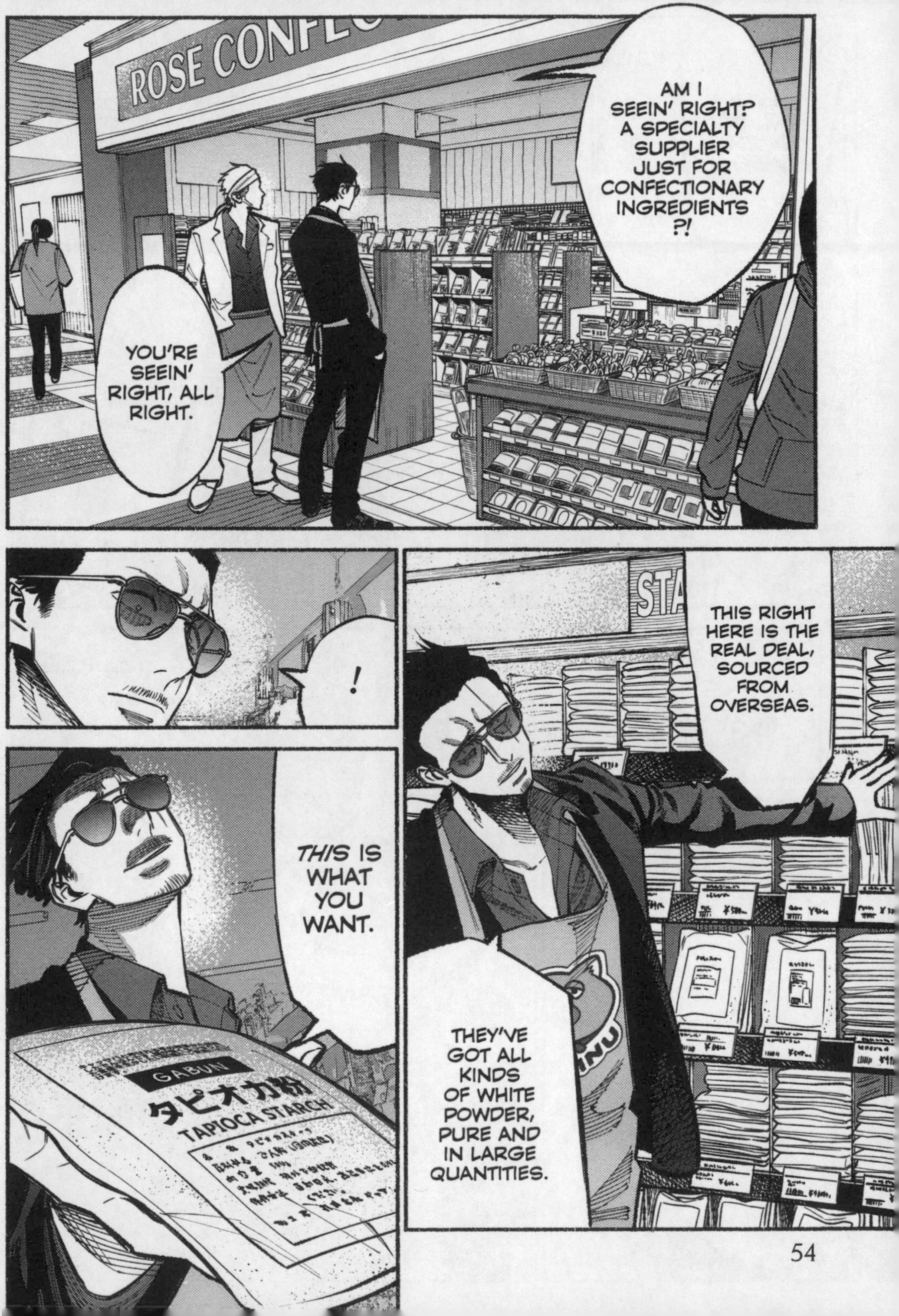
AM I SEEIN' RIGHT? A SPECIALTY SUPPLIER JUST FOR CONFECTIONARY INGREDIENTS ?!
YOU'RE SEEIN' RIGHT, ALL RIGHT.
THIS RIGHT HERE IS THE REAL DEAL, SOURCED FROM OVERSEAS.
THEY'VE GOT ALL KINDS OF WHITE POWDER, PURE AND IN LARGE QUANTITIES.
!
THIS IS WHAT YOU WANT.
GABUN
タピオカ粉
TAPIOCA STARCH

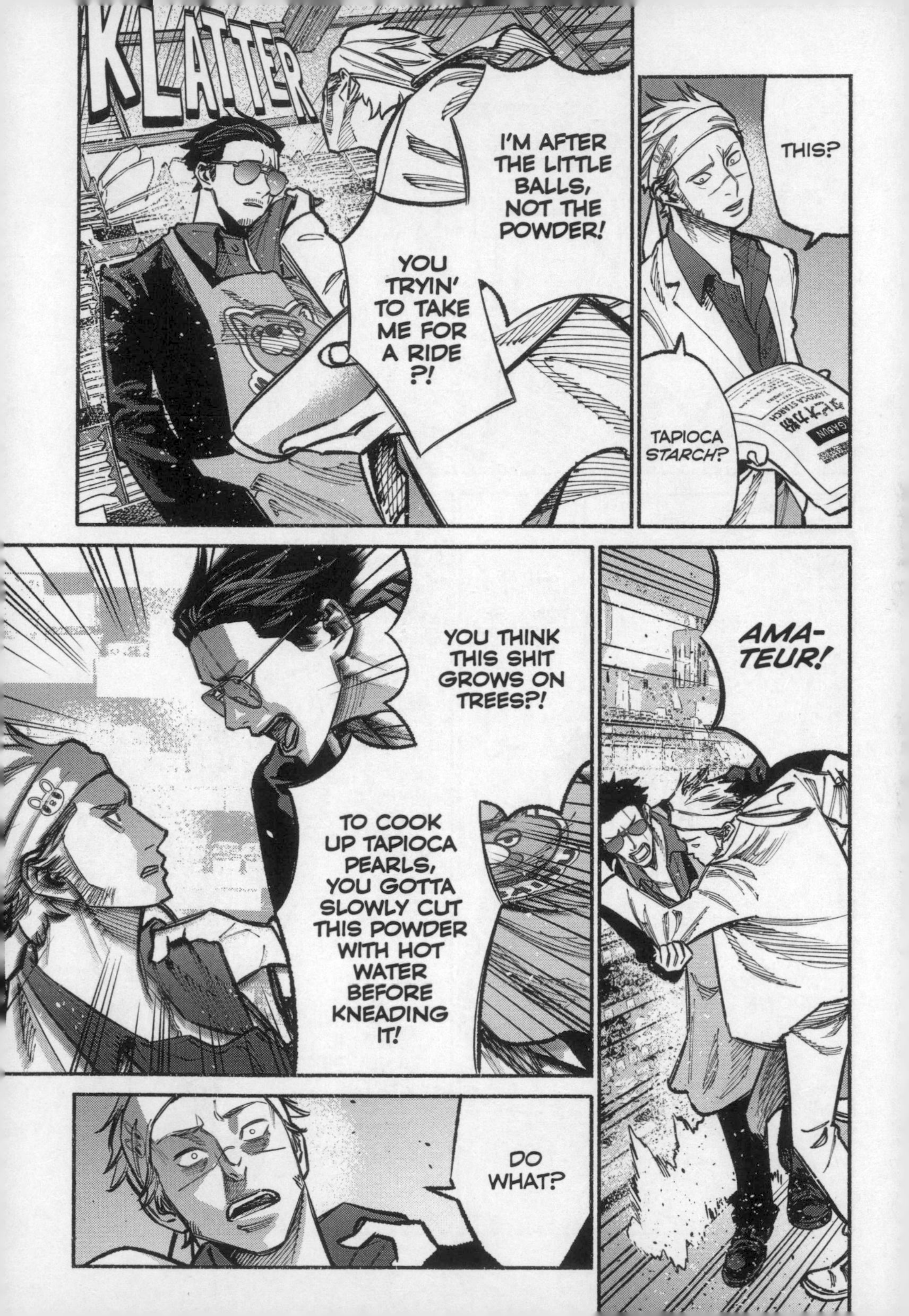
THIS?
TAPIOCA STARCH?
KLATTER
I'M AFTER THE LITTLE BALLS, NOT THE POWDER!
YOU TRYIN' TO TAKE ME FOR A RIDE ?!
AMA-TEUR!
YOU THINK THIS SHIT GROWS ON TREES?!
TO COOK UP TAPIOCA PEARLS, YOU GOTTA SLOWLY CUT THIS POWDER WITH HOT WATER BEFORE KNEADING IT!
DO WHAT?

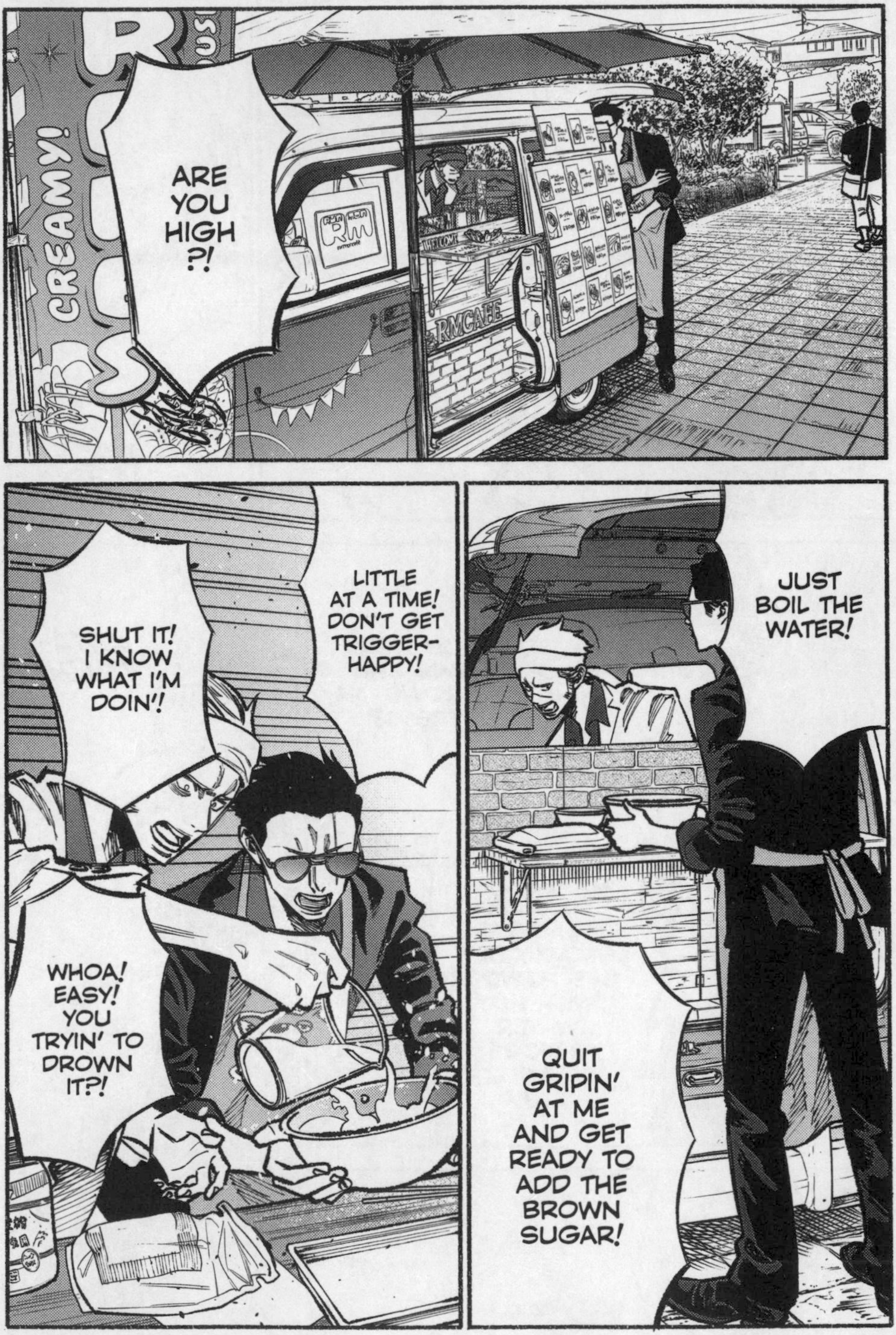
CREAMY!
ARE YOU HIGH ?!
RMCAFE
JUST BOIL THE WATER!
QUIT GRIPIN' AT ME AND GET READY TO ADD THE BROWN SUGAR!
LITTLE AT A TIME! DON'T GET TRIGGER-HAPPY!
SHUT IT! I KNOW WHAT I'M DOIN'!
WHOA! EASY! YOU TRYIN' TO DROWN IT?!

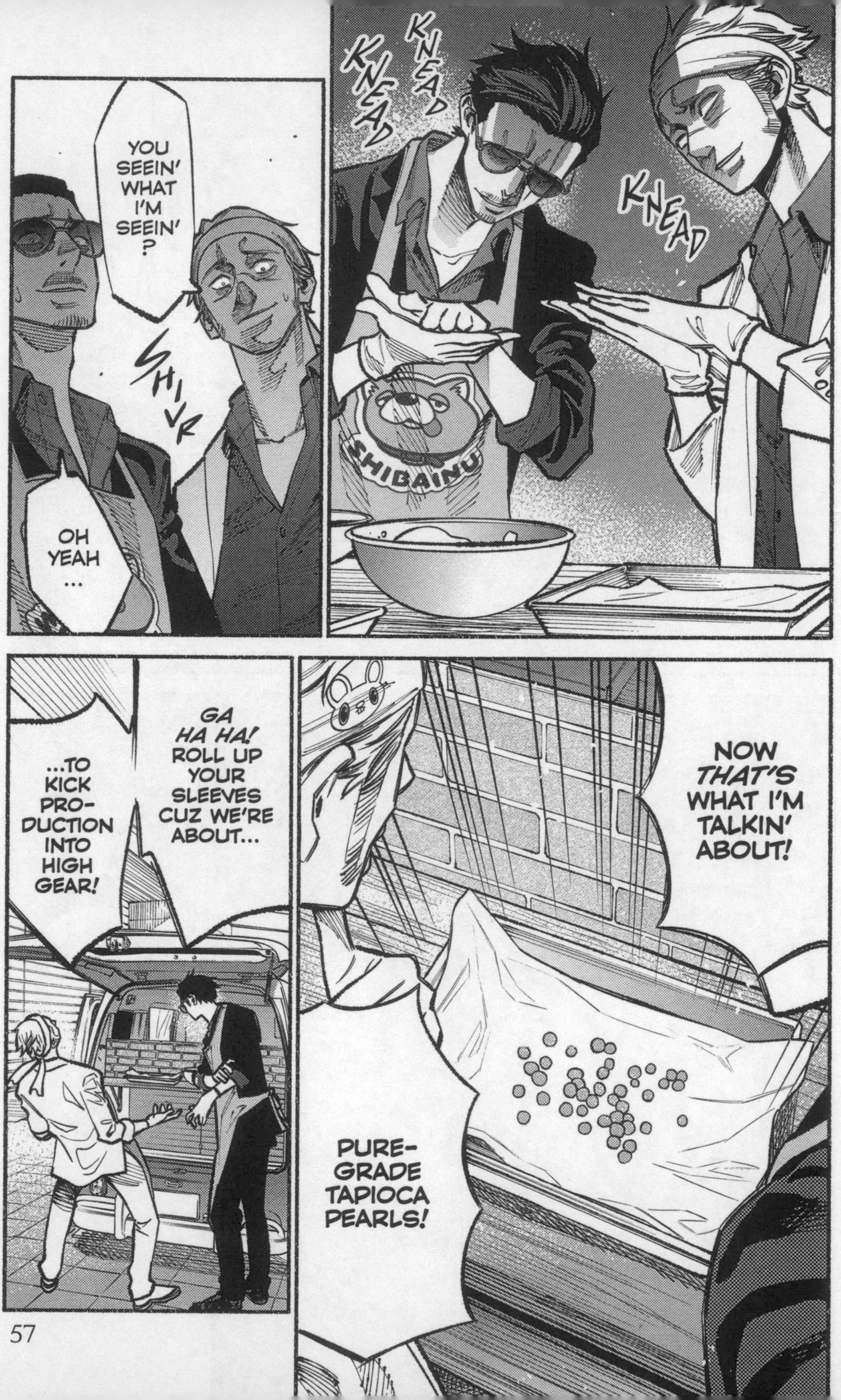
KNEAD KNEAD
KNEAD
YOU SEEIN' WHAT I'M SEEIN'?
SHIVR
OH YEAH...
SHIBAINU
NOW *THAT'S* WHAT I'M TALKIN' ABOUT!
PURE-GRADE TAPIOCA PEARLS!
GA HA HA! ROLL UP YOUR SLEEVES CUZ WE'RE ABOUT...
...TO KICK PRO-DUCTION INTO HIGH GEAR!

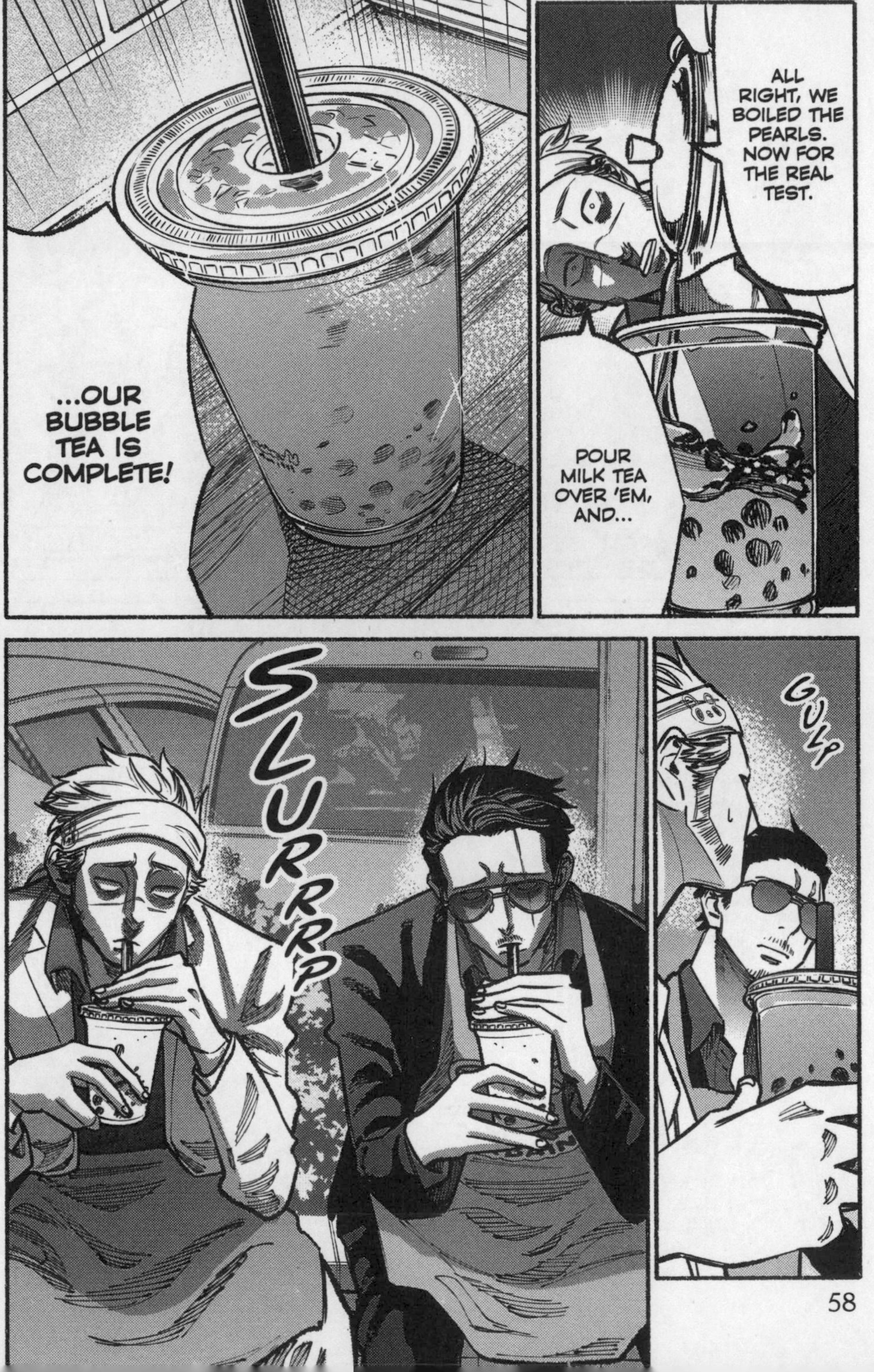
ALL RIGHT, WE BOILED THE PEARLS. NOW FOR THE REAL TEST.
POUR MILK TEA OVER 'EM, AND...
...OUR BUBBLE TEA IS COMPLETE!
GULP
SLURRRP

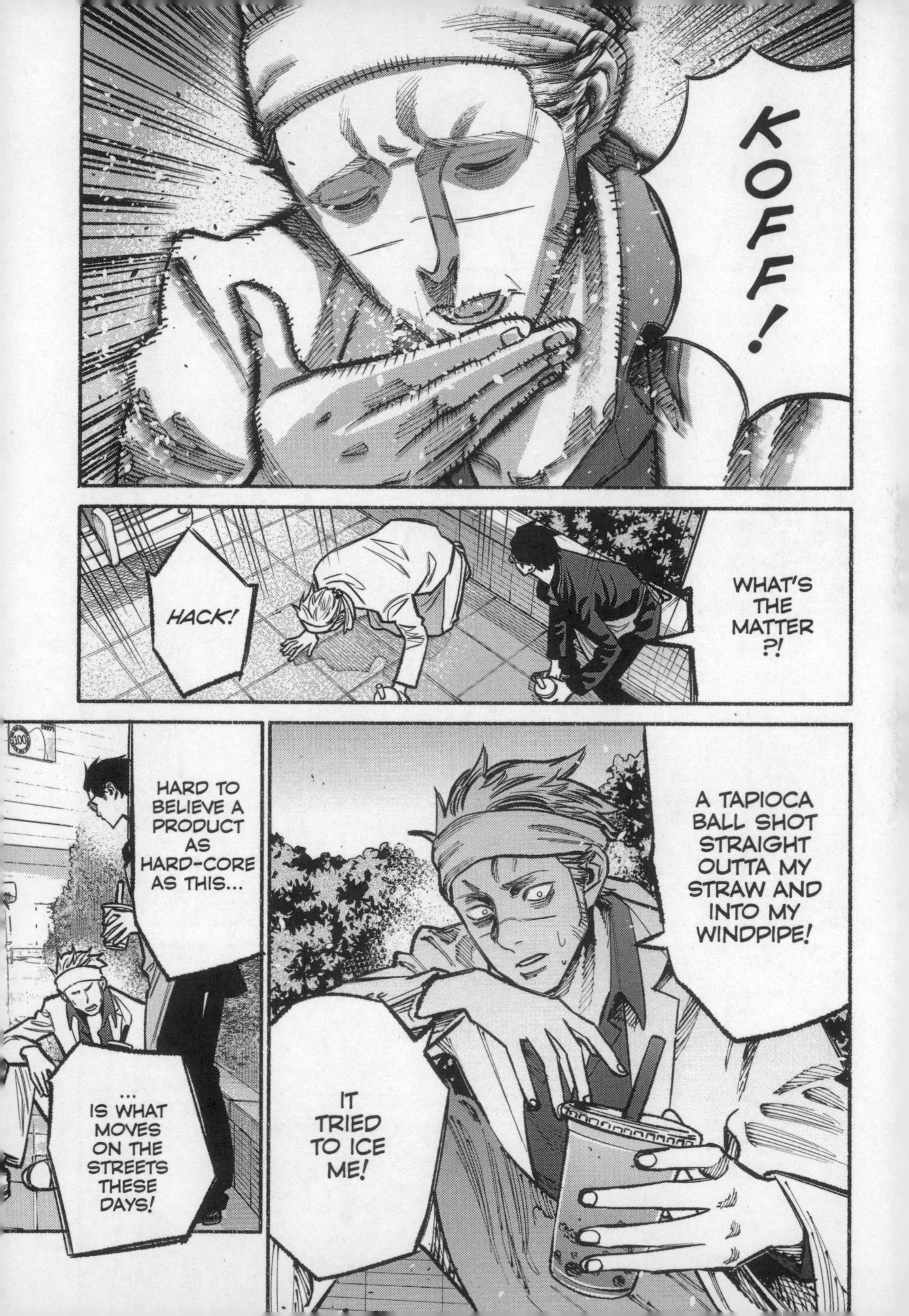
KOFF!
WHAT'S THE MATTER?!
HACK!
A TAPIOCA BALL SHOT STRAIGHT OUTTA MY STRAW AND INTO MY WINDPIPE!
IT TRIED TO ICE ME!
HARD TO BELIEVE A PRODUCT AS HARD-CORE AS THIS...
...IS WHAT MOVES ON THE STREETS THESE DAYS!

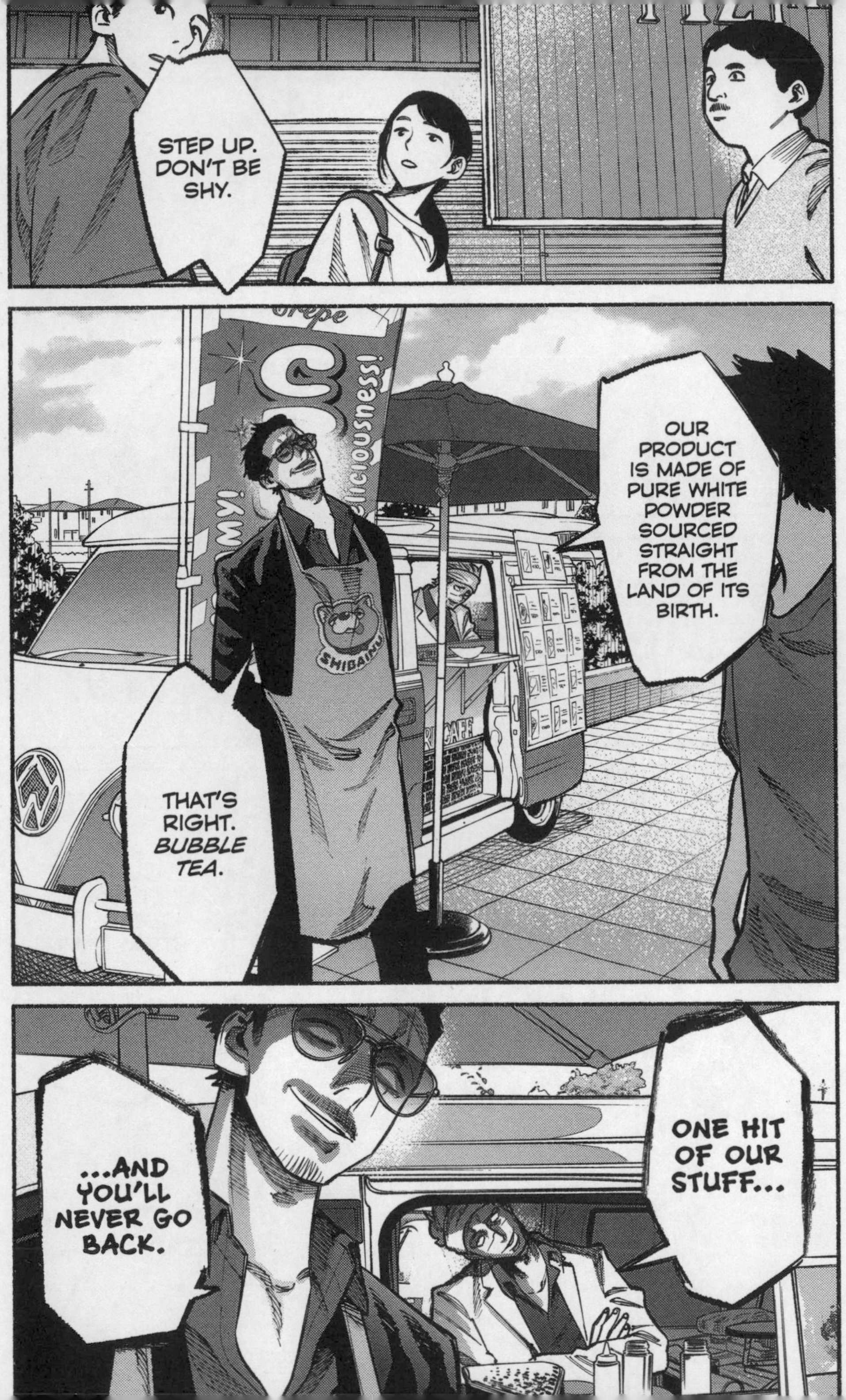
STEP UP. DON'T BE SHY.
OUR PRODUCT IS MADE OF PURE WHITE POWDER SOURCED STRAIGHT FROM THE LAND OF ITS BIRTH.
SHIBAINU
THAT'S RIGHT. *BUBBLE TEA.*
ONE HIT OF OUR STUFF...
...AND YOU'LL NEVER GO BACK.

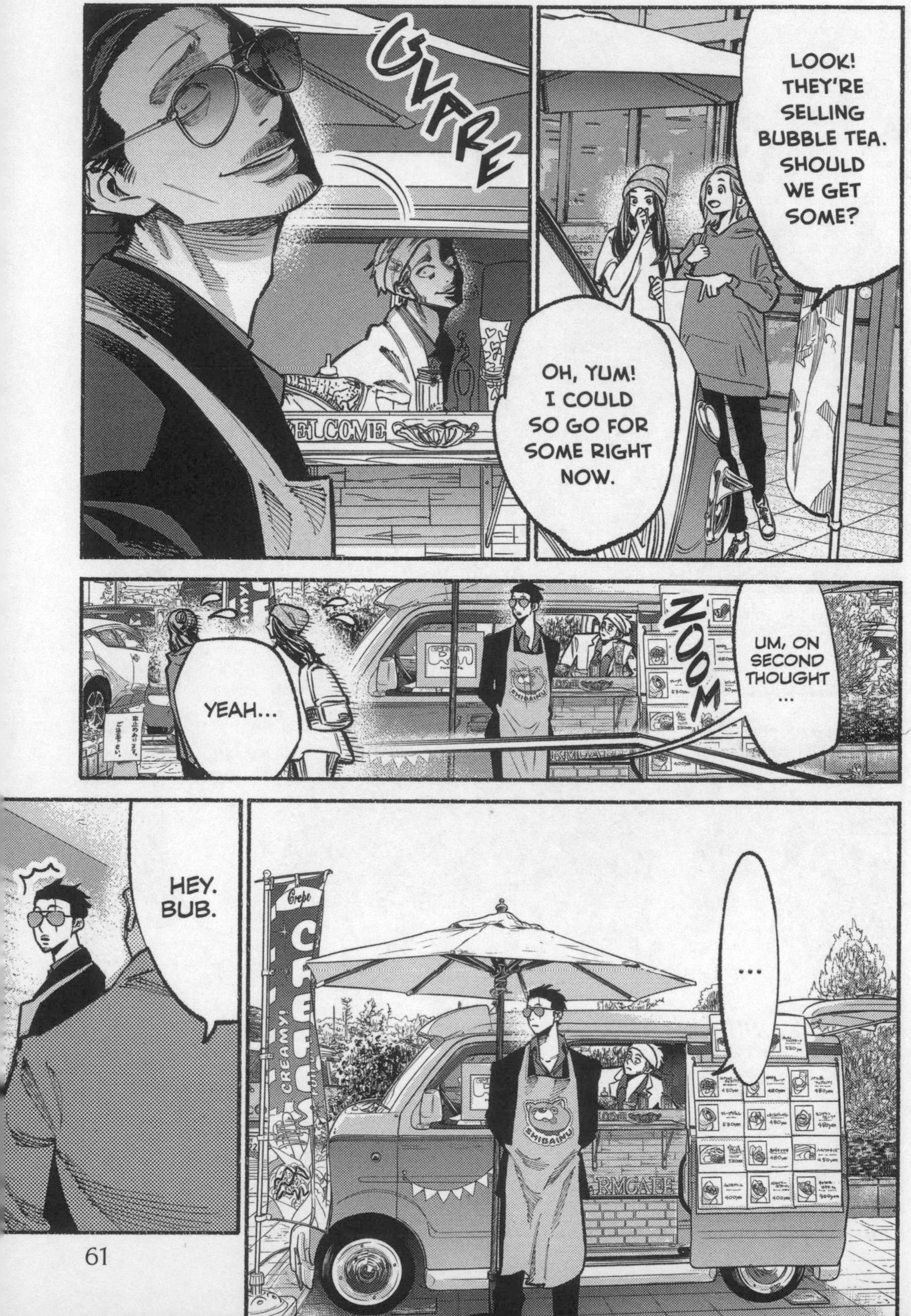
LOOK! THEY'RE SELLING BUBBLE TEA. SHOULD WE GET SOME?
OH, YUM! I COULD SO GO FOR SOME RIGHT NOW.
GLARE
UM, ON SECOND THOUGHT ...
ZOOM
YEAH...
...
HEY. BUB.

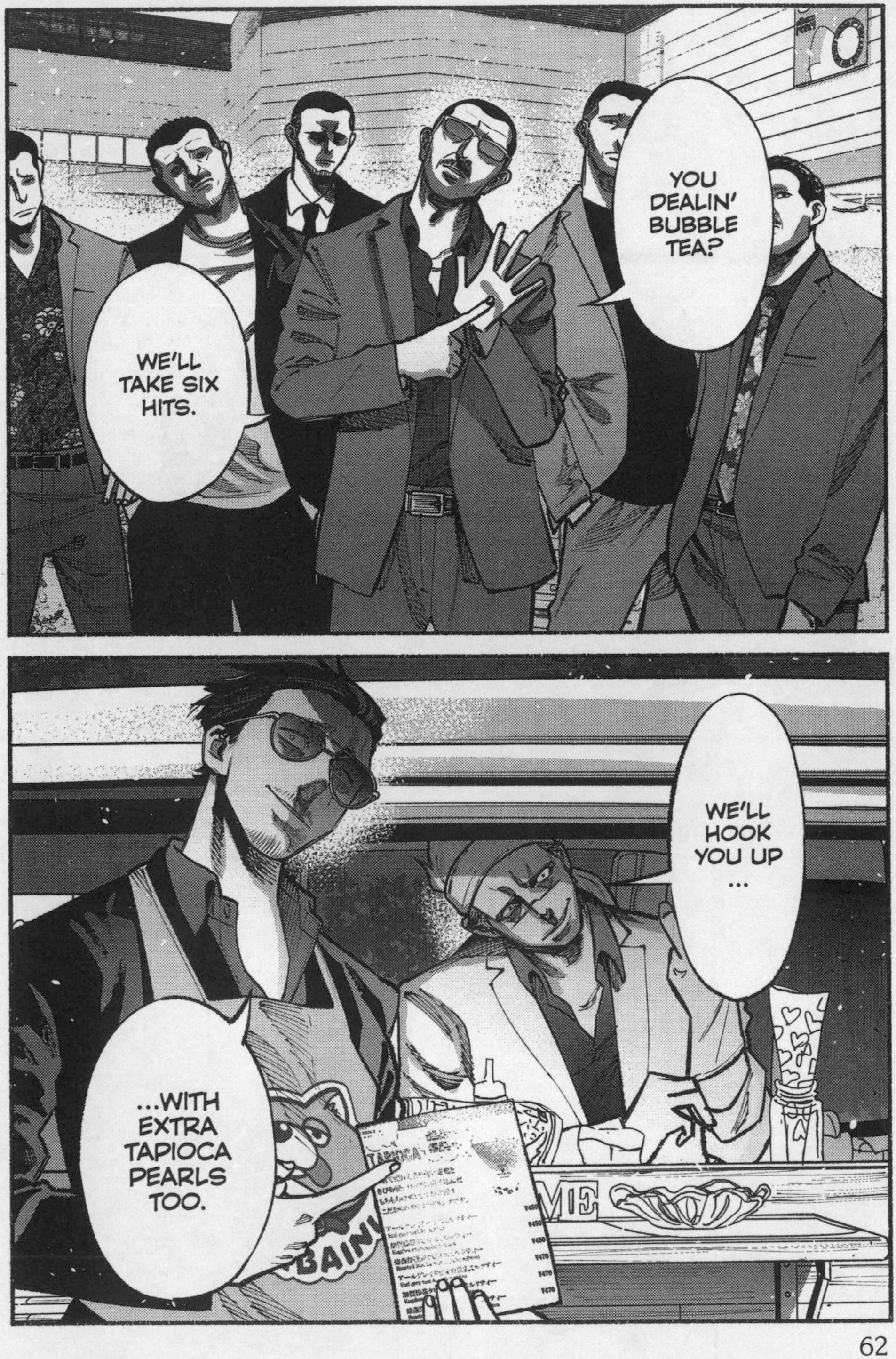
YOU DEALIN' BUBBLE TEA?
WE'LL TAKE SIX HITS.
WE'LL HOOK YOU UP ...
...WITH EXTRA TAPIOCA PEARLS TOO.

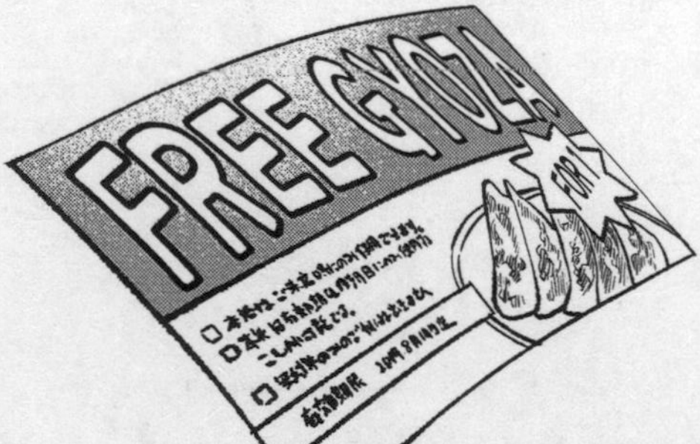
FREE GYOZA
FOR 1

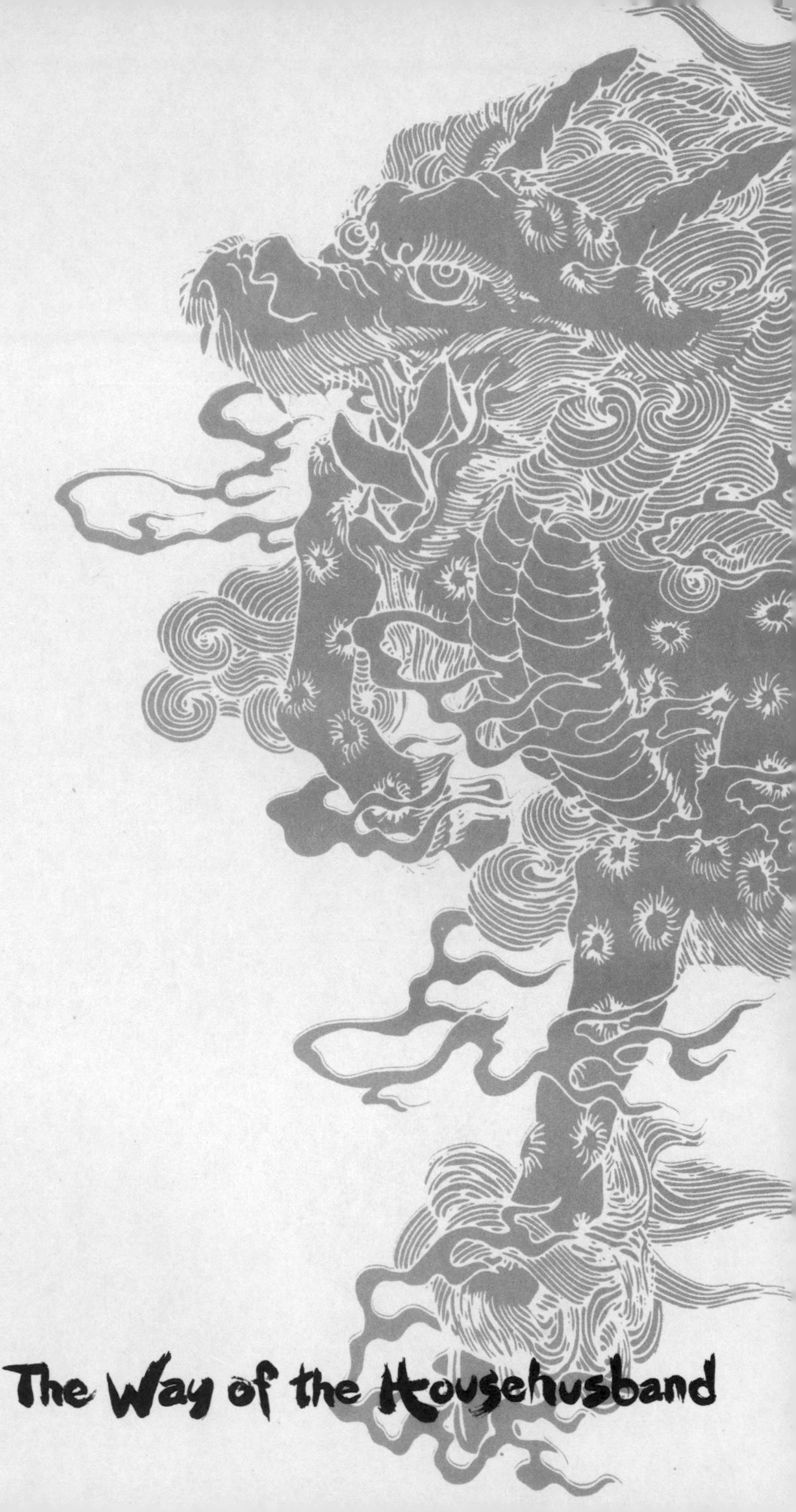
The Way of the Househusband

CHAPTER 32

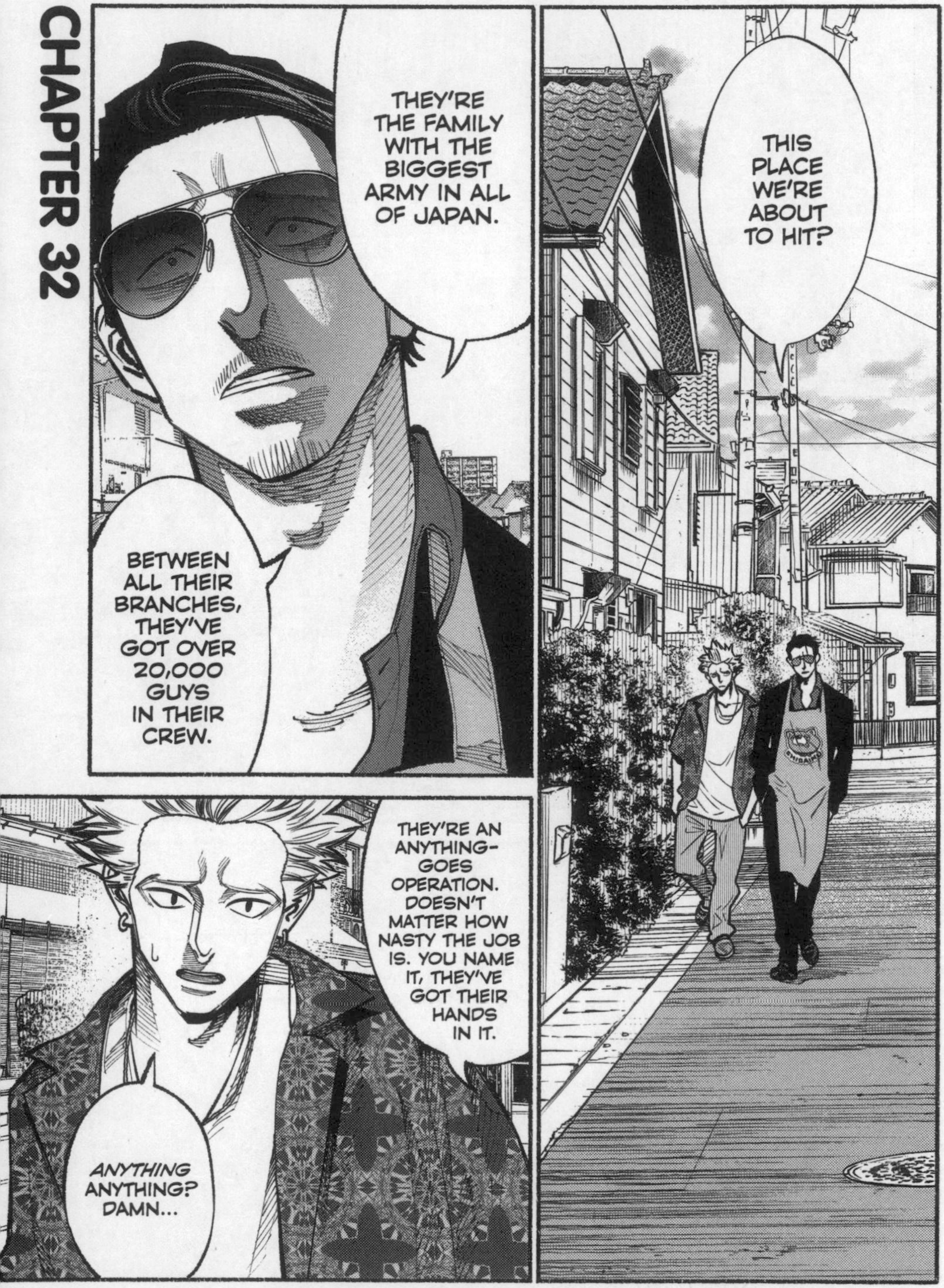
THIS PLACE WE'RE ABOUT TO HIT?
THEY'RE THE FAMILY WITH THE BIGGEST ARMY IN ALL OF JAPAN.
BETWEEN ALL THEIR BRANCHES, THEY'VE GOT OVER 20,000 GUYS IN THEIR CREW.
THEY'RE AN ANYTHING-GOES OPERATION. DOESN'T MATTER HOW NASTY THE JOB IS. YOU NAME IT, THEY'VE GOT THEIR HANDS IN IT.
ANYTHING ANYTHING? DAMN...

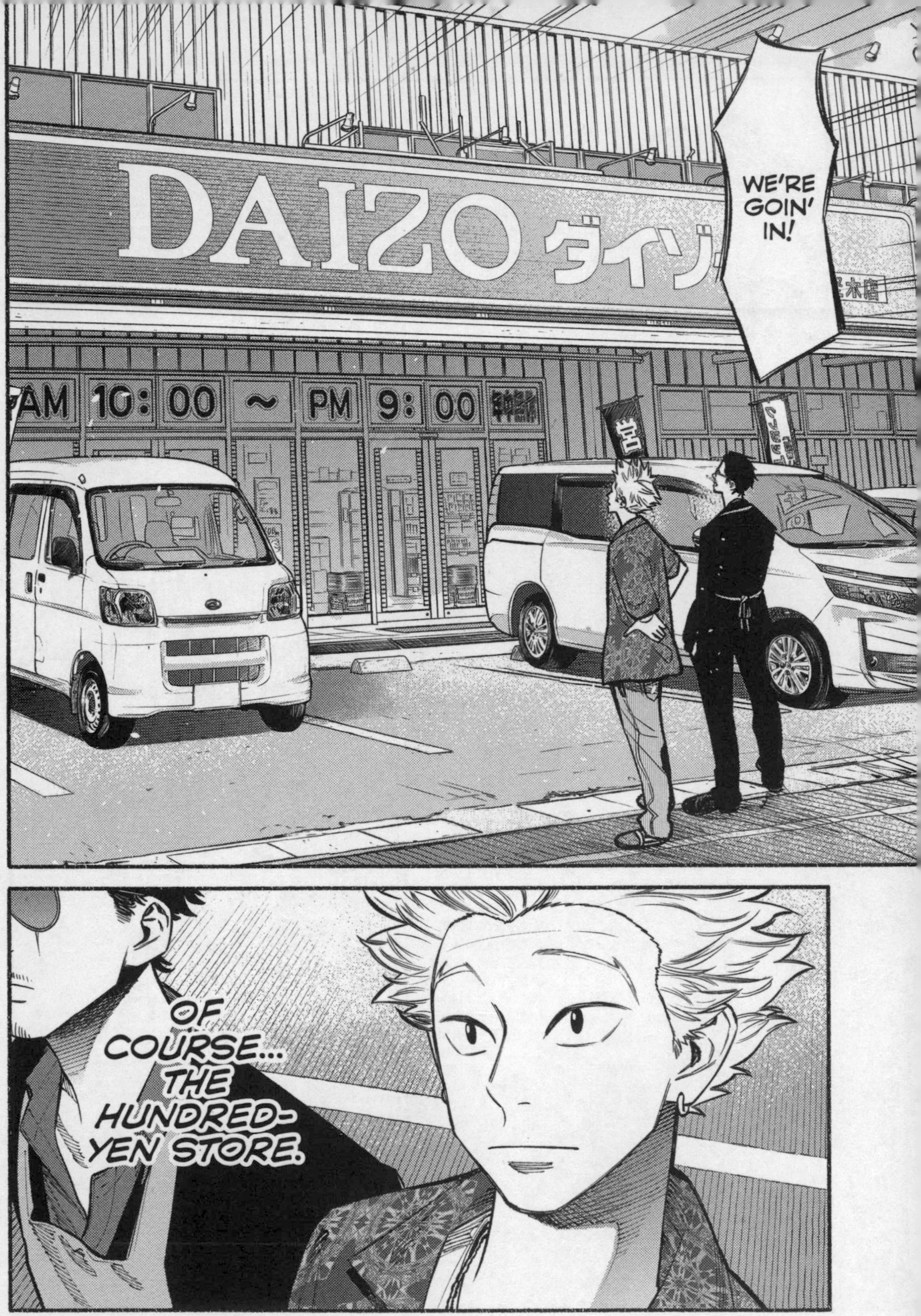
DAIZO ダイソ
AM 10:00 ~ PM 9:00
WE'RE GOIN' IN!
OF COURSE... THE HUNDRED-YEN STORE.

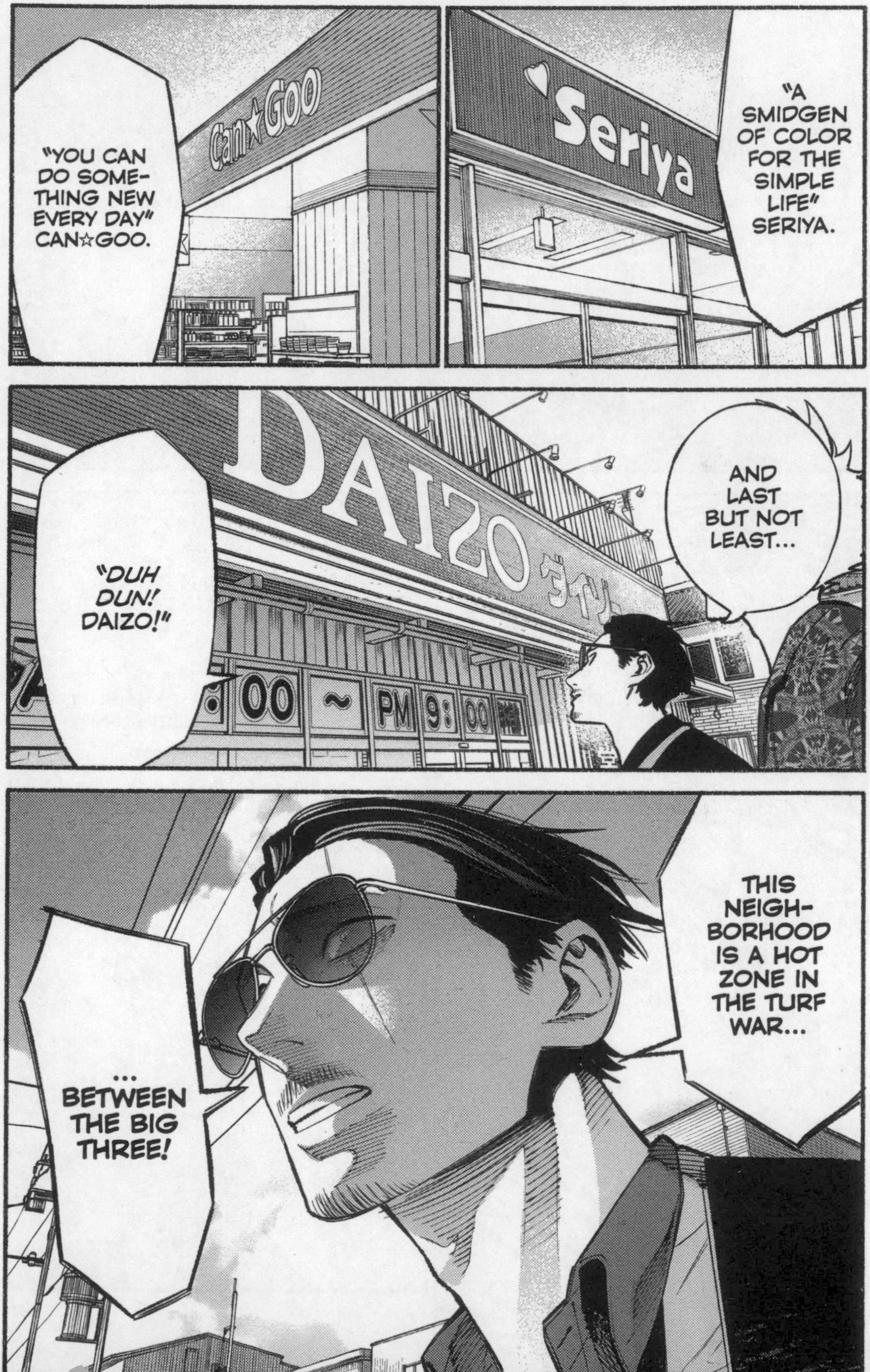
Seriya
"A SMIDGEN OF COLOR FOR THE SIMPLE LIFE" SERIYA.
Can☆Goo
"YOU CAN DO SOME-THING NEW EVERY DAY" CAN☆GOO.
AND LAST BUT NOT LEAST...
DAIZO
"DUH DUN! DAIZO!"
00 ~ PM 9:00
THIS NEIGH-BORHOOD IS A HOT ZONE IN THE TURF WAR...
...BETWEEN THE BIG THREE!

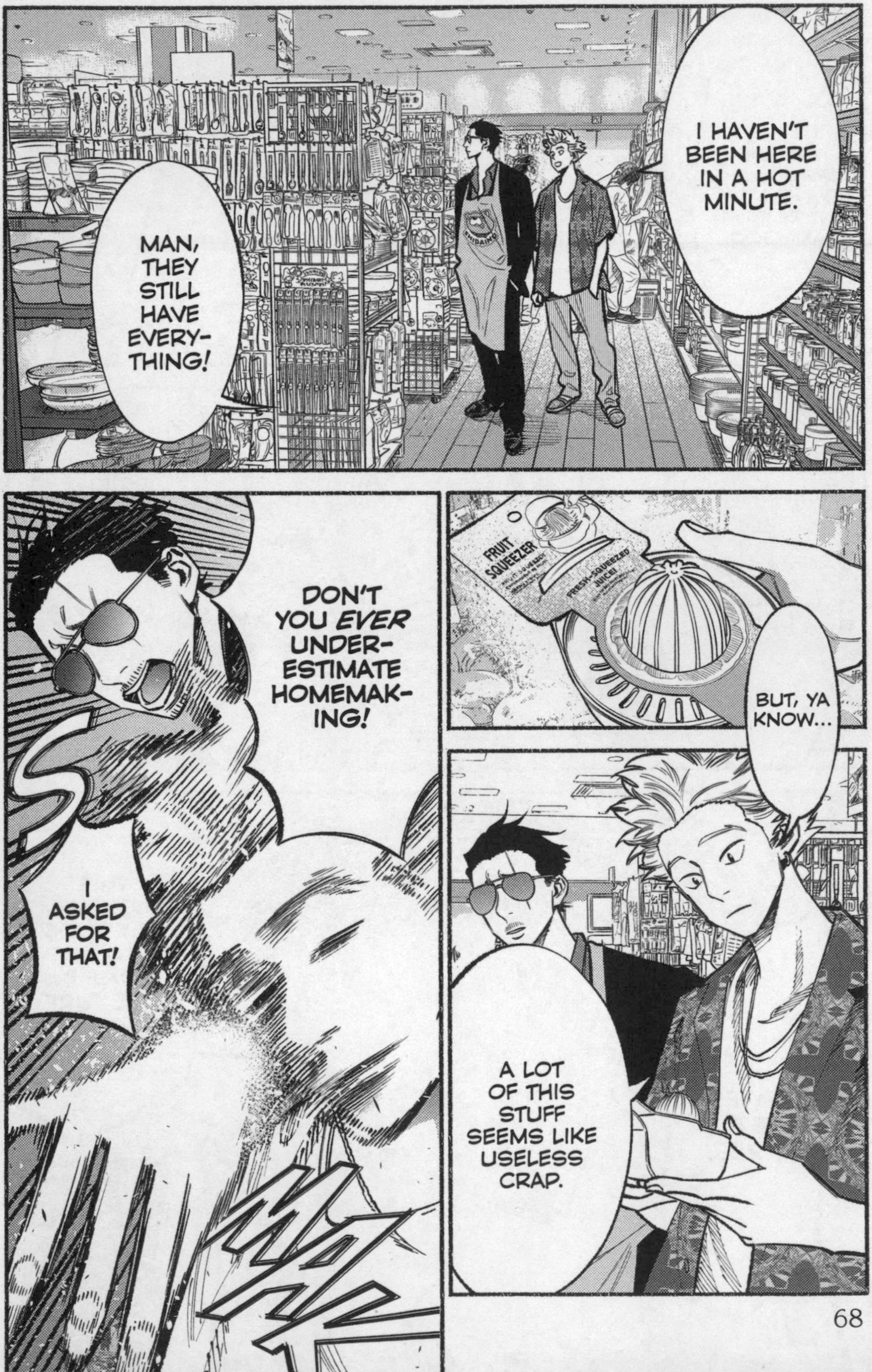
I HAVEN'T BEEN HERE IN A HOT MINUTE.
MAN, THEY STILL HAVE EVERYTHING!
FRUIT SQUEEZER
FRESH-SQUEEZED JUICE!
BUT, YA KNOW...
A LOT OF THIS STUFF SEEMS LIKE USELESS CRAP.
DON'T YOU *EVER* UNDER-ESTIMATE HOMEMAK-ING!
I ASKED FOR THAT!

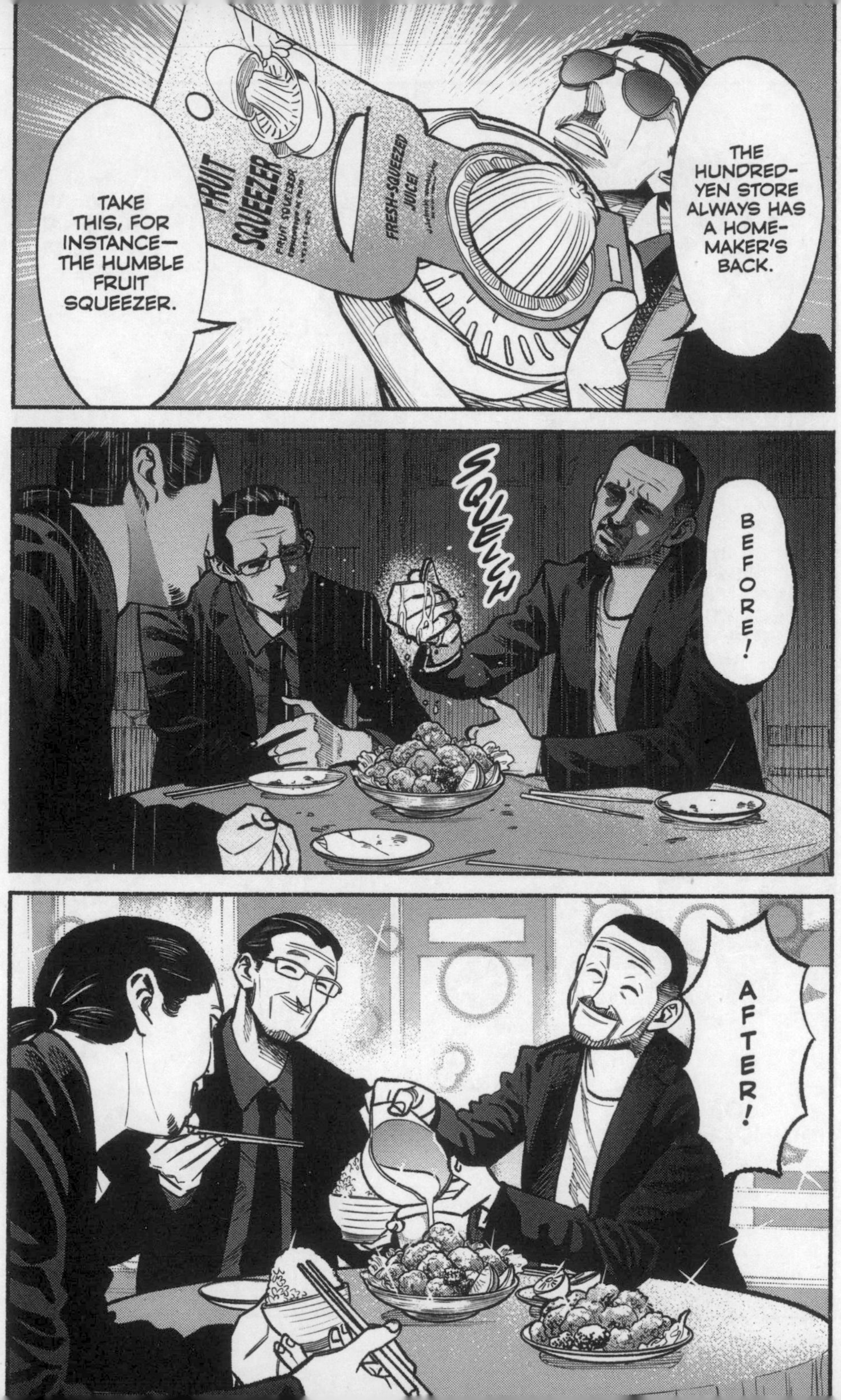
THE HUNDRED-YEN STORE ALWAYS HAS A HOME-MAKER'S BACK.
TAKE THIS, FOR INSTANCE—THE HUMBLE FRUIT SQUEEZER.
FRUIT SQUEEZER
FRESH-SQUEEZED JUICE!
BEFORE!
AFTER!

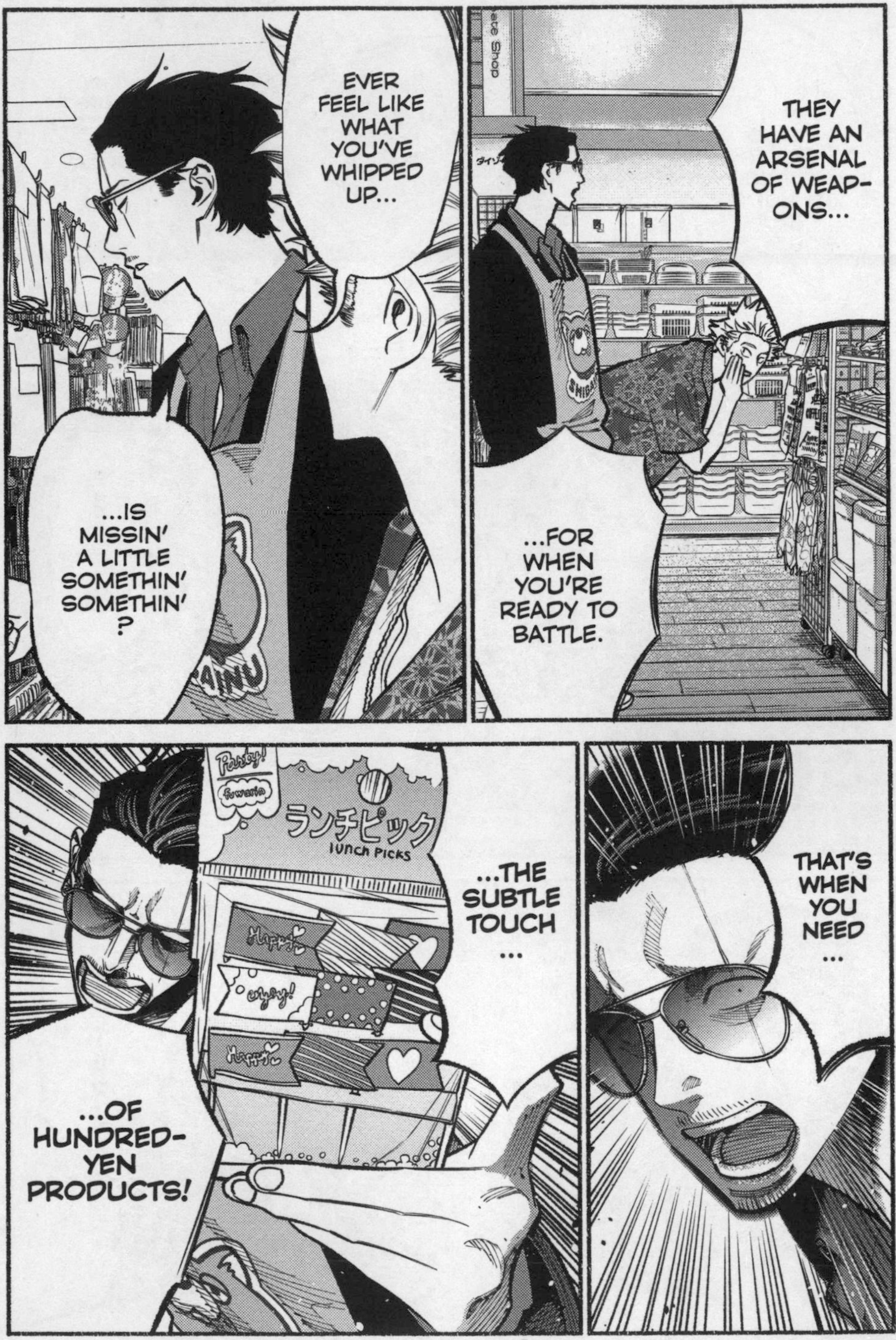
ate Shop
THEY HAVE AN ARSENAL OF WEAP-ONS...
...FOR WHEN YOU'RE READY TO BATTLE.
EVER FEEL LIKE WHAT YOU'VE WHIPPED UP...
...IS MISSIN' A LITTLE SOMETHIN' SOMETHIN'?
THAT'S WHEN YOU NEED...
Party!
fuwario
ランチピック
lunch picks
...THE SUBTLE TOUCH...
...OF HUNDRED-YEN PRODUCTS!

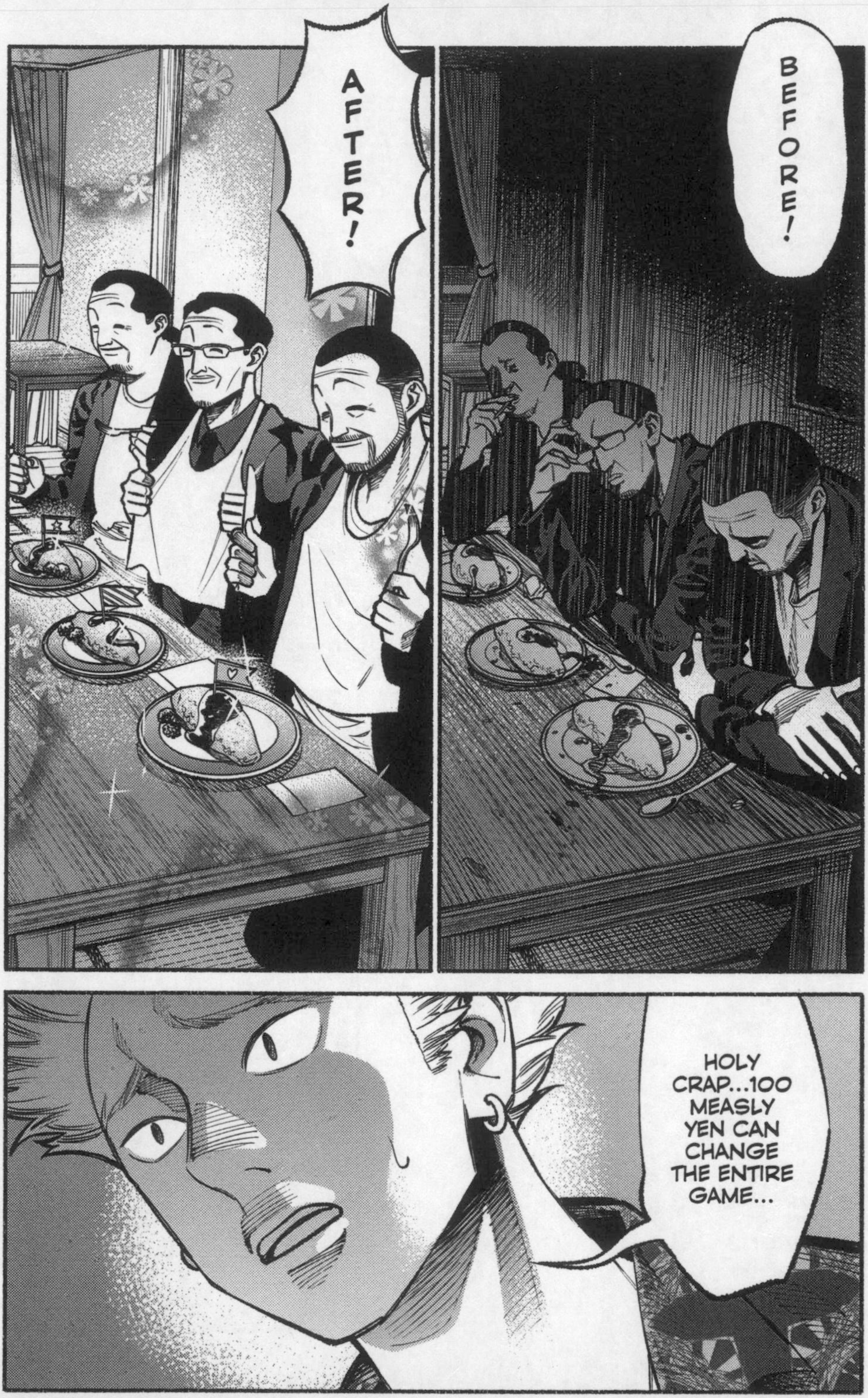
BEFORE!
AFTER!
HOLY CRAP...100 MEASLY YEN CAN CHANGE THE ENTIRE GAME...

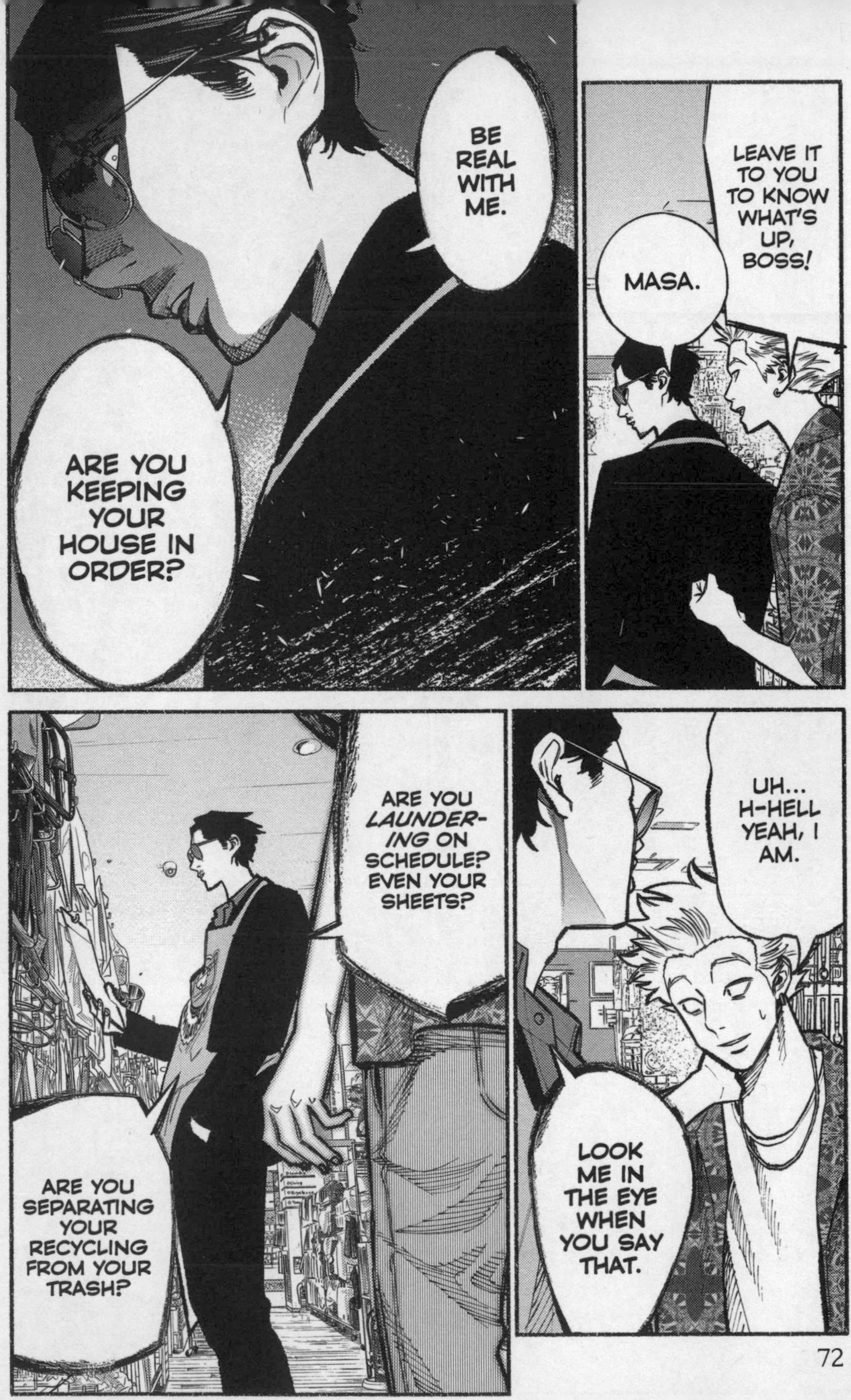
LEAVE IT TO YOU TO KNOW WHAT'S UP, BOSS!
MASA.
BE REAL WITH ME.
ARE YOU KEEPING YOUR HOUSE IN ORDER?
UH... H-HELL YEAH, I AM.
LOOK ME IN THE EYE WHEN YOU SAY THAT.
ARE YOU *LAUNDERING* ON SCHEDULE? EVEN YOUR SHEETS?
ARE YOU SEPARATING YOUR RECYCLING FROM YOUR TRASH?

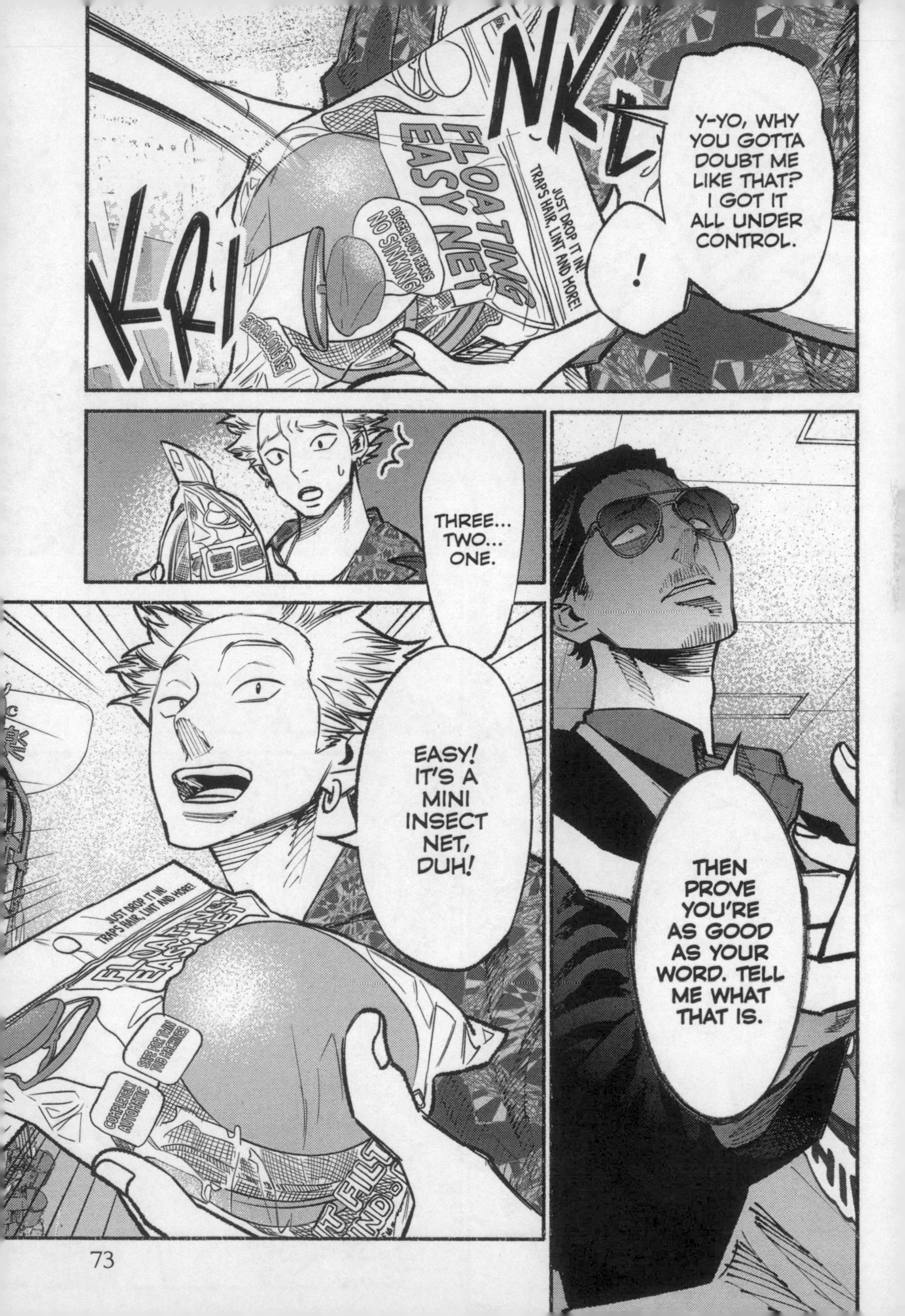
KRI
NK
FLOATING EASY NET!
JUST DROP IT IN! TRAPS HAIR, LINT AND MORE!
BIGGER BUOY MEANS NO SINKING!
Y-YO, WHY YOU GOTTA DOUBT ME LIKE THAT? I GOT IT ALL UNDER CONTROL.
!
THEN PROVE YOU'RE AS GOOD AS YOUR WORD. TELL ME WHAT THAT IS.
THREE... TWO... ONE.
EASY! IT'S A MINI INSECT NET, DUH!
JUST DROP IT IN! TRAPS HAIR, LINT AND MORE!
FLOATING EASY NET!
COMPLETELY AUTOMATIC

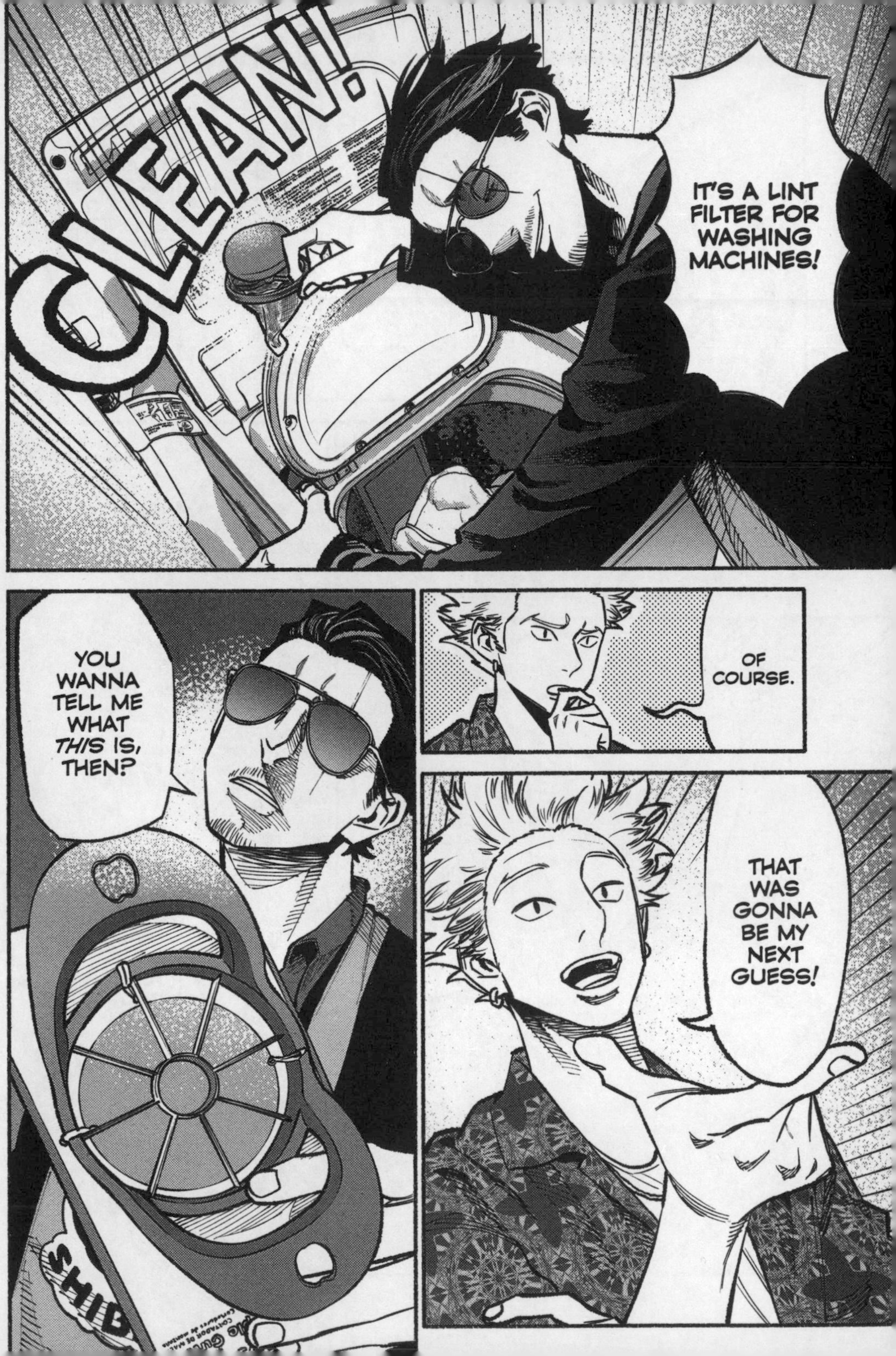
CLEAN!
IT'S A LINT FILTER FOR WASHING MACHINES!
OF COURSE.
THAT WAS GONNA BE MY NEXT GUESS!
YOU WANNA TELL ME WHAT *THIS* IS, THEN?
SHIB

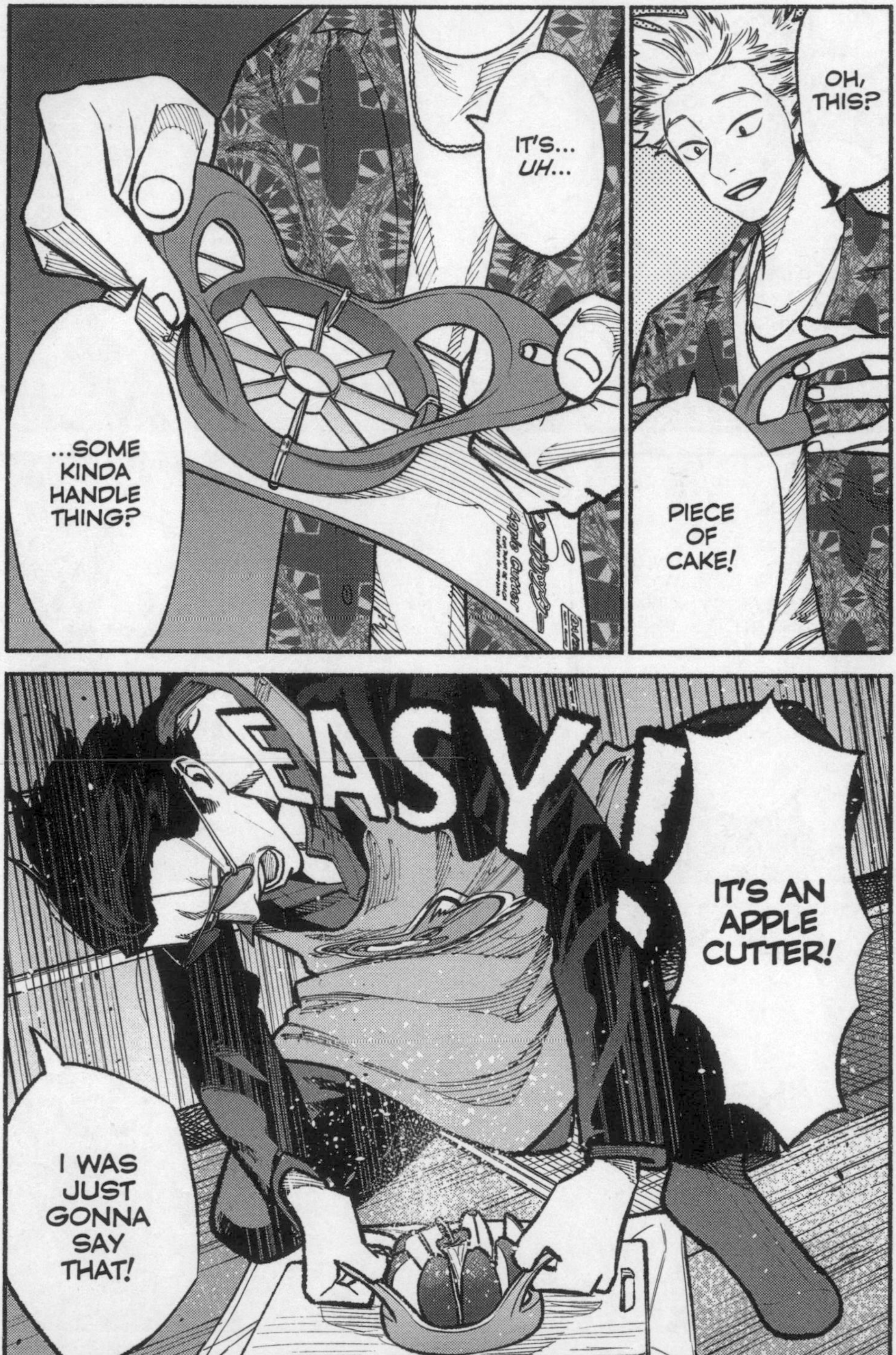
OH, THIS?
PIECE OF CAKE!
IT'S... UH...
...SOME KINDA HANDLE THING?
EASY!!
IT'S AN APPLE CUTTER!
I WAS JUST GONNA SAY THAT!

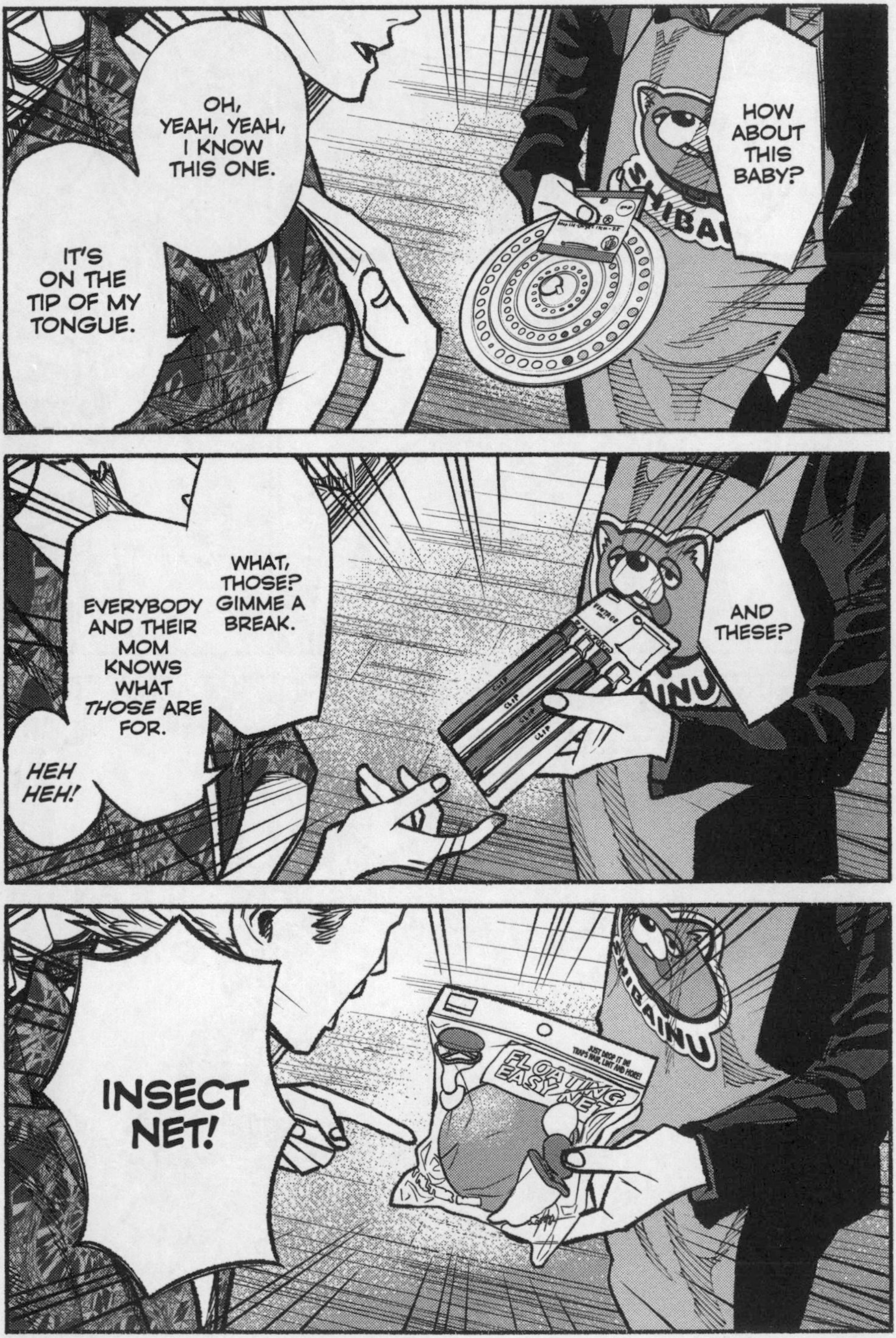
HOW ABOUT THIS BABY?
OH, YEAH, YEAH, I KNOW THIS ONE.
IT'S ON THE TIP OF MY TONGUE.
AND THESE?
WHAT, THOSE? GIMME A BREAK.
EVERYBODY AND THEIR MOM KNOWS WHAT *THOSE* ARE FOR.
HEH HEH!
SHIBAINU
FLOATING EASY NET
INSECT NET!

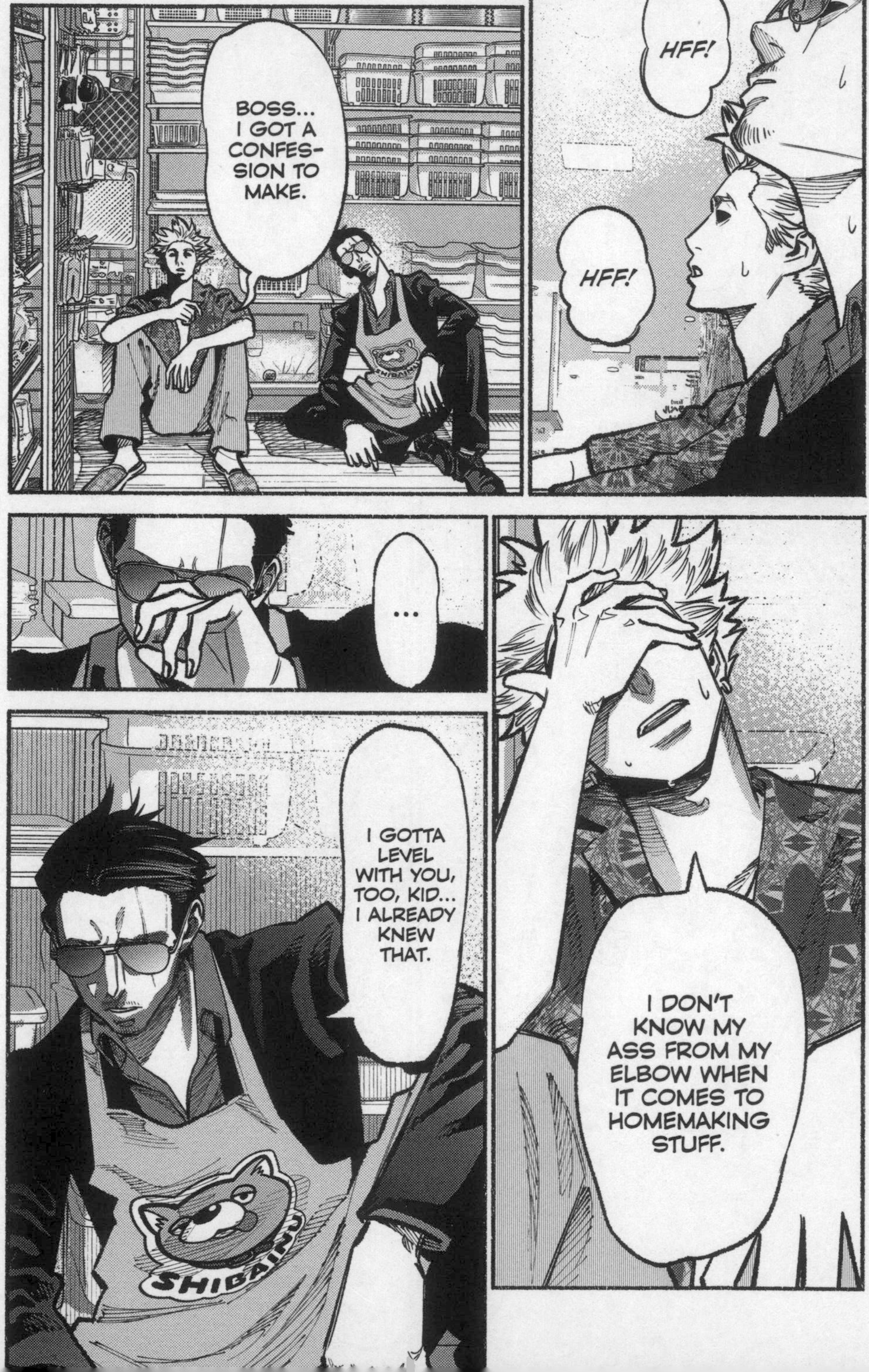
HFF!
HFF!
BOSS... I GOT A CONFES-SION TO MAKE.
I DON'T KNOW MY ASS FROM MY ELBOW WHEN IT COMES TO HOMEMAKING STUFF.
...
I GOTTA LEVEL WITH YOU, TOO, KID... I ALREADY KNEW THAT.

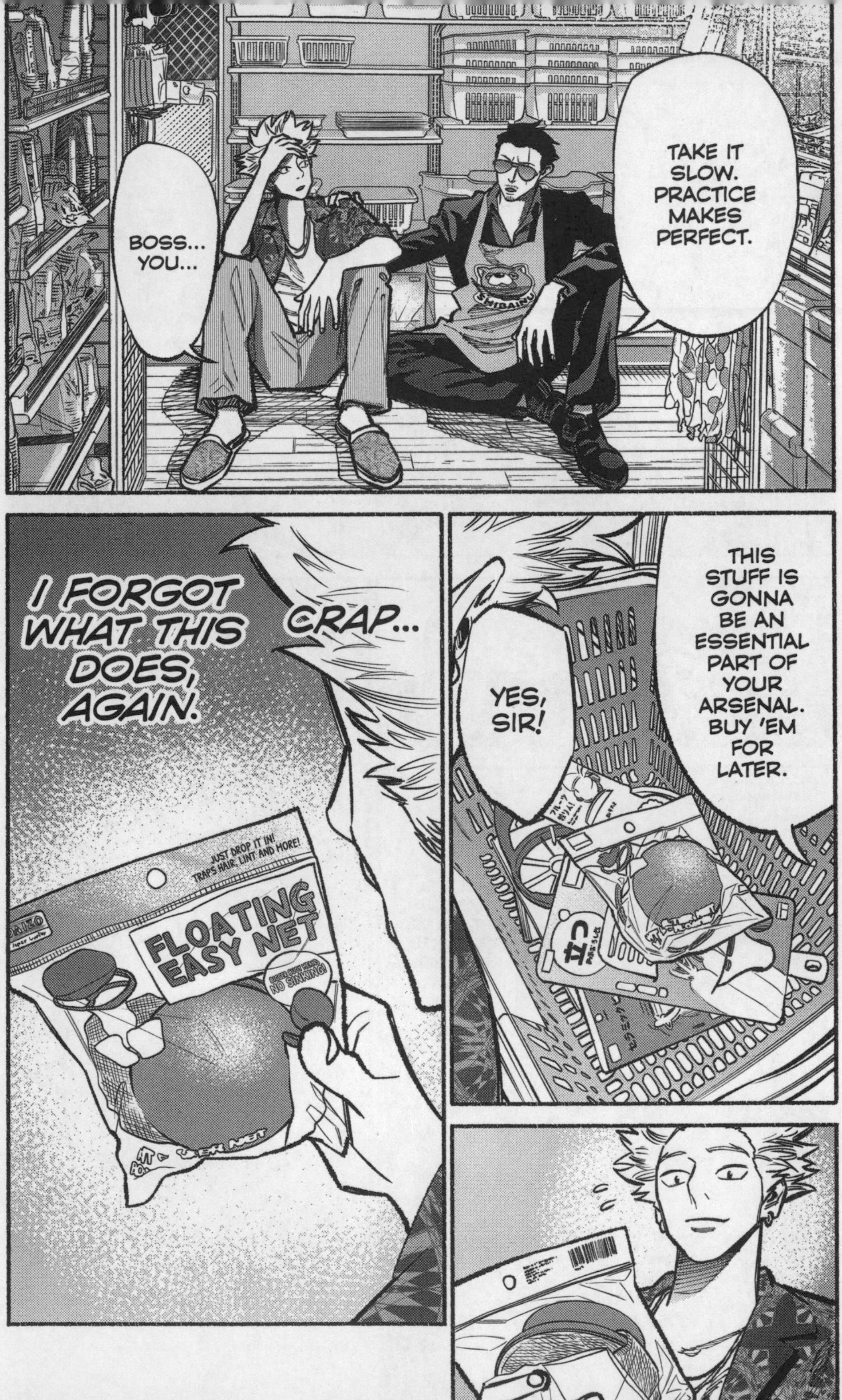
TAKE IT SLOW. PRACTICE MAKES PERFECT.
BOSS... YOU...
SHIBAINU
THIS STUFF IS GONNA BE AN ESSENTIAL PART OF YOUR ARSENAL. BUY 'EM FOR LATER.
YES, SIR!
CRAP...
I FORGOT WHAT THIS DOES, AGAIN.
JUST DROP IT IN! TRAPS HAIR, LINT AND MORE!
FLOATING EASY NET
NO SINKING!

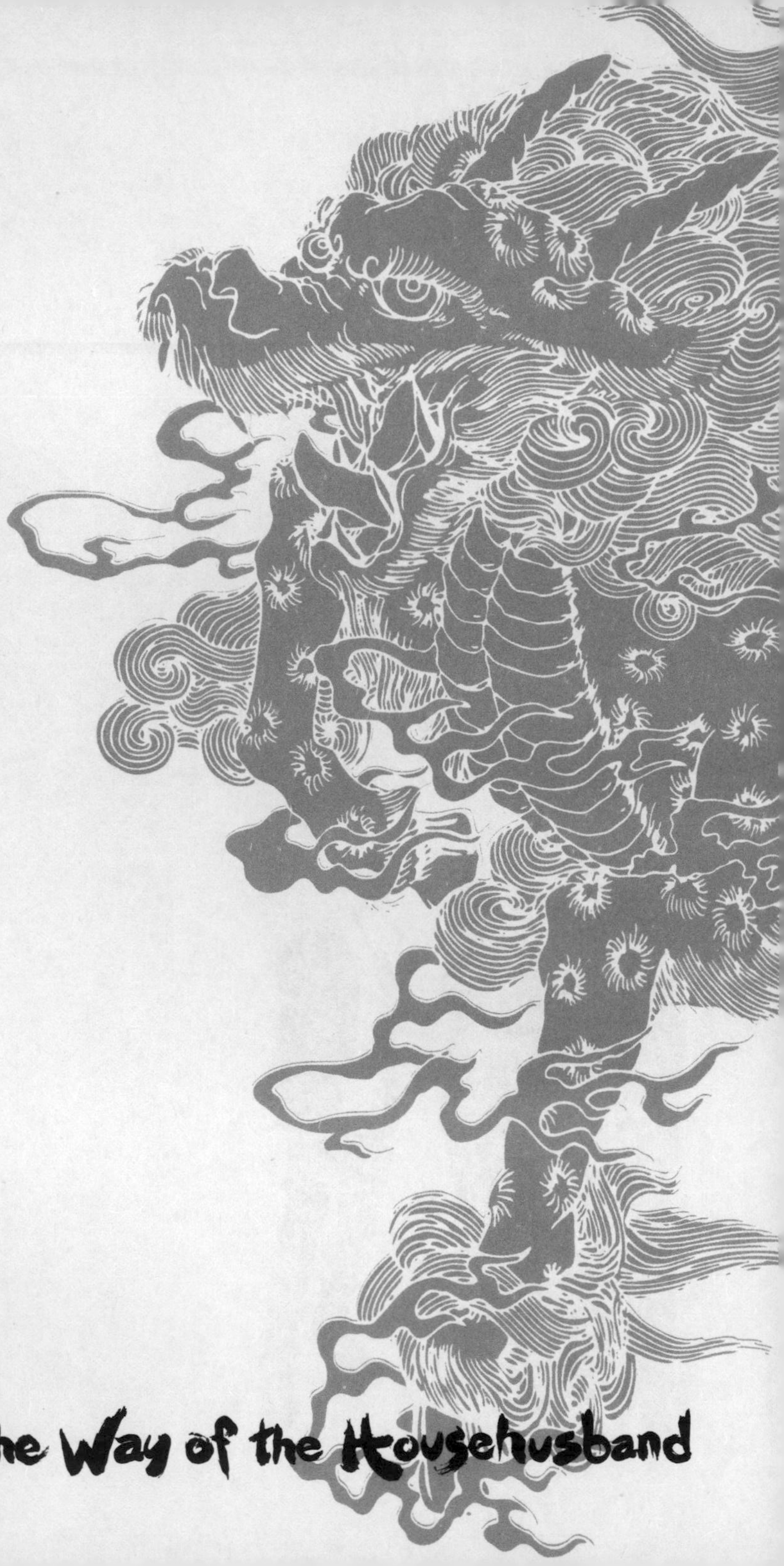
The Way of the Househusband

CHAPTER 33

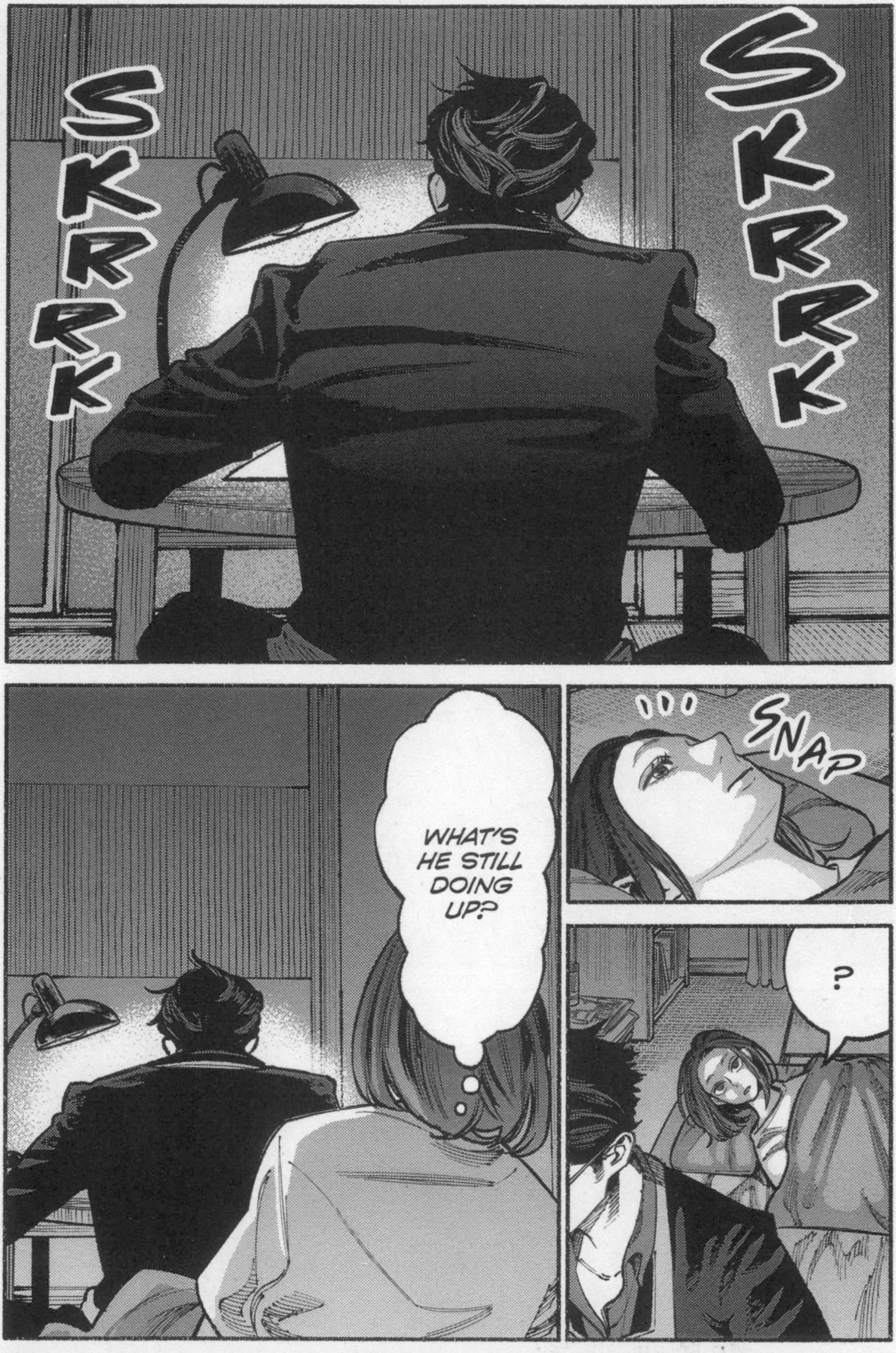
SKRRK
SKRRK
!!!
SNAP
?
WHAT'S HE STILL DOING UP?

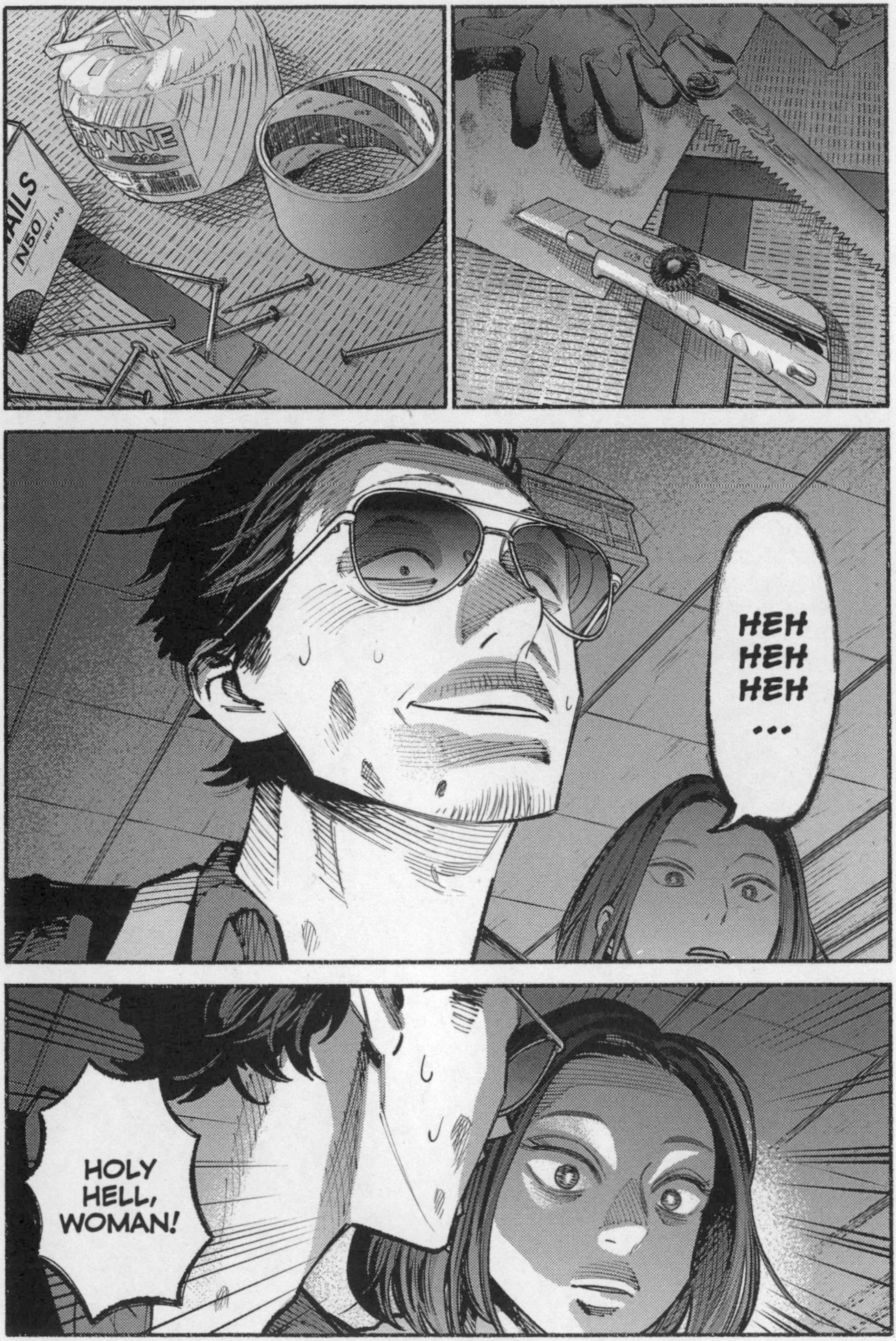
HEH HEH HEH ...
HOLY HELL, WOMAN!

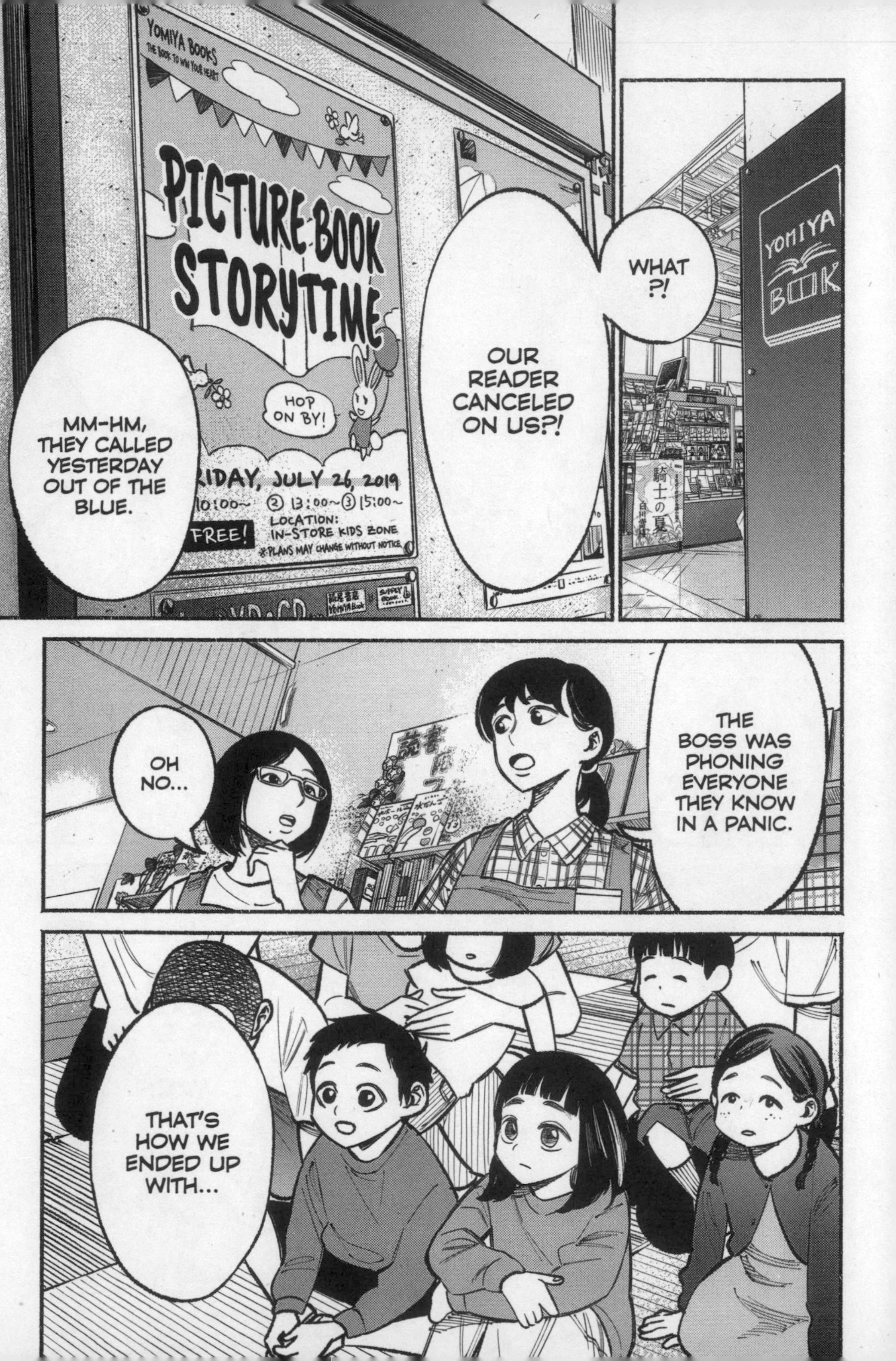
YOMIYA BOOK
WHAT ?!
OUR READER CANCELED ON US?!
騎士の夏
YOMIYA BOOKS
THE BOOK TO WIN YOUR HEART
PICTURE BOOK STORYTIME
HOP ON BY!
RIDAY, JULY 26, 2019
10:00~ ② 13:00~ ③ 15:00~
FREE!
LOCATION: IN-STORE KIDS ZONE
※PLANS MAY CHANGE WITHOUT NOTICE
MM-HM, THEY CALLED YESTERDAY OUT OF THE BLUE.
THE BOSS WAS PHONING EVERYONE THEY KNOW IN A PANIC.
OH NO...
THAT'S HOW WE ENDED UP WITH...

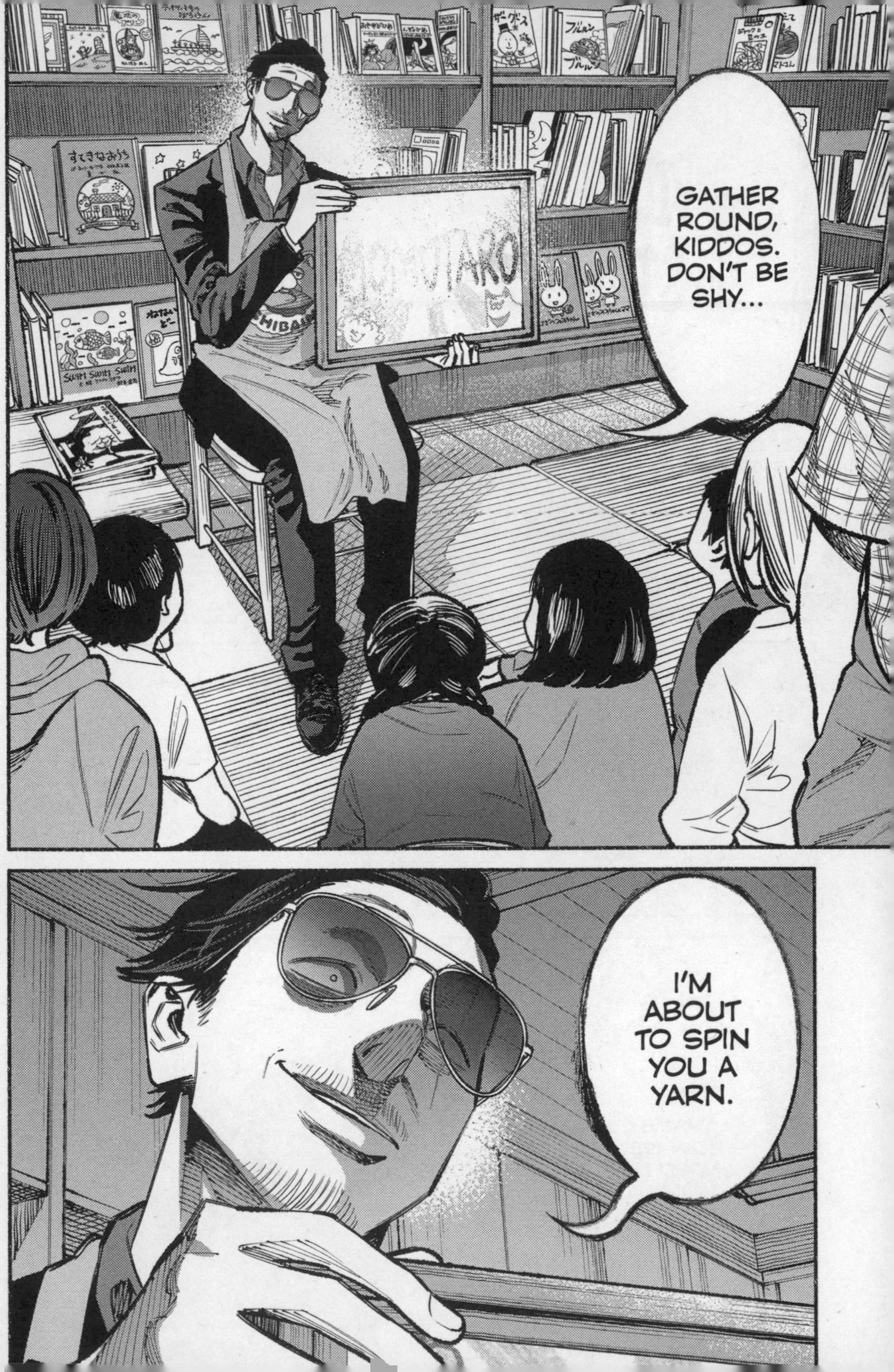
GATHER ROUND, KIDDOS. DON'T BE SHY...
I'M ABOUT TO SPIN YOU A YARN.

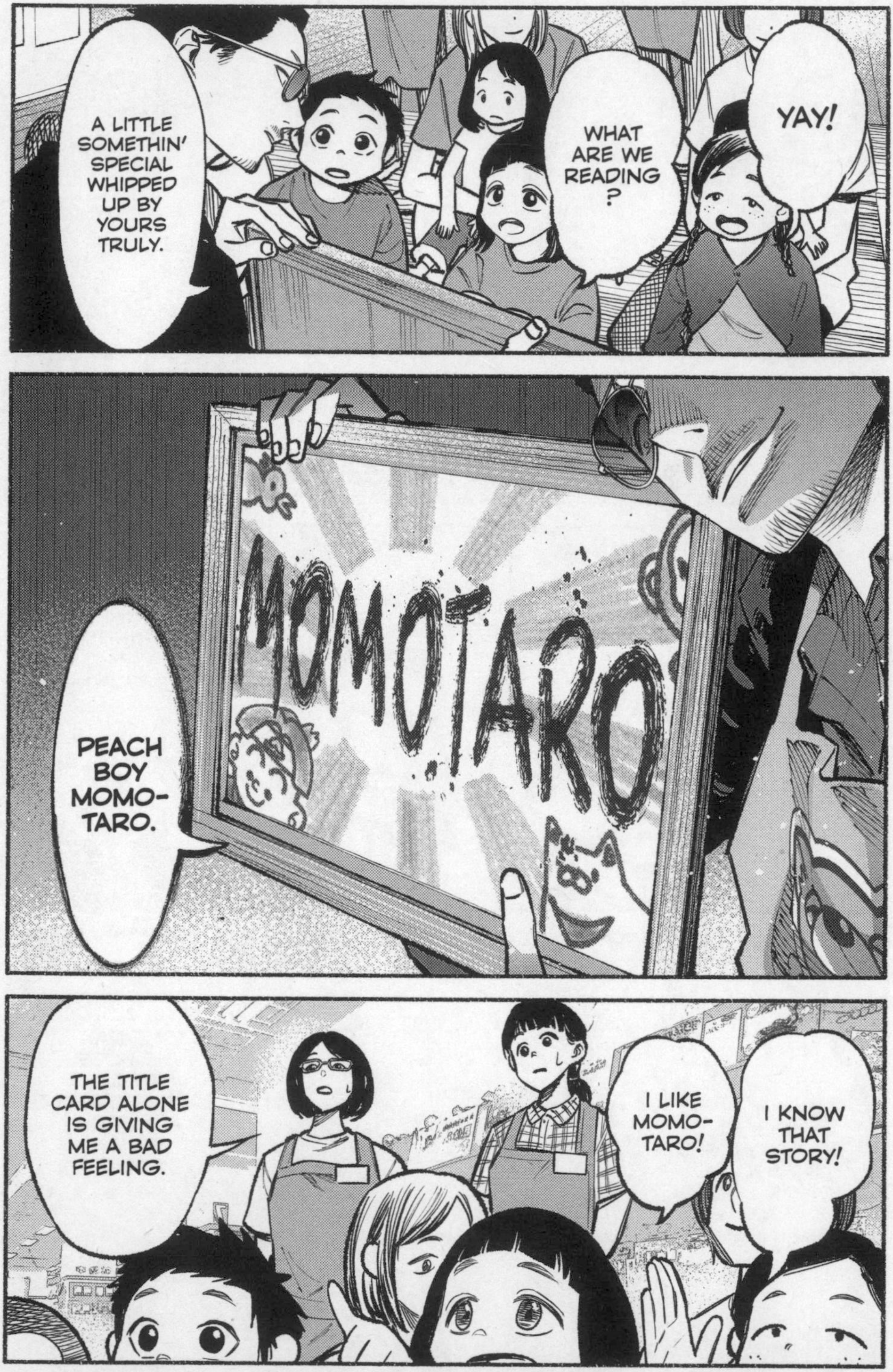
YAY!
WHAT ARE WE READING?
A LITTLE SOMETHIN' SPECIAL WHIPPED UP BY YOURS TRULY.
MOMOTARO
PEACH BOY MOMO-TARO.
I KNOW THAT STORY!
I LIKE MOMO-TARO!
THE TITLE CARD ALONE IS GIVING ME A BAD FEELING.

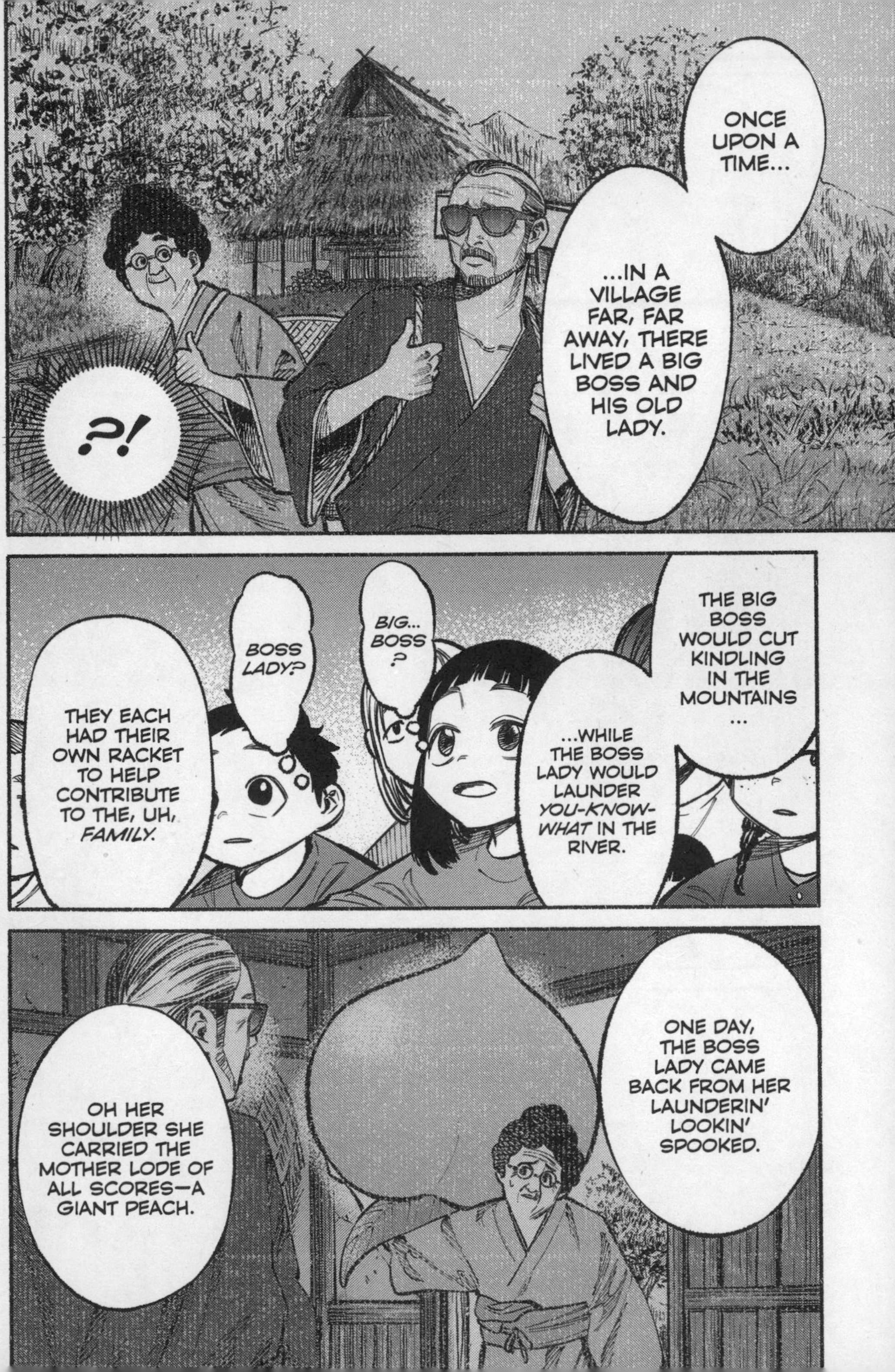
ONCE UPON A TIME...
...IN A VILLAGE FAR, FAR AWAY, THERE LIVED A BIG BOSS AND HIS OLD LADY.
?!
THE BIG BOSS WOULD CUT KINDLING IN THE MOUNTAINS ...
...WHILE THE BOSS LADY WOULD LAUNDER *YOU-KNOW-WHAT* IN THE RIVER.
BIG... BOSS?
BOSS LADY?
THEY EACH HAD THEIR OWN RACKET TO HELP CONTRIBUTE TO THE, UH, *FAMILY*.
ONE DAY, THE BOSS LADY CAME BACK FROM HER LAUNDERIN' LOOKIN' SPOOKED.
OH HER SHOULDER SHE CARRIED THE MOTHER LODE OF ALL SCORES—A GIANT PEACH.

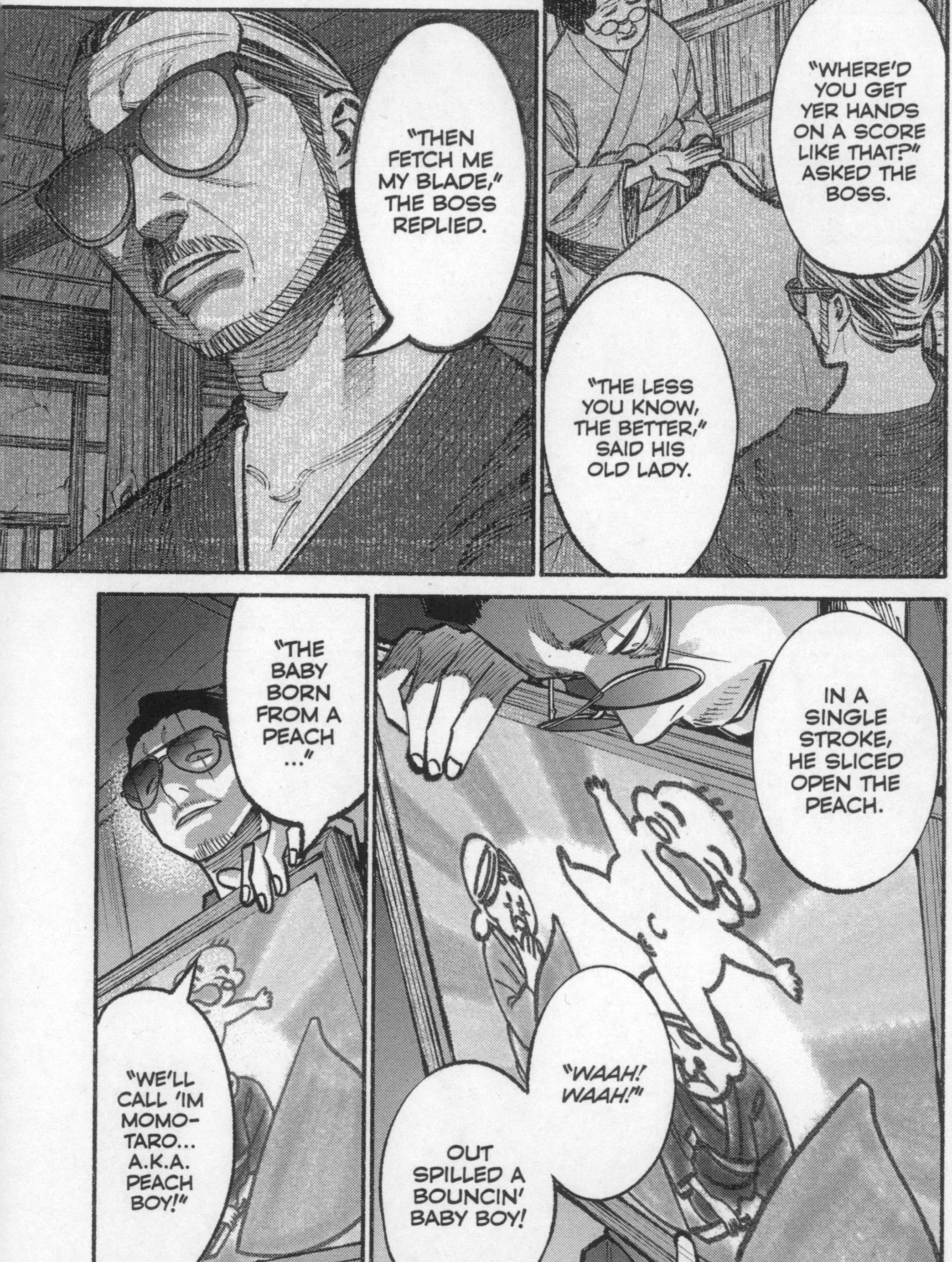
"WHERE'D YOU GET YER HANDS ON A SCORE LIKE THAT?" ASKED THE BOSS.
"THE LESS YOU KNOW, THE BETTER," SAID HIS OLD LADY.
"THEN FETCH ME MY BLADE," THE BOSS REPLIED.
IN A SINGLE STROKE, HE SLICED OPEN THE PEACH.
"WAAH! WAAH!"
OUT SPILLED A BOUNCIN' BABY BOY!
"THE BABY BORN FROM A PEACH..."
"WE'LL CALL 'IM MOMOTARO... A.K.A. PEACH BOY!"

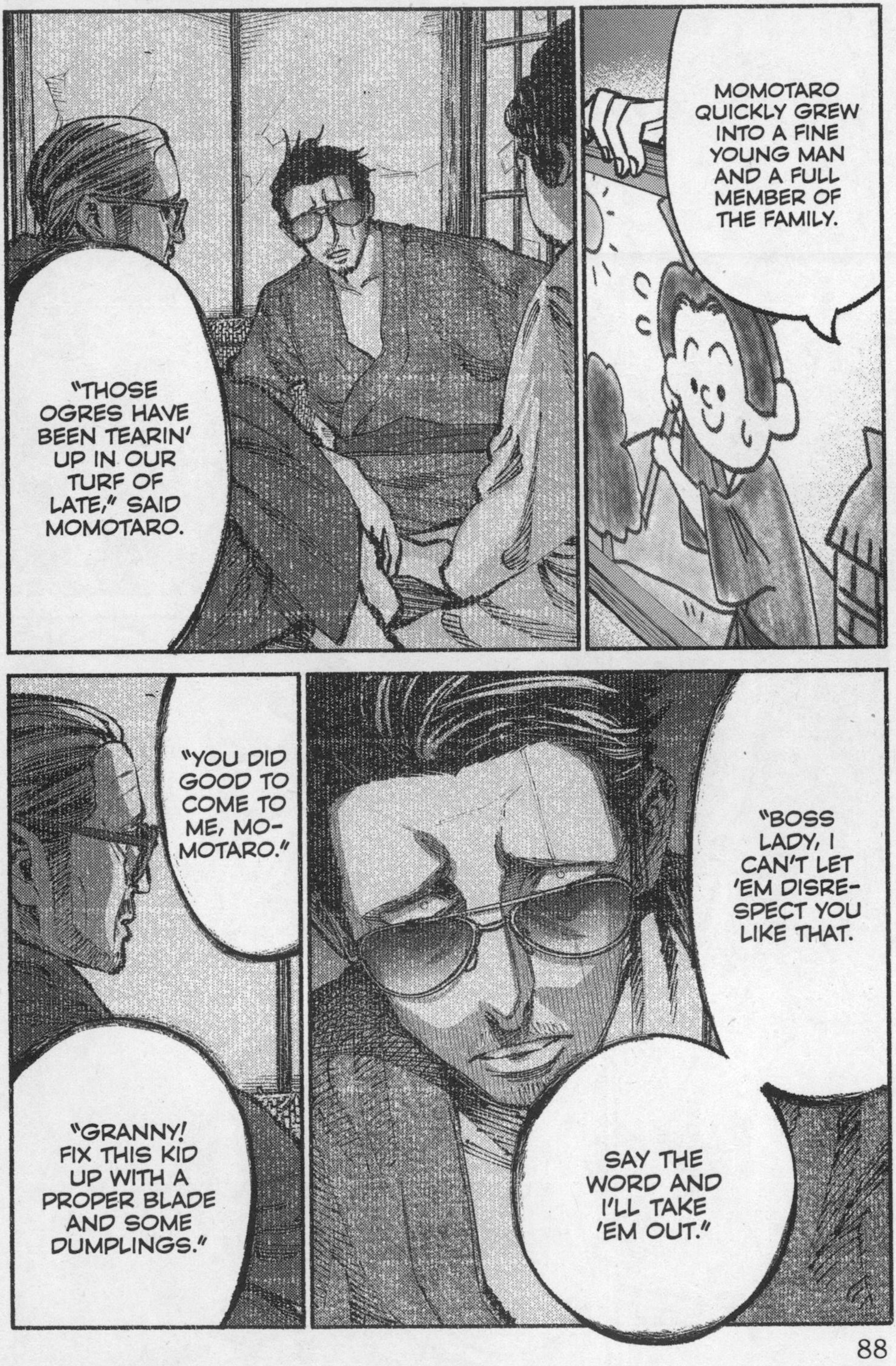
MOMOTARO QUICKLY GREW INTO A FINE YOUNG MAN AND A FULL MEMBER OF THE FAMILY.
"THOSE OGRES HAVE BEEN TEARIN' UP IN OUR TURF OF LATE," SAID MOMOTARO.
"BOSS LADY, I CAN'T LET 'EM DISRE-SPECT YOU LIKE THAT.
SAY THE WORD AND I'LL TAKE 'EM OUT."
"YOU DID GOOD TO COME TO ME, MO-MOTARO."
"GRANNY! FIX THIS KID UP WITH A PROPER BLADE AND SOME DUMPLINGS."

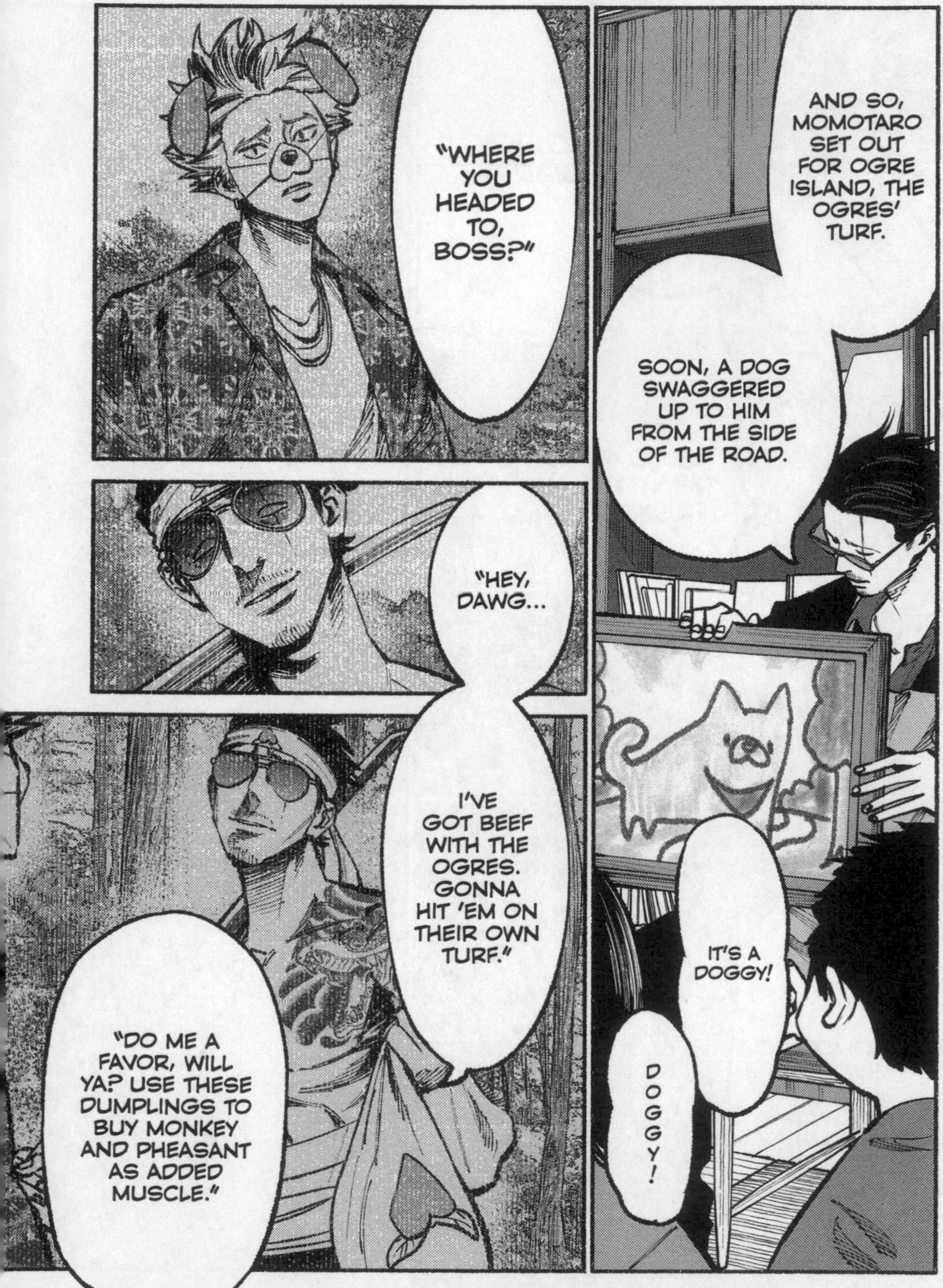
AND SO, MOMOTARO SET OUT FOR OGRE ISLAND, THE OGRES' TURF.
SOON, A DOG SWAGGERED UP TO HIM FROM THE SIDE OF THE ROAD.
IT'S A DOGGY!
DOGGY!
"WHERE YOU HEADED TO, BOSS?"
"HEY, DAWG...
I'VE GOT BEEF WITH THE OGRES. GONNA HIT 'EM ON THEIR OWN TURF."
"DO ME A FAVOR, WILL YA? USE THESE DUMPLINGS TO BUY MONKEY AND PHEASANT AS ADDED MUSCLE."

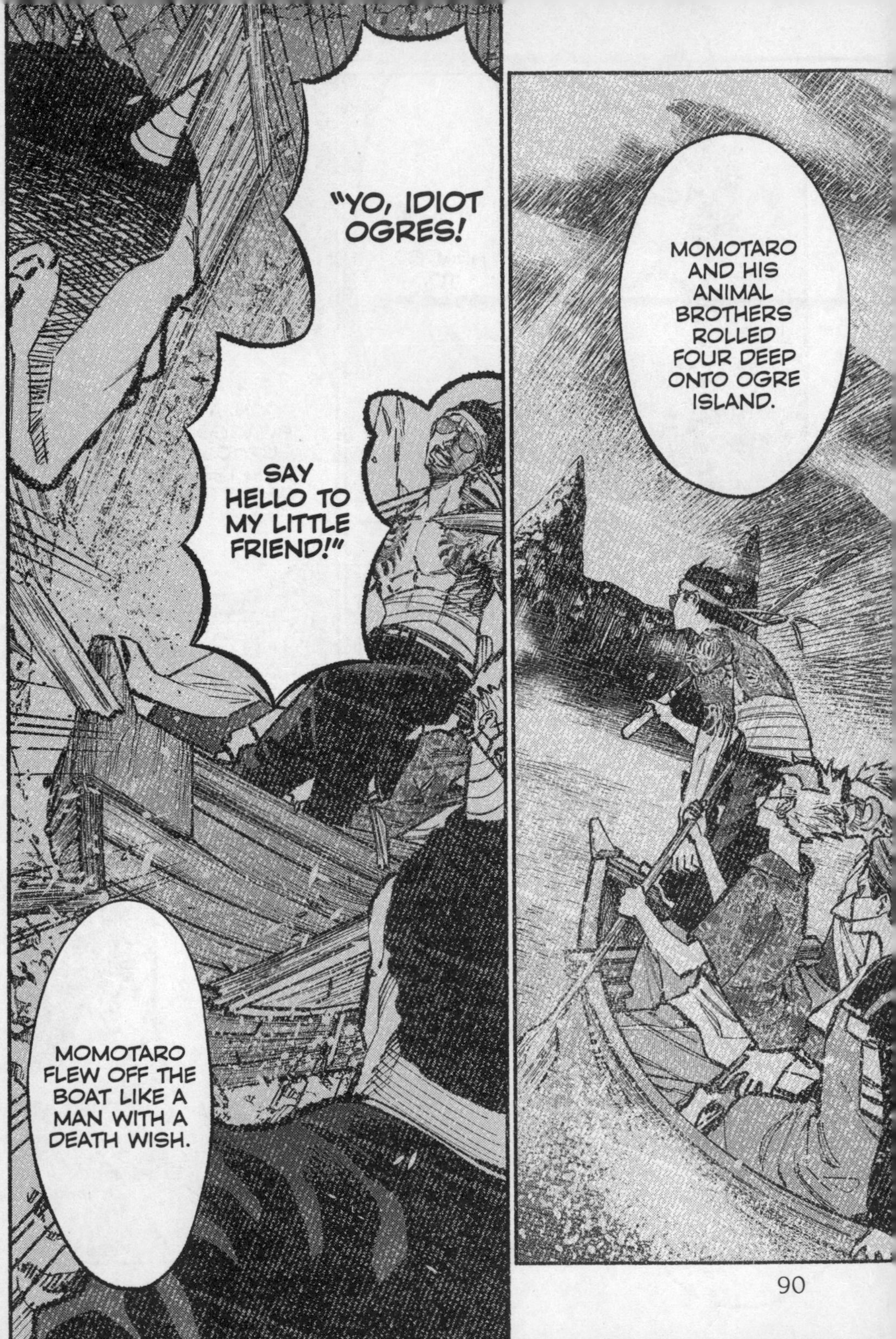
MOMOTARO AND HIS ANIMAL BROTHERS ROLLED FOUR DEEP ONTO OGRE ISLAND.
"YO, IDIOT OGRES!
SAY HELLO TO MY LITTLE FRIEND!"
MOMOTARO FLEW OFF THE BOAT LIKE A MAN WITH A DEATH WISH.

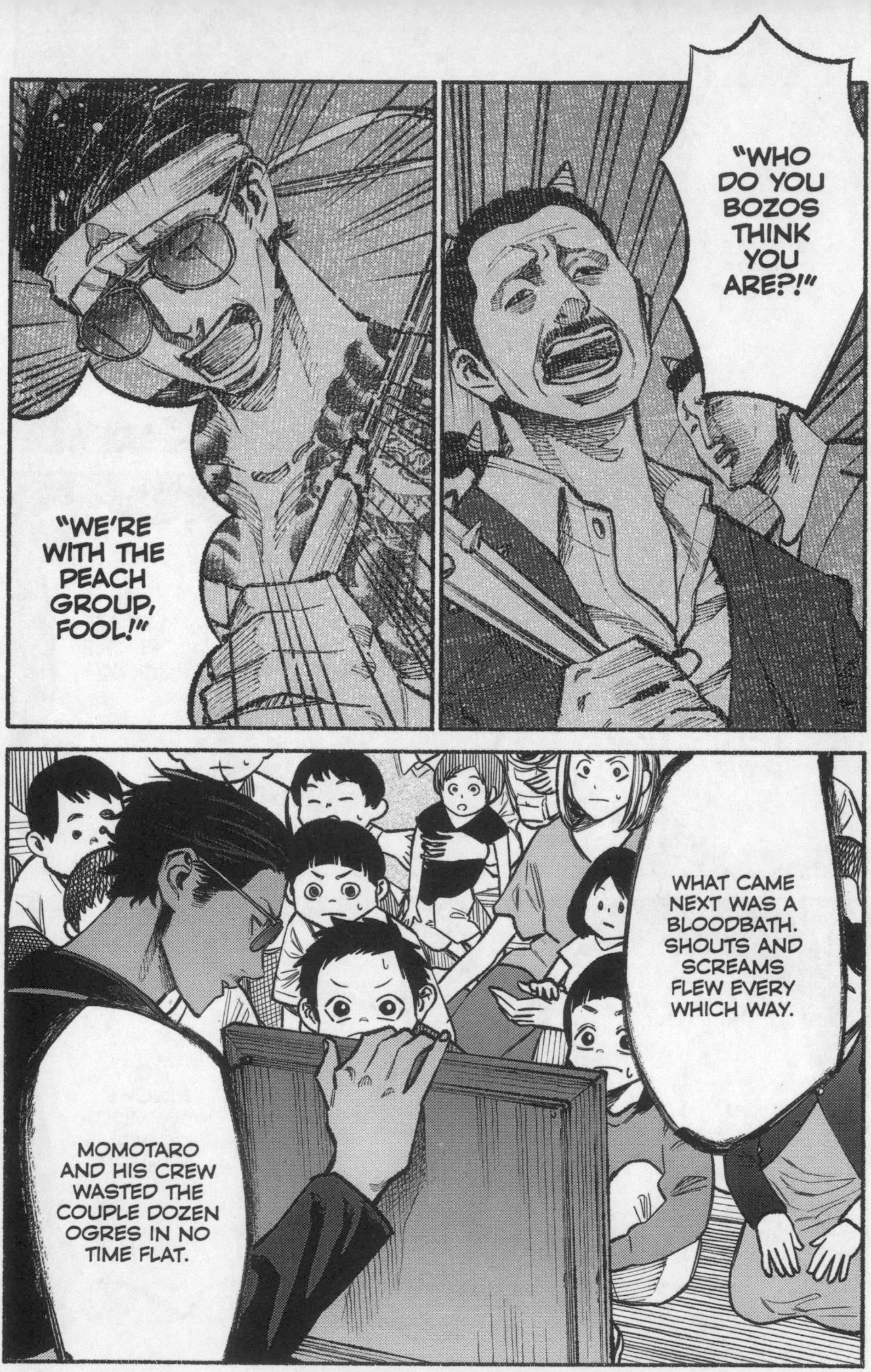
"WHO DO YOU BOZOS THINK YOU ARE?!"
"WE'RE WITH THE PEACH GROUP, FOOL!"
WHAT CAME NEXT WAS A BLOODBATH. SHOUTS AND SCREAMS FLEW EVERY WHICH WAY.
MOMOTARO AND HIS CREW WASTED THE COUPLE DOZEN OGRES IN NO TIME FLAT.

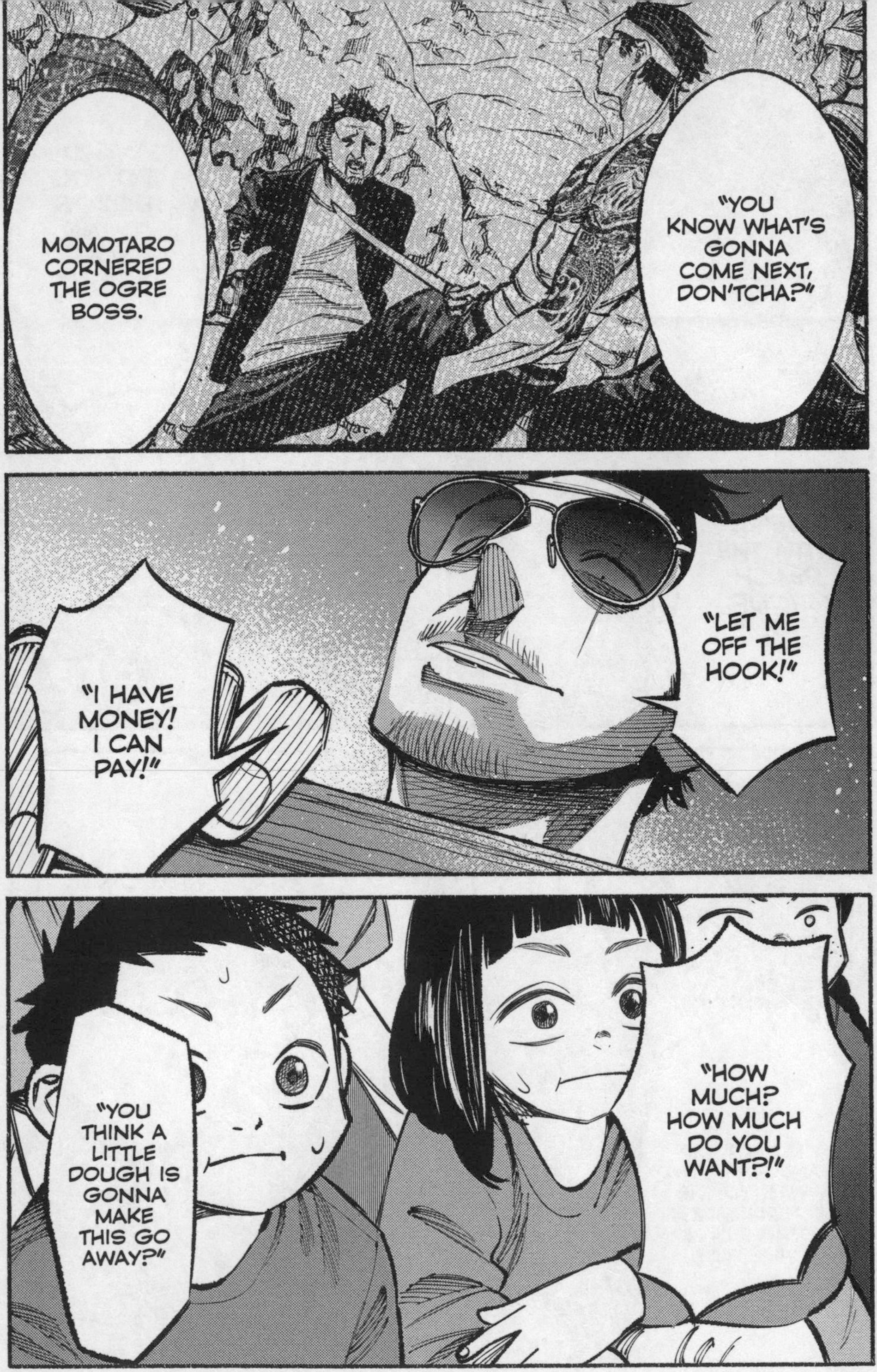
"YOU KNOW WHAT'S GONNA COME NEXT, DON'TCHA?"
MOMOTARO CORNERED THE OGRE BOSS.
"LET ME OFF THE HOOK!"
"I HAVE MONEY! I CAN PAY!"
"HOW MUCH? HOW MUCH DO YOU WANT?!"
"YOU THINK A LITTLE DOUGH IS GONNA MAKE THIS GO AWAY?"

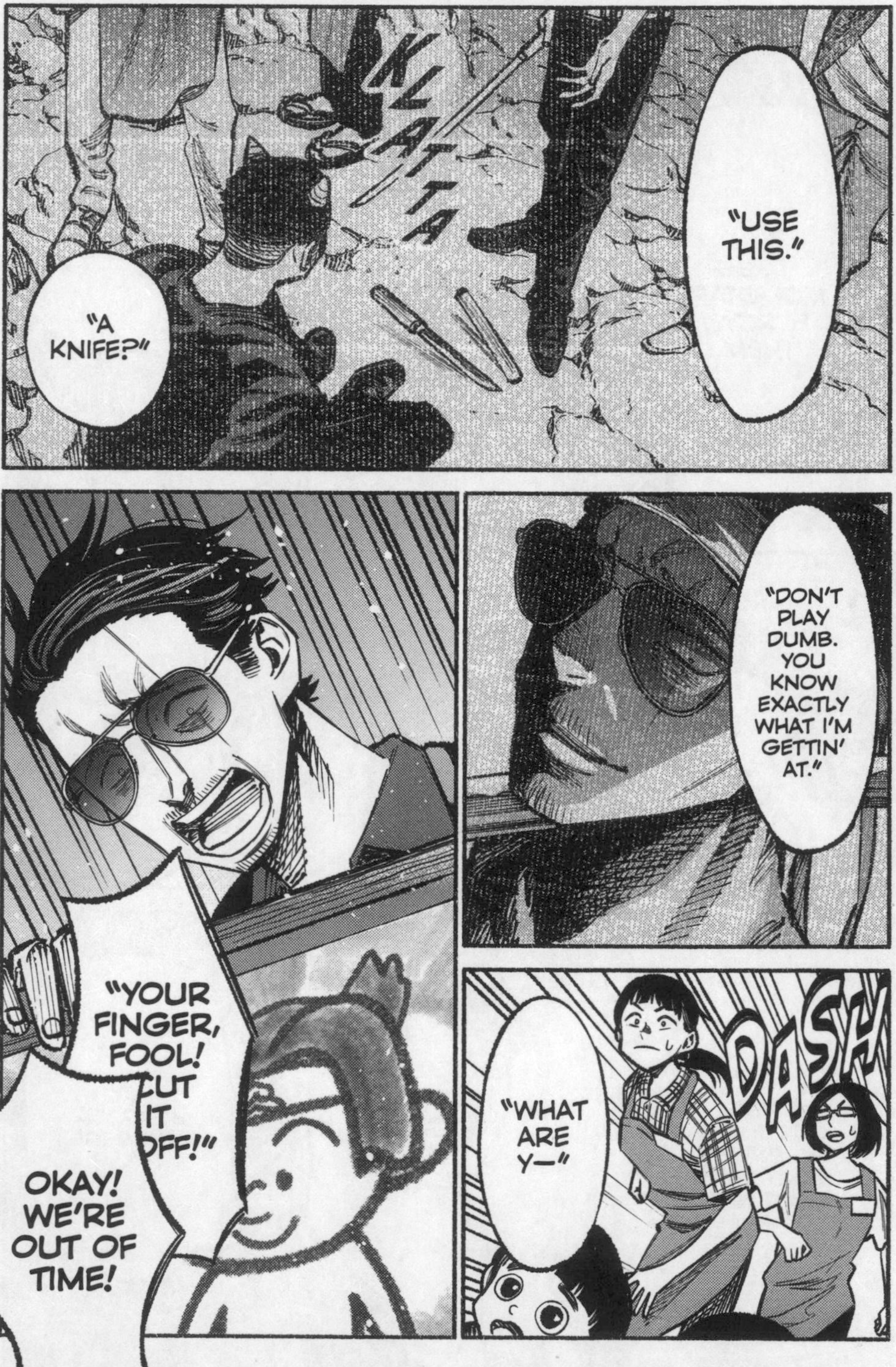
"USE THIS."
KLATTA
"A KNIFE?"
"DON'T PLAY DUMB. YOU KNOW EXACTLY WHAT I'M GETTIN' AT."
DASH
"WHAT ARE Y—"
"YOUR FINGER, FOOL! CUT IT OFF!"
OKAY! WE'RE OUT OF TIME!

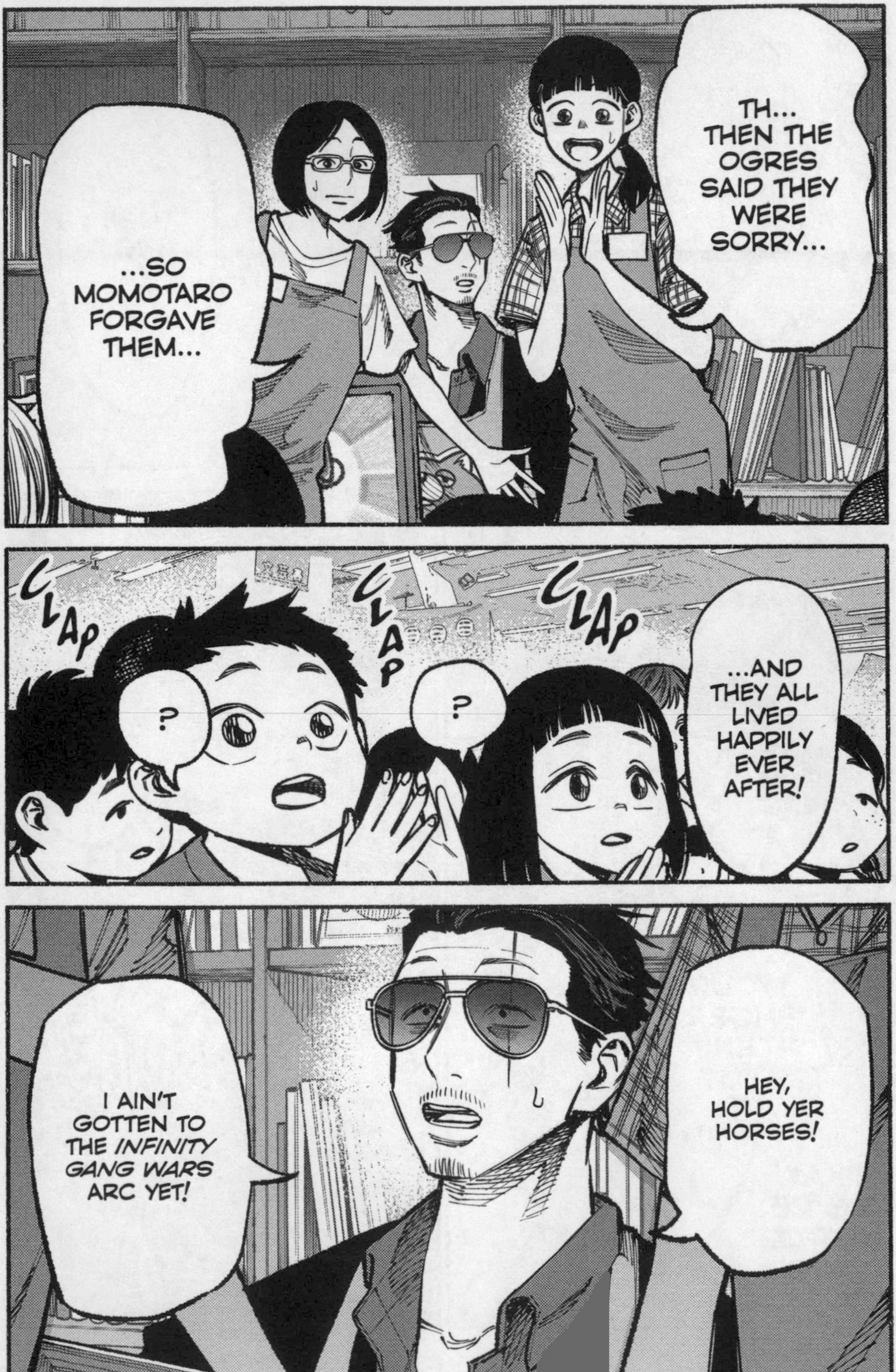
TH... THEN THE OGRES SAID THEY WERE SORRY...
...SO MOMOTARO FORGAVE THEM...
CLAP
CLAP
CLAP
...AND THEY ALL LIVED HAPPILY EVER AFTER!
?
?
HEY, HOLD YER HORSES!
I AIN'T GOTTEN TO THE *INFINITY GANG WARS* ARC YET!

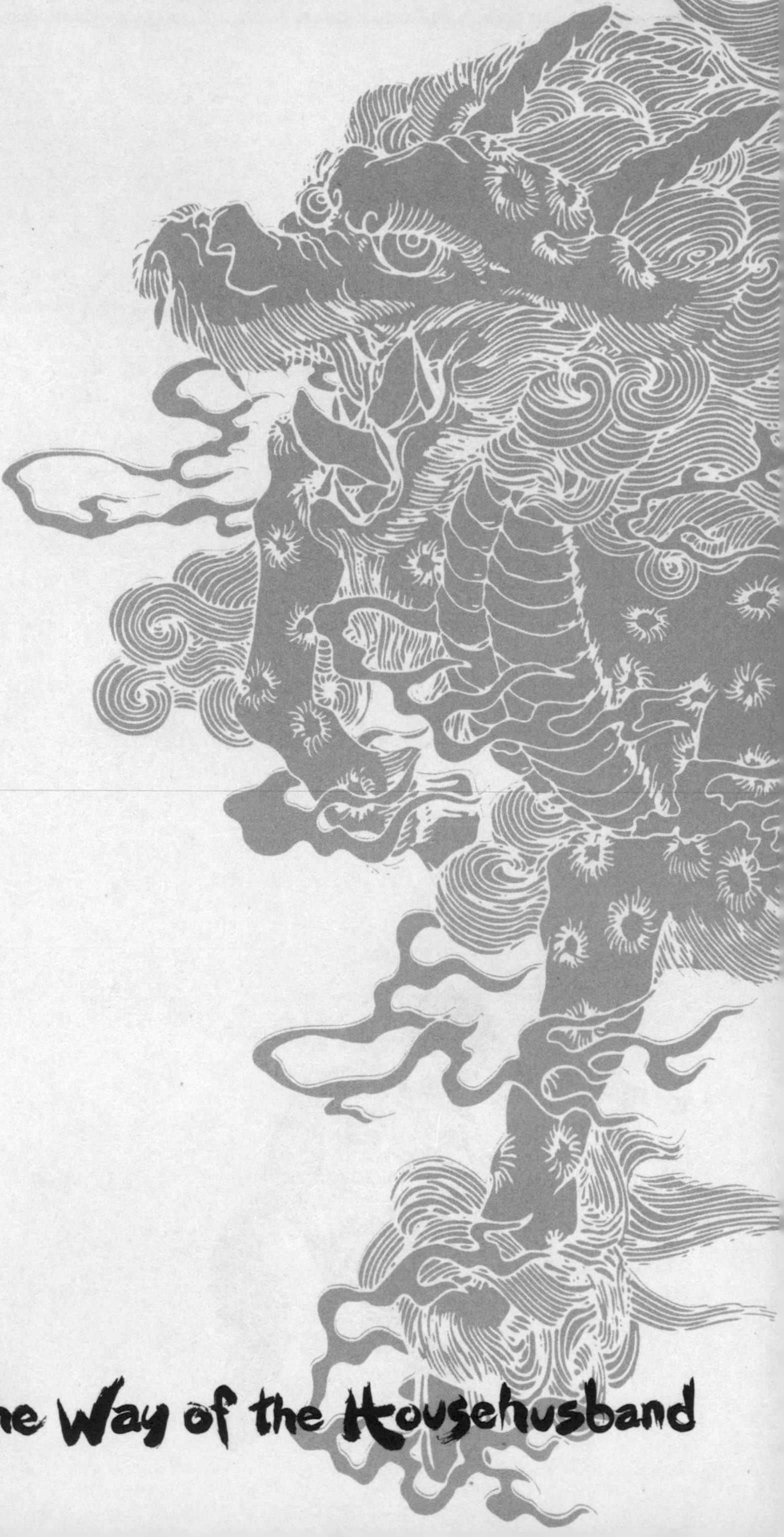

The Way of the Househusband

CHAPTER 34

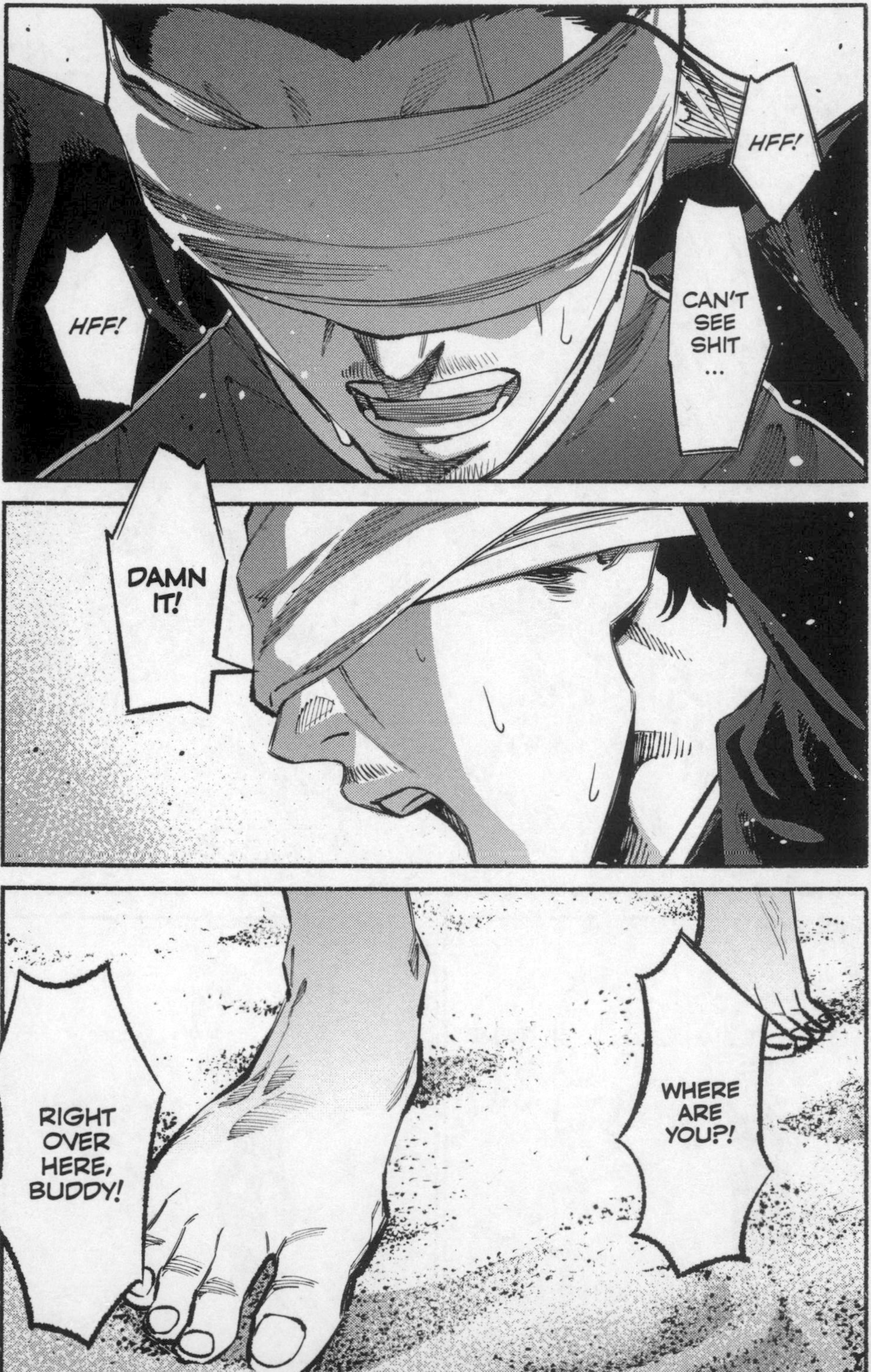
HFF!
CAN'T SEE SHIT ...
HFF!
DAMN IT!
WHERE ARE YOU?!
RIGHT OVER HERE, BUDDY!

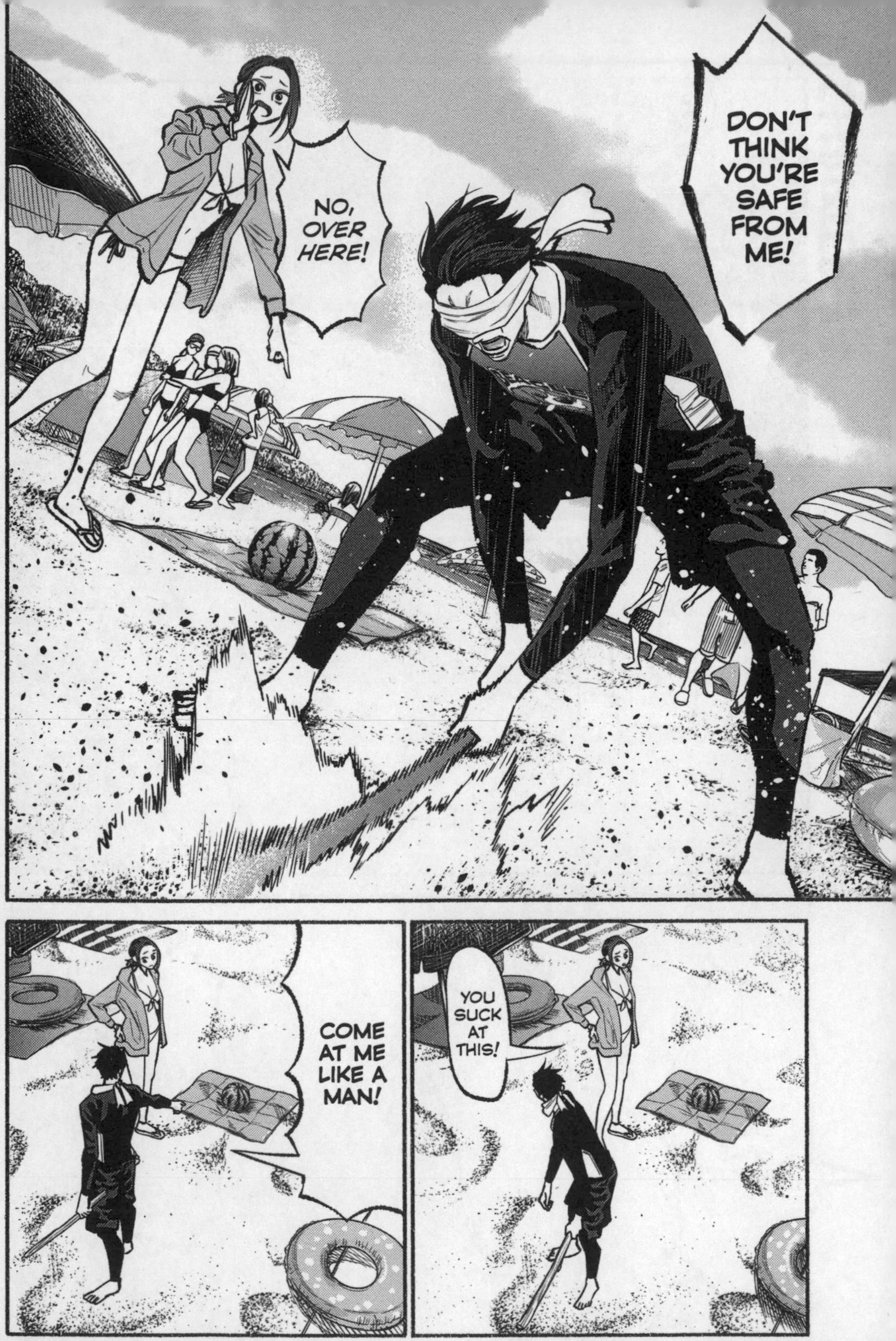
DON'T THINK YOU'RE SAFE FROM ME!
NO, OVER HERE!
YOU SUCK AT THIS!
COME AT ME LIKE A MAN!

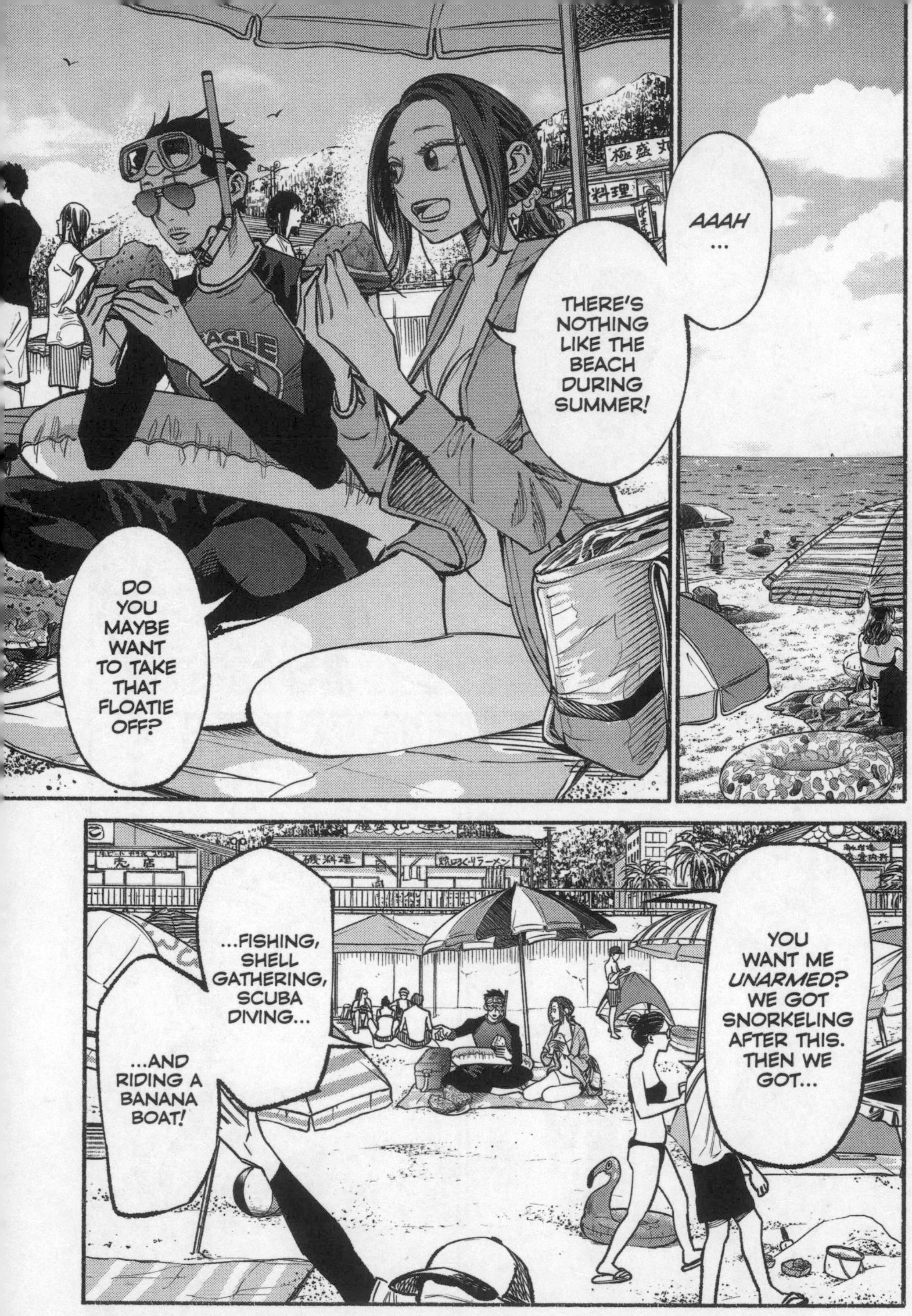
AAAH ...
THERE'S NOTHING LIKE THE BEACH DURING SUMMER!
DO YOU MAYBE WANT TO TAKE THAT FLOATIE OFF?
YOU WANT ME *UNARMED*? WE GOT SNORKELING AFTER THIS. THEN WE GOT...
...FISHING, SHELL GATHERING, SCUBA DIVING...
...AND RIDING A BANANA BOAT!

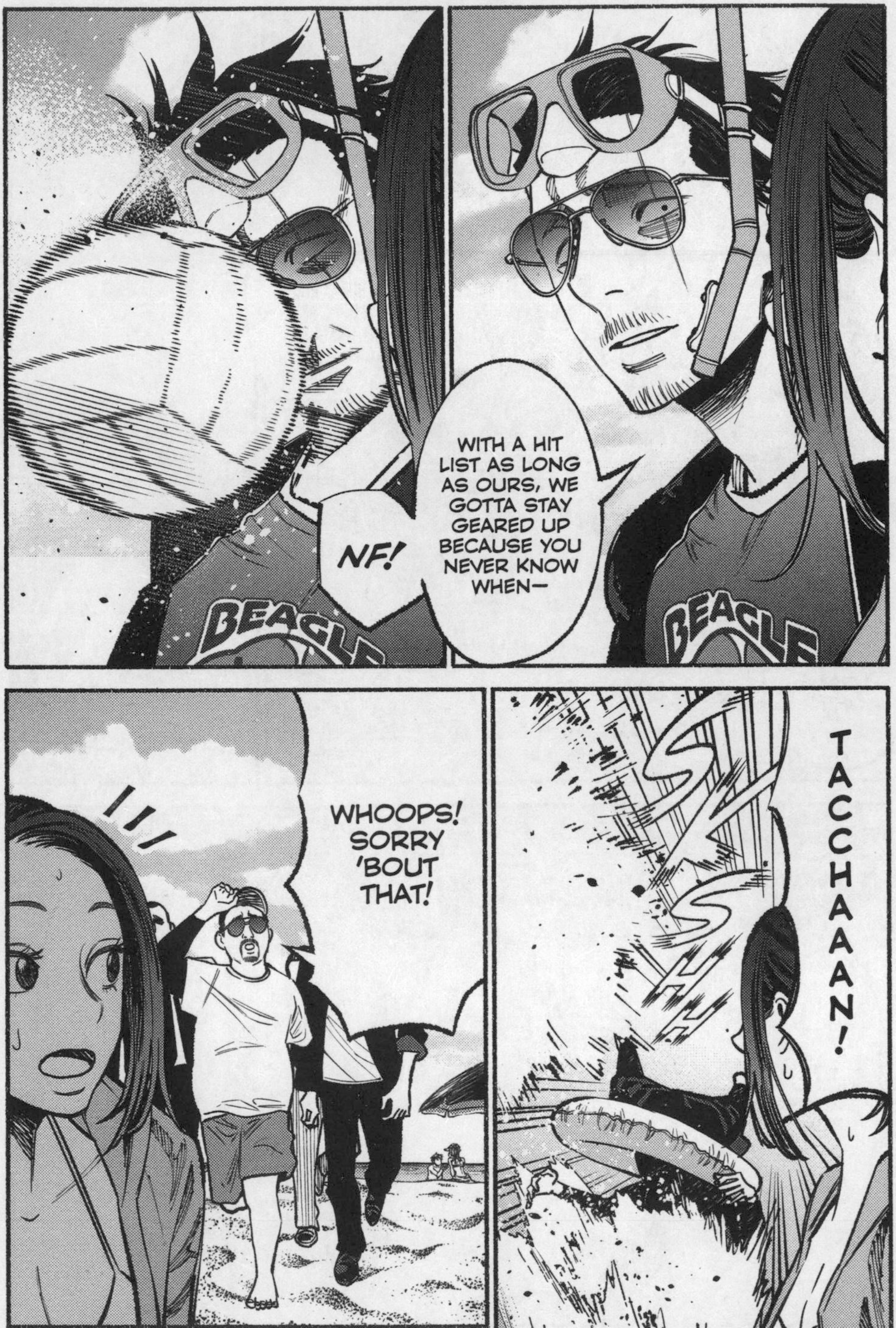
WITH A HIT LIST AS LONG AS OURS, WE GOTTA STAY GEARED UP BECAUSE YOU NEVER KNOW WHEN—
NF!
TACCHAAAN!
WHOOPS! SORRY 'BOUT THAT!

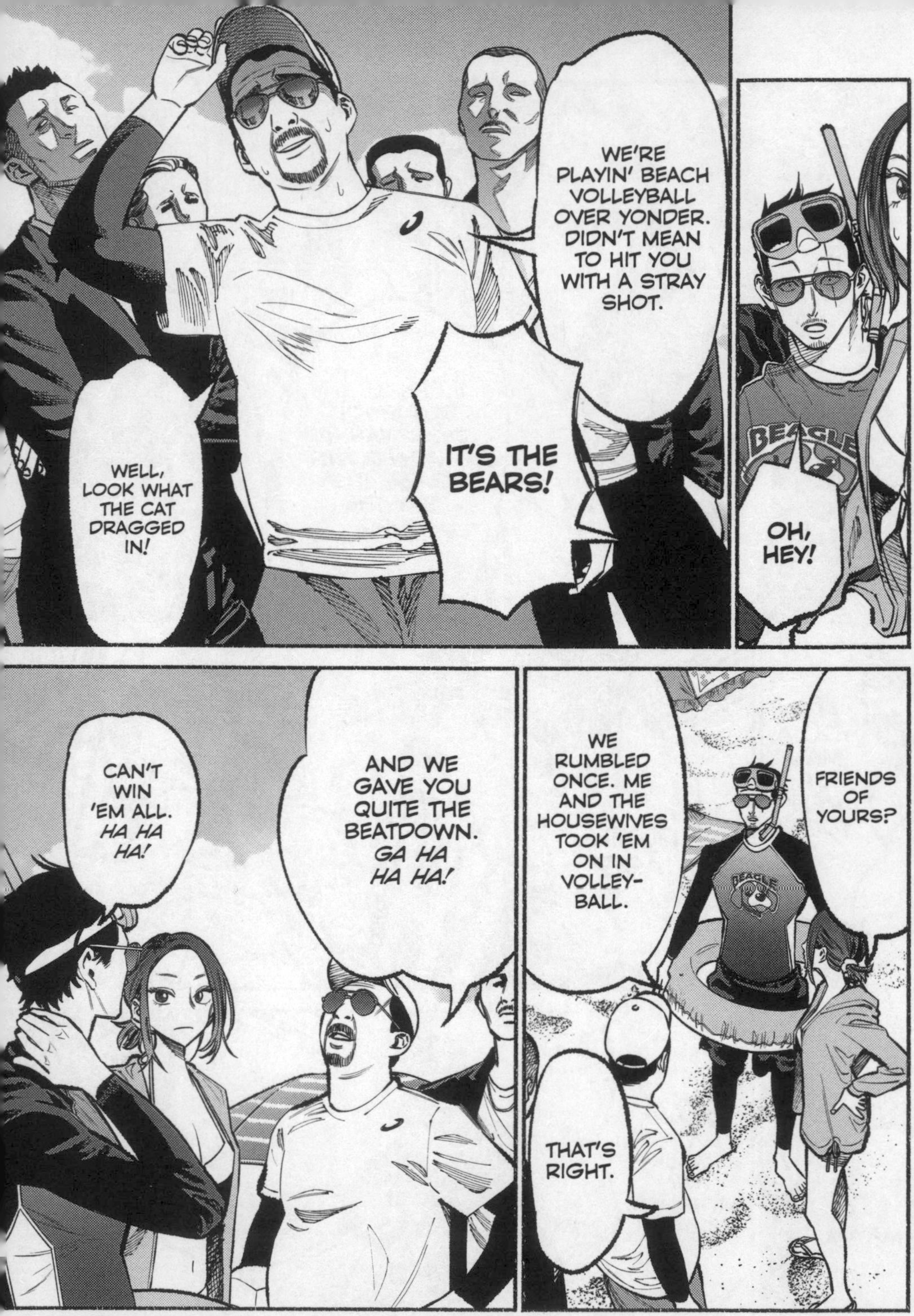
OH, HEY!
WE'RE PLAYIN' BEACH VOLLEYBALL OVER YONDER. DIDN'T MEAN TO HIT YOU WITH A STRAY SHOT.
IT'S THE BEARS!
WELL, LOOK WHAT THE CAT DRAGGED IN!
FRIENDS OF YOURS?
WE RUMBLED ONCE. ME AND THE HOUSEWIVES TOOK 'EM ON IN VOLLEY-BALL.
THAT'S RIGHT.
AND WE GAVE YOU QUITE THE BEATDOWN. *GA HA HA HA!*
CAN'T WIN 'EM ALL. *HA HA HA!*

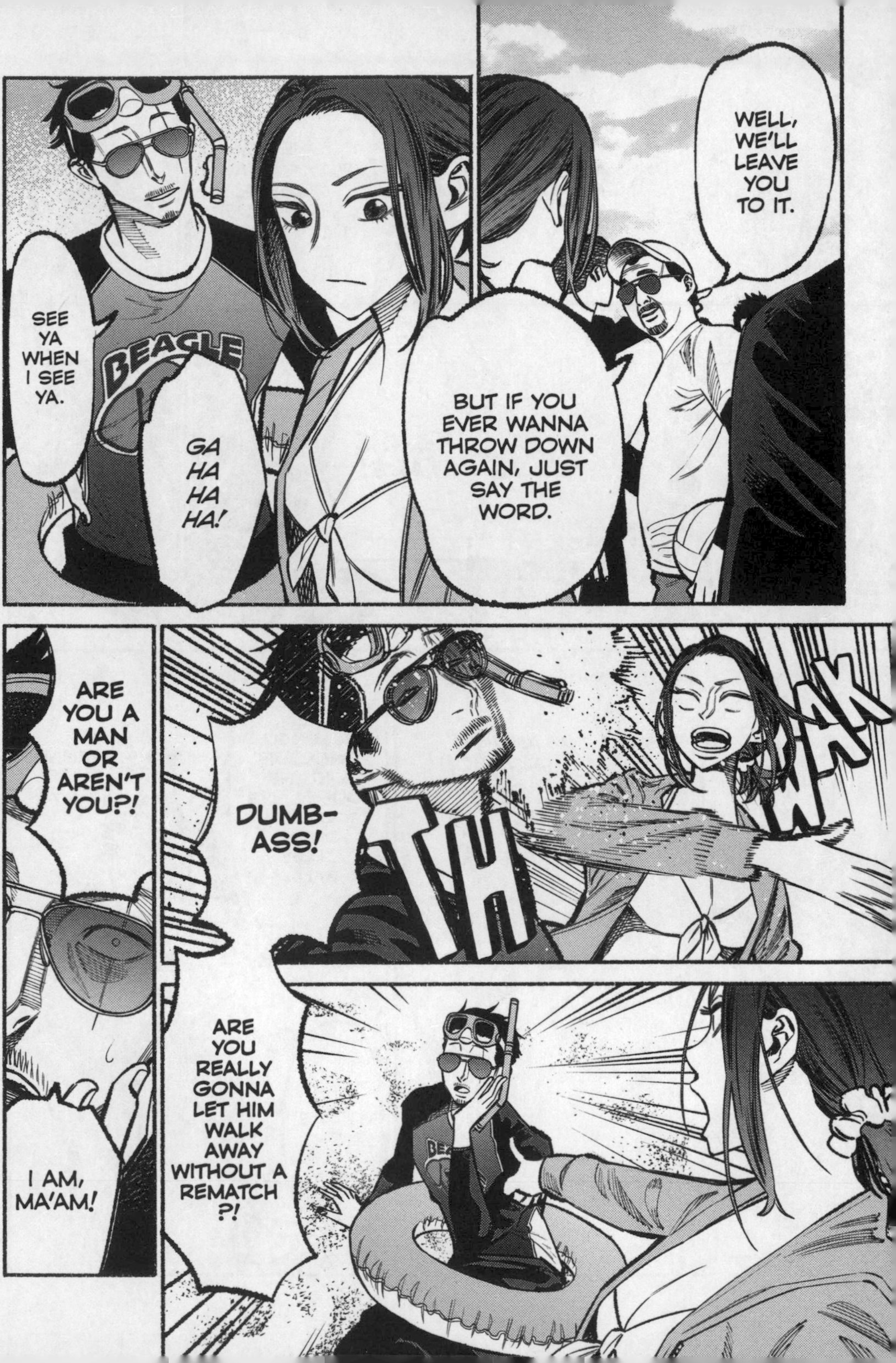
WELL, WE'LL LEAVE YOU TO IT.
BUT IF YOU EVER WANNA THROW DOWN AGAIN, JUST SAY THE WORD.
GA HA HA HA!
SEE YA WHEN I SEE YA.
DUMB-ASS!
TH
ARE YOU REALLY GONNA LET HIM WALK AWAY WITHOUT A REMATCH?!
ARE YOU A MAN OR AREN'T YOU?!
I AM, MA'AM!

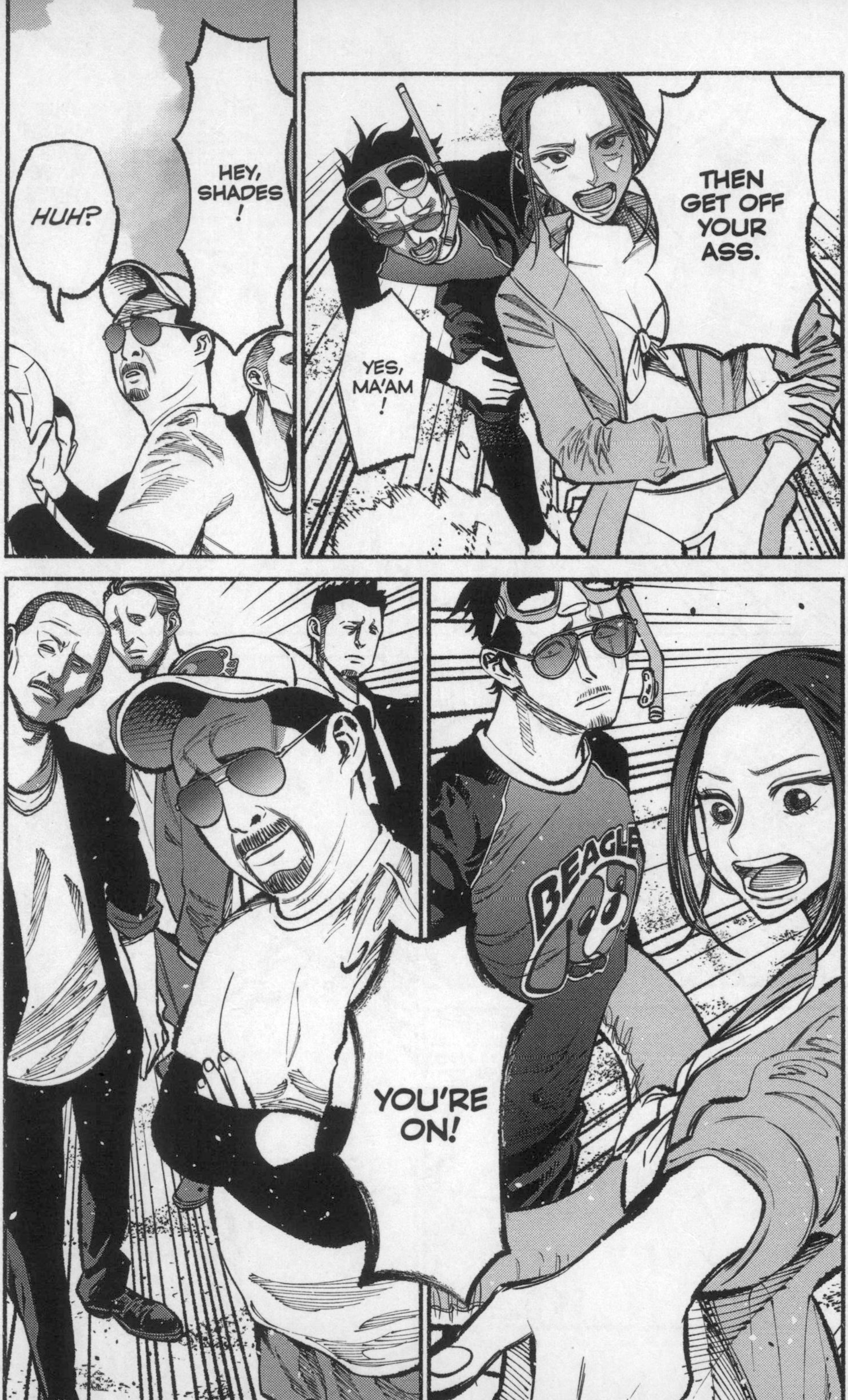
THEN GET OFF YOUR ASS.
YES, MA'AM!
HEY, SHADES!
HUH?
YOU'RE ON!

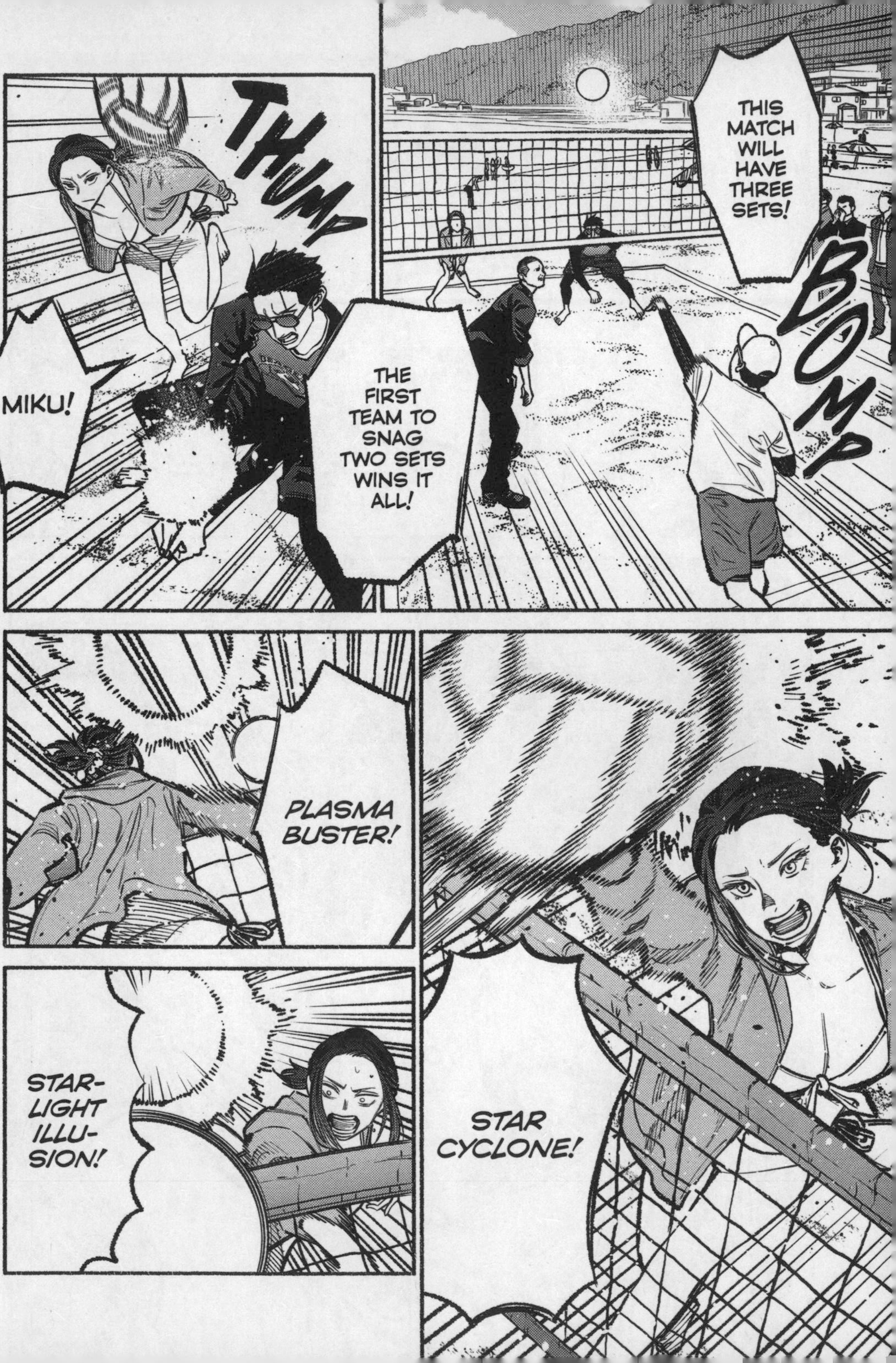
THIS MATCH WILL HAVE THREE SETS!
BOOMP!
THE FIRST TEAM TO SNAG TWO SETS WINS IT ALL!
THUMP
MIKU!
STAR CYCLONE!
PLASMA BUSTER!
STAR-LIGHT ILLU-SION!

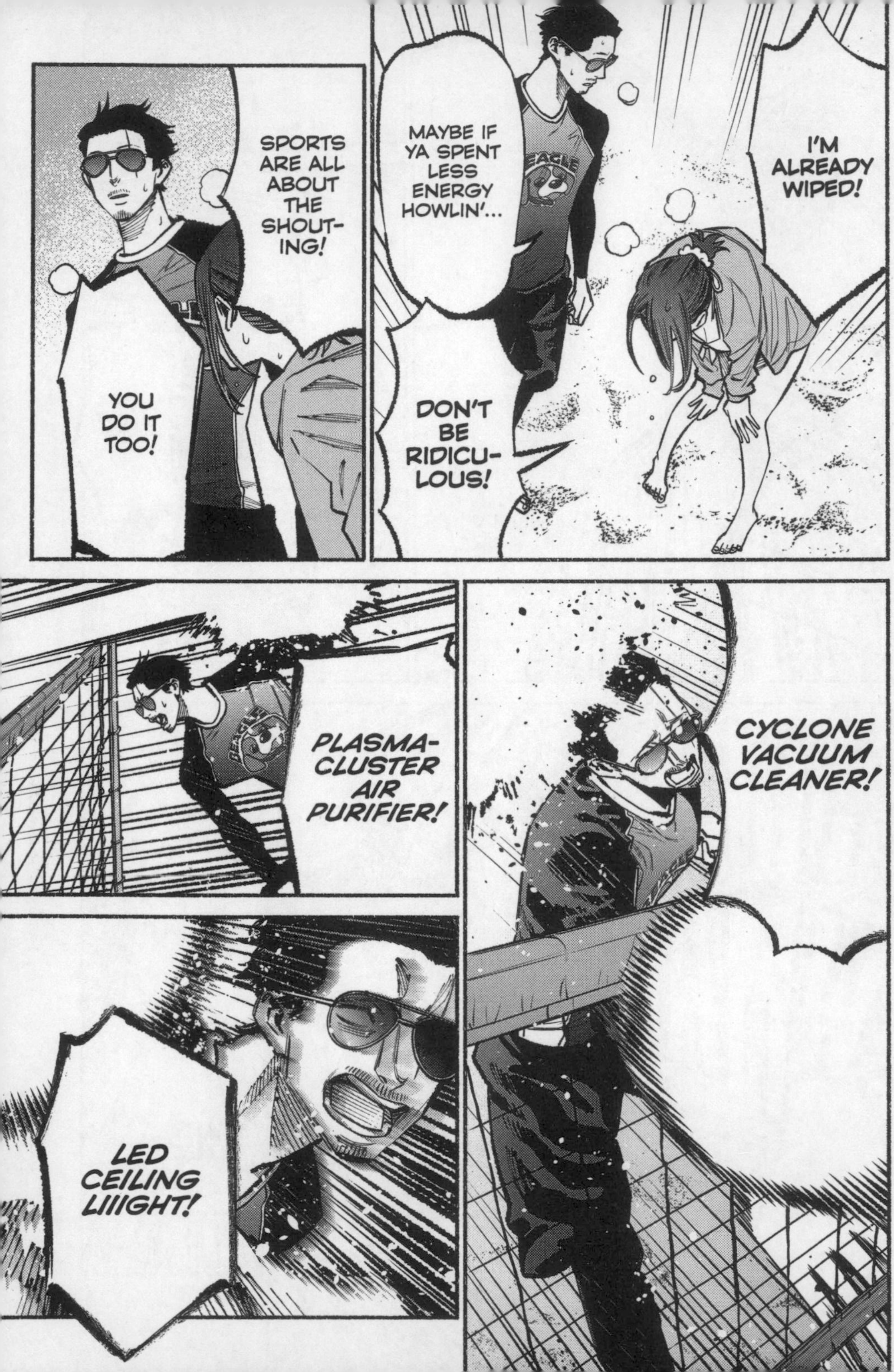
I'M ALREADY WIPED!
MAYBE IF YA SPENT LESS ENERGY HOWLIN'...
DON'T BE RIDICULOUS!
SPORTS ARE ALL ABOUT THE SHOUTING!
YOU DO IT TOO!
CYCLONE VACUUM CLEANER!
PLASMA-CLUSTER AIR PURIFIER!
LED CEILING LIIIGHT!

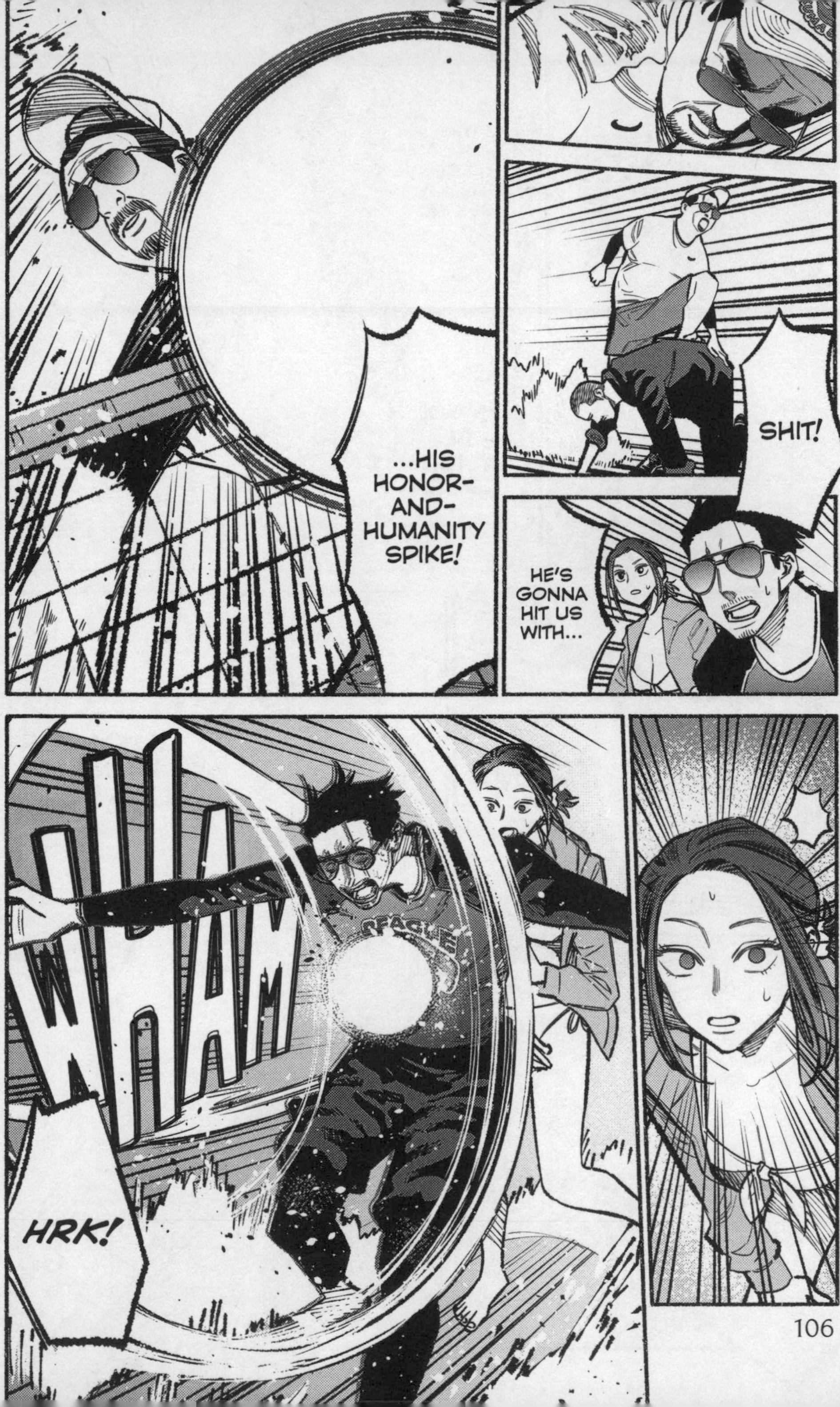
SHIT!
HE'S GONNA HIT US WITH...
...HIS HONOR-AND-HUMANITY SPIKE!
WHAM
HRK!

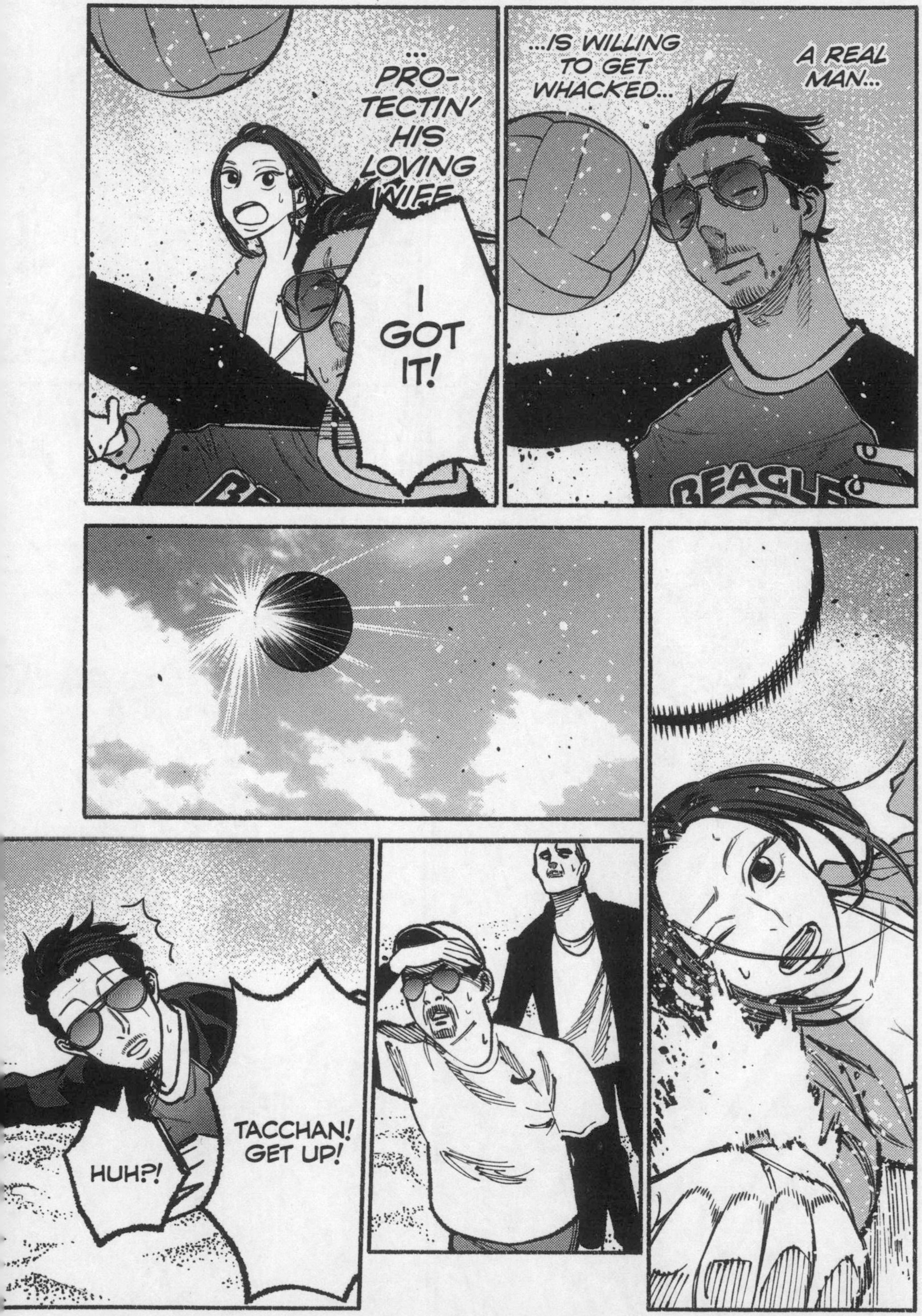
A REAL MAN...
...IS WILLING TO GET WHACKED...
... PROTECTIN' HIS LOVING WIFE
I GOT IT!
TACCHAN! GET UP!
HUH?!

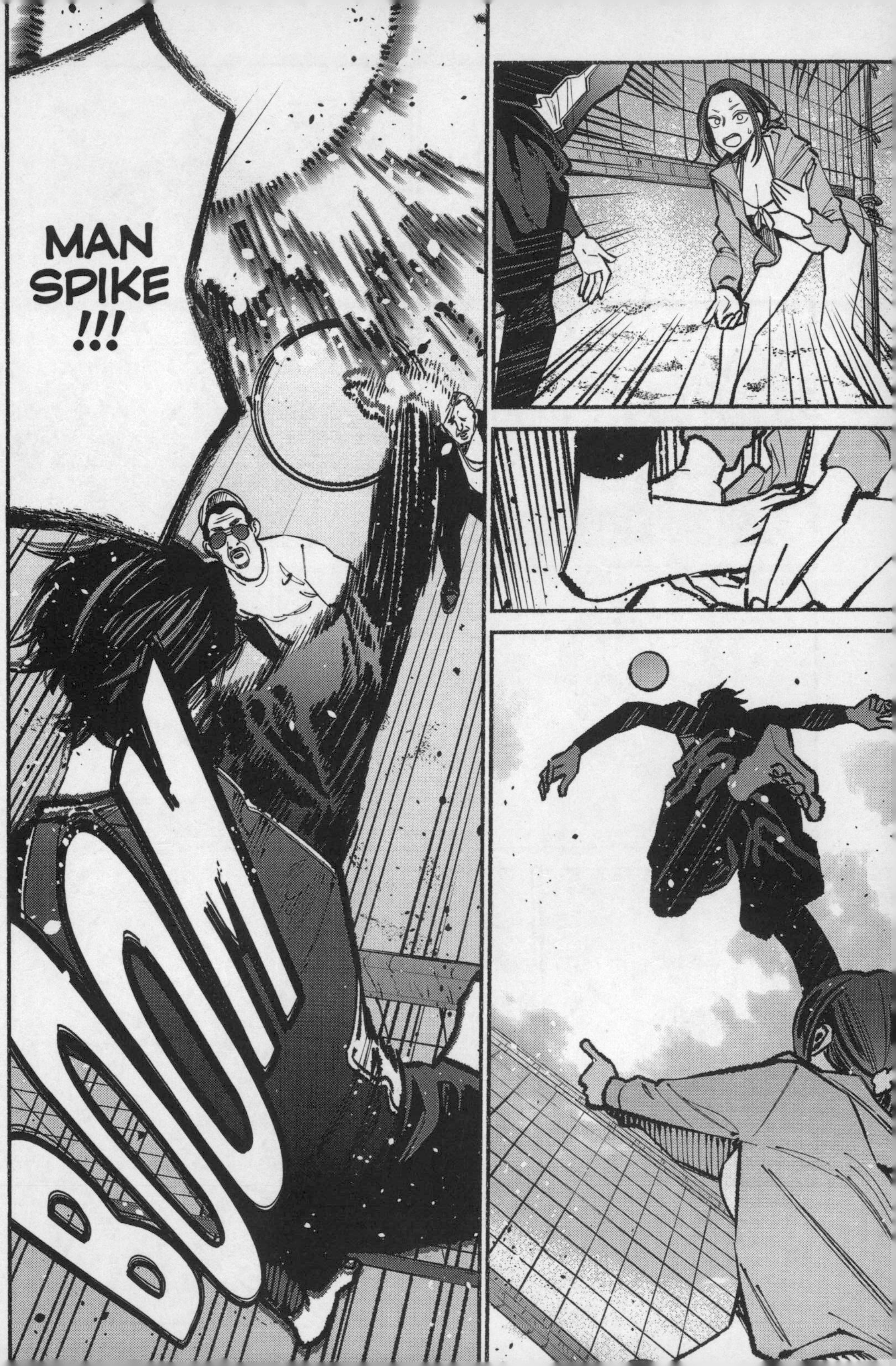
MAN SPIKE !!!
BOOM

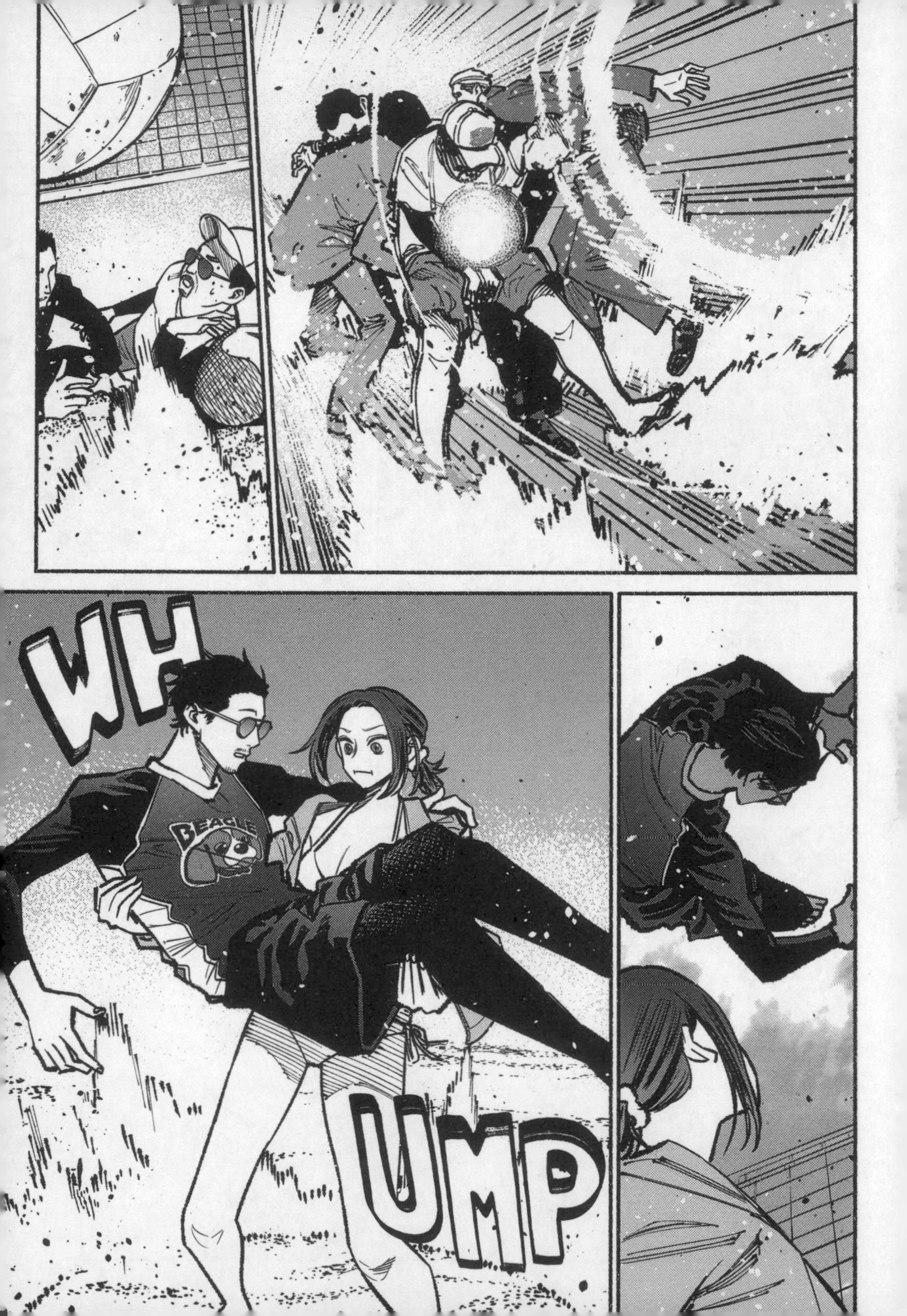
WH
BEAGLE
UMP

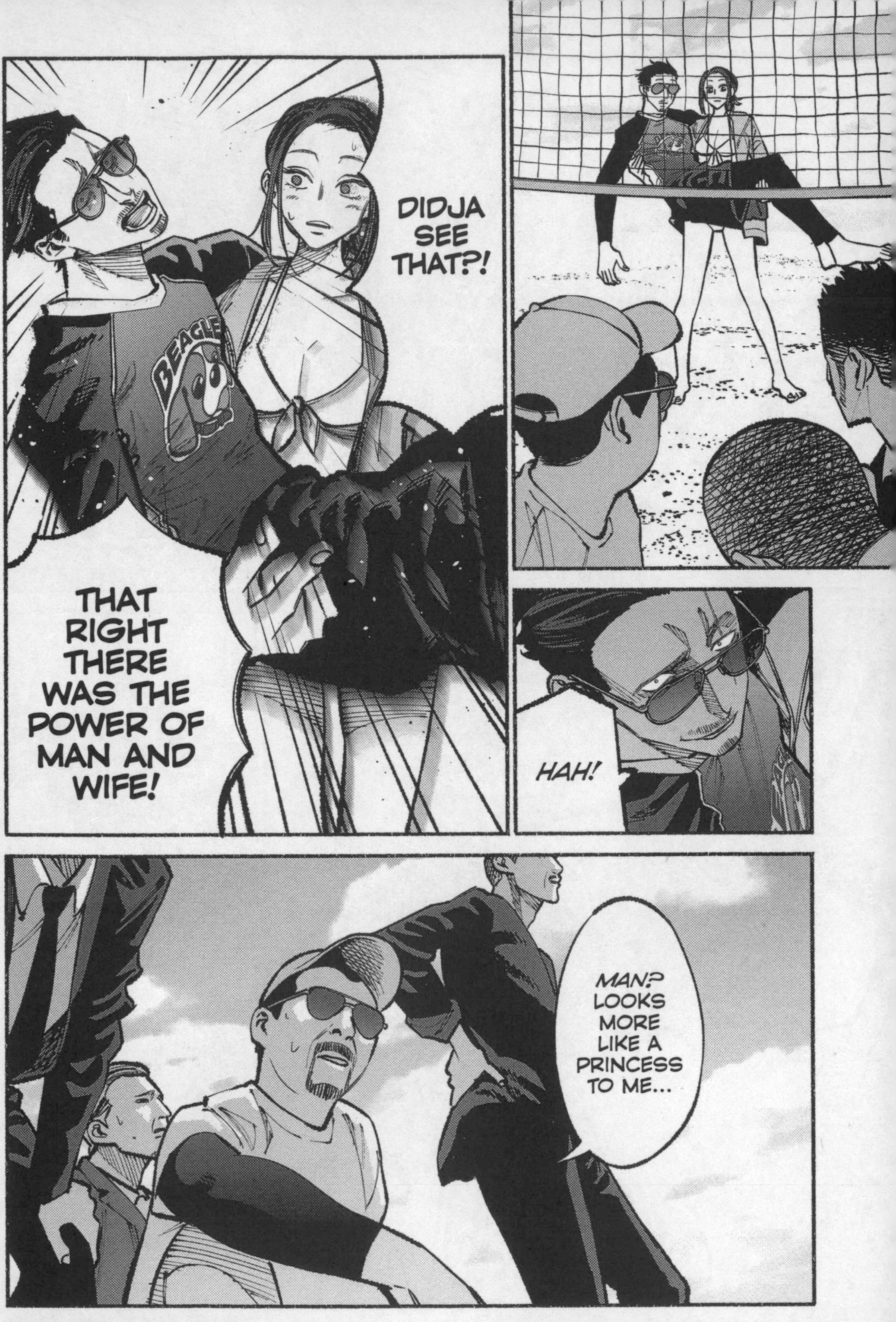
HAH!
DIDJA SEE THAT?!
BEAGLE
THAT RIGHT THERE WAS THE POWER OF MAN AND WIFE!
MAN? LOOKS MORE LIKE A PRINCESS TO ME...

BEAGLE

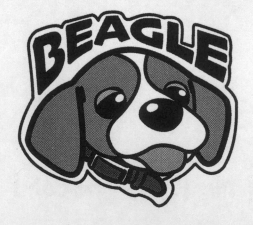

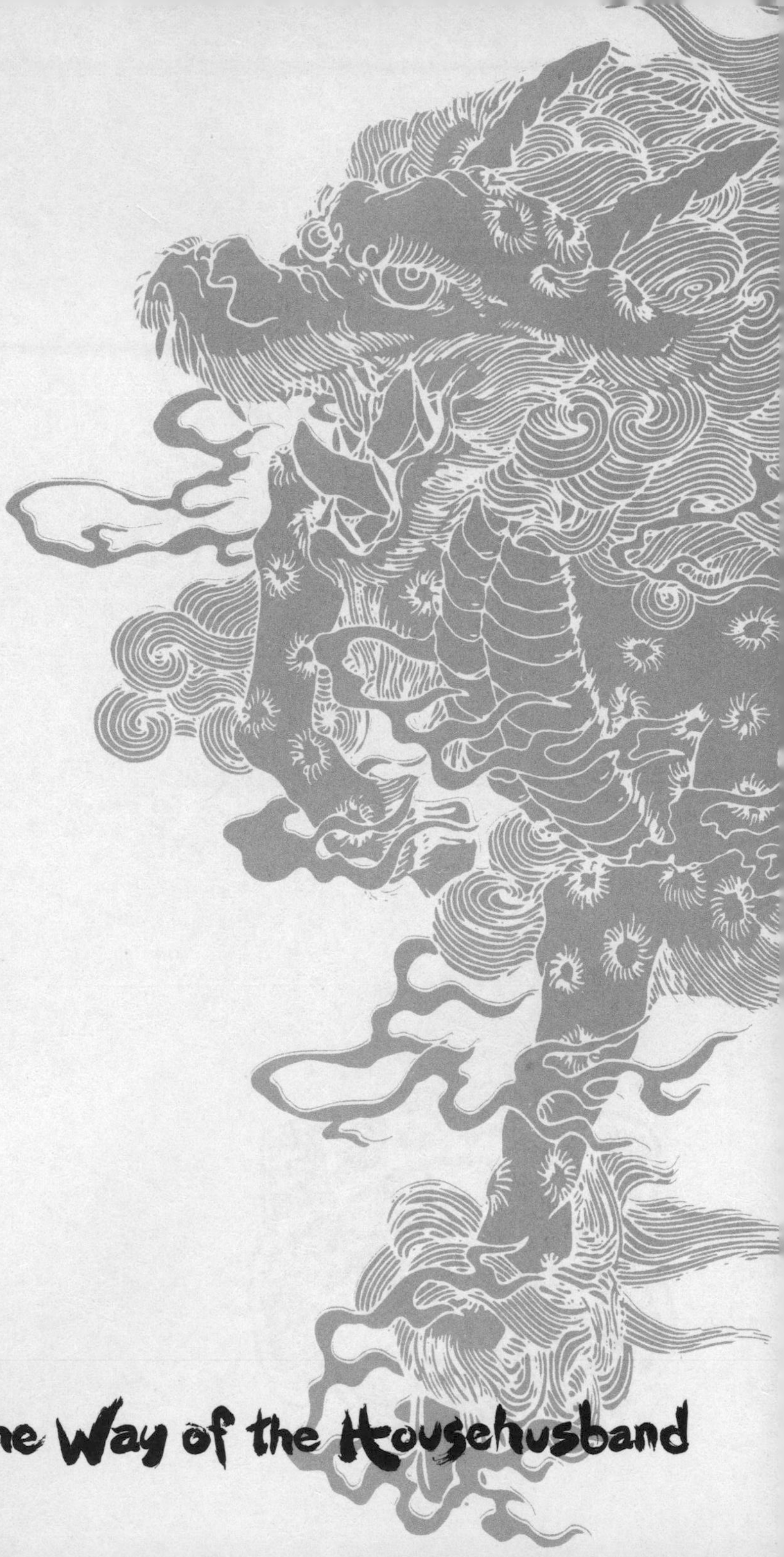

The Way of the Househusband

CHAPTER 35

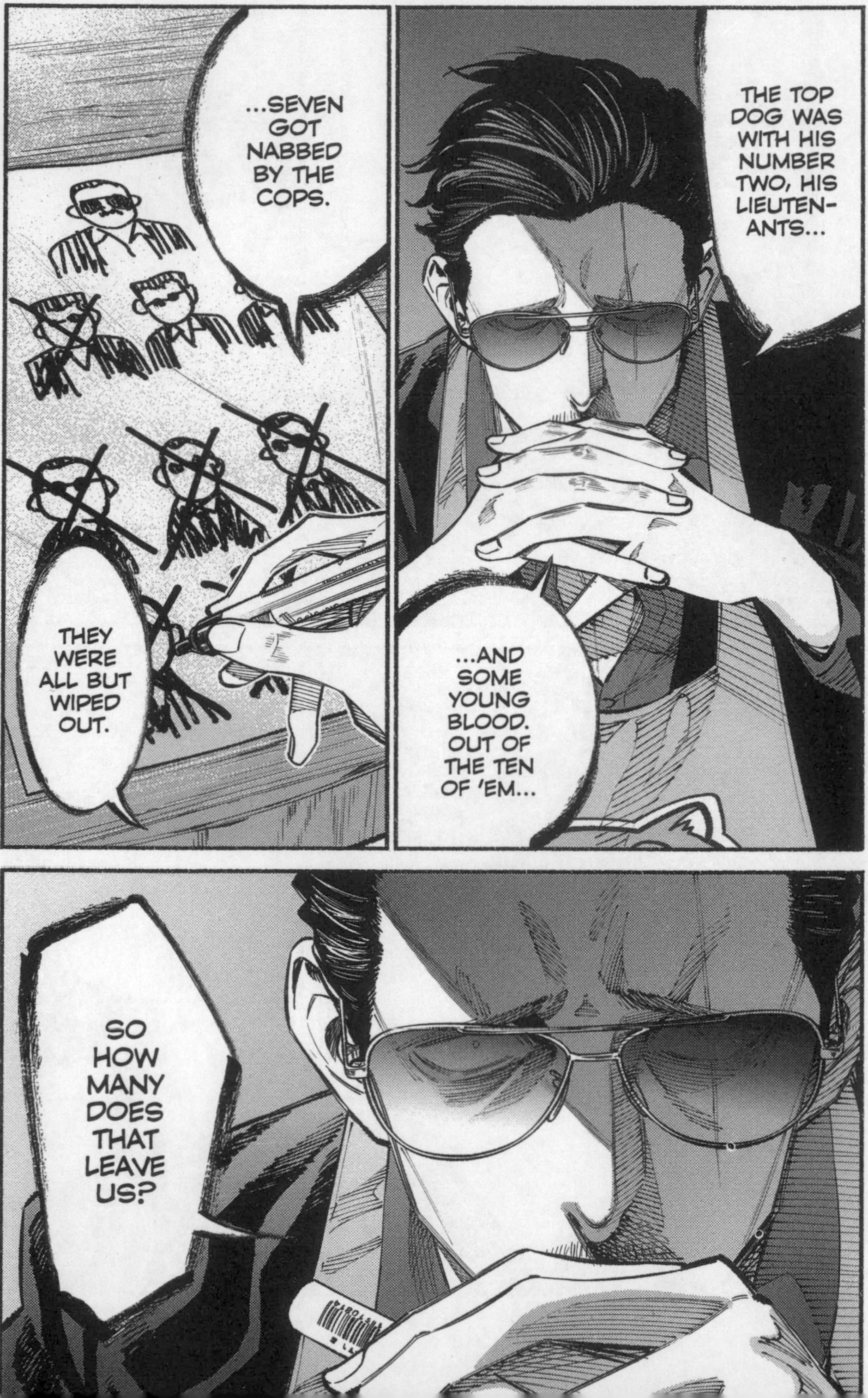
THE TOP DOG WAS WITH HIS NUMBER TWO, HIS LIEUTEN-ANTS...
...AND SOME YOUNG BLOOD. OUT OF THE TEN OF 'EM...
...SEVEN GOT NABBED BY THE COPS.
THEY WERE ALL BUT WIPED OUT.
SO HOW MANY DOES THAT LEAVE US?

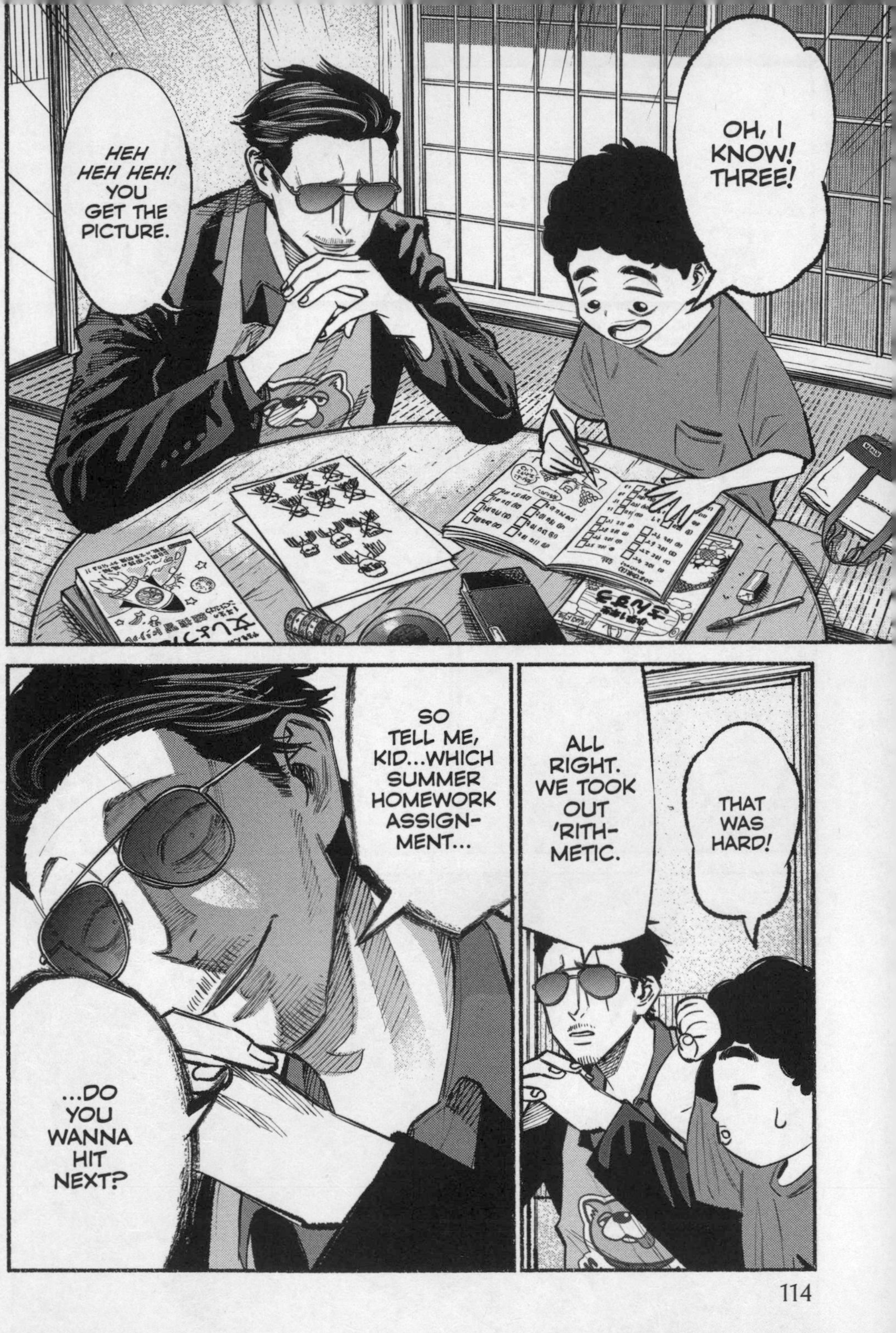
OH, I KNOW! THREE!
HEH HEH HEH! YOU GET THE PICTURE.
ALL RIGHT. WE TOOK OUT 'RITH-METIC.
THAT WAS HARD!
SO TELL ME, KID...WHICH SUMMER HOMEWORK ASSIGN-MENT...
...DO YOU WANNA HIT NEXT?

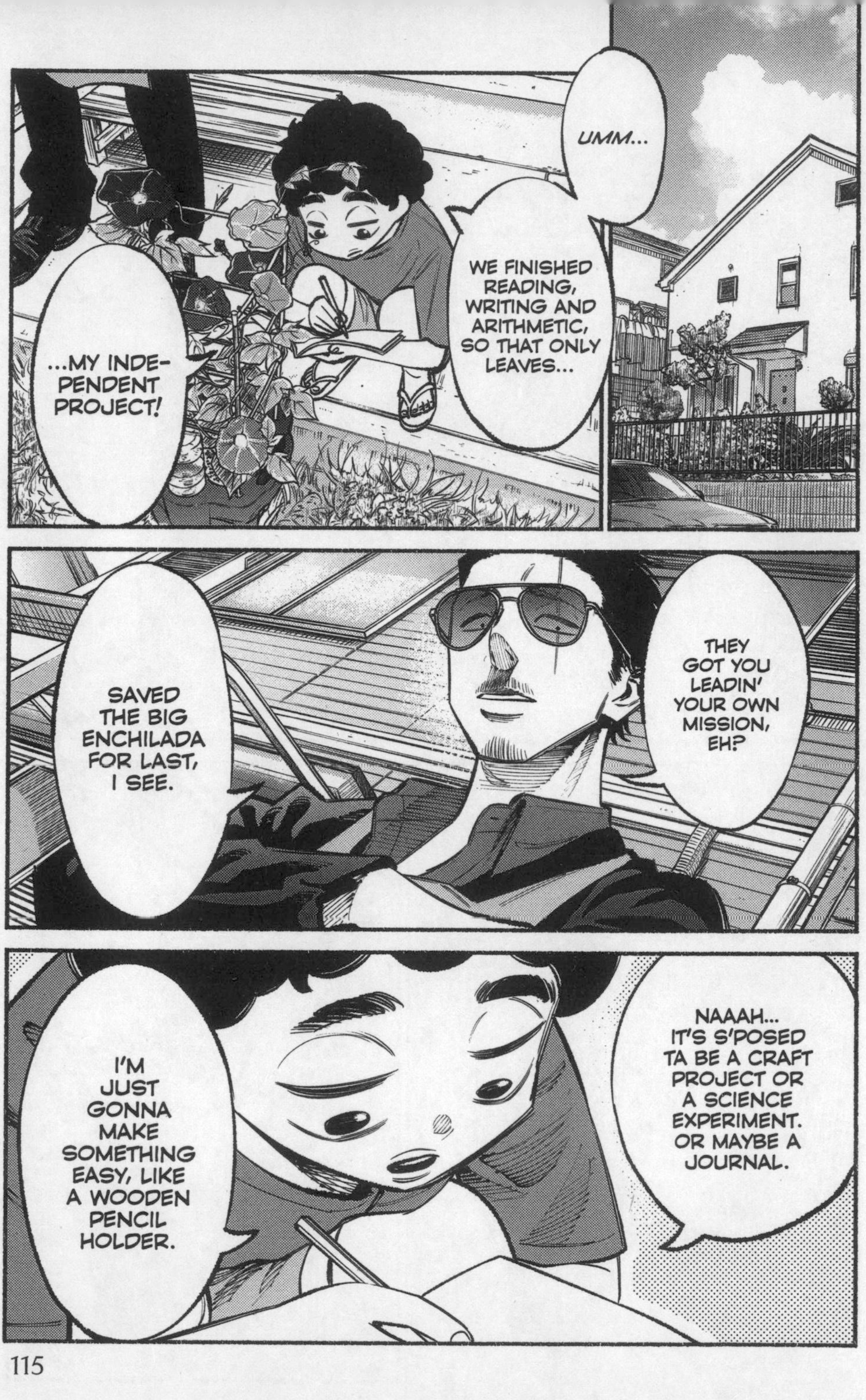
UMM...
WE FINISHED READING, WRITING AND ARITHMETIC, SO THAT ONLY LEAVES...
...MY INDE-PENDENT PROJECT!
THEY GOT YOU LEADIN' YOUR OWN MISSION, EH?
SAVED THE BIG ENCHILADA FOR LAST, I SEE.
NAAAH... IT'S S'POSED TA BE A CRAFT PROJECT OR A SCIENCE EXPERIMENT. OR MAYBE A JOURNAL.
I'M JUST GONNA MAKE SOMETHING EASY, LIKE A WOODEN PENCIL HOLDER.

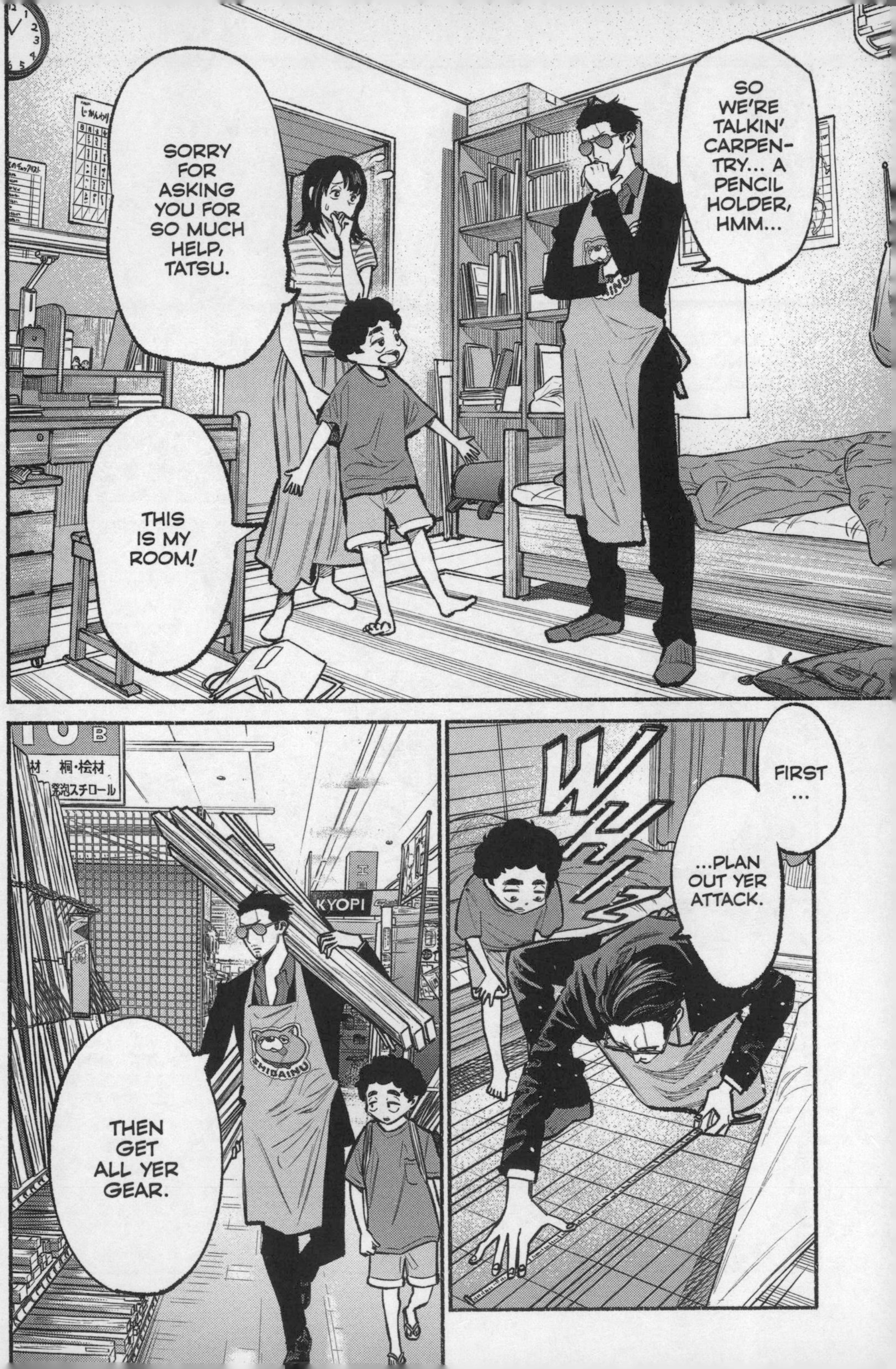
SO WE'RE TALKIN' CARPENTRY... A PENCIL HOLDER, HMM...
SORRY FOR ASKING YOU FOR SO MUCH HELP, TATSU.
THIS IS MY ROOM!
FIRST ...
...PLAN OUT YER ATTACK.
桐・桧材
発泡スチロール
KYOPI
THEN GET ALL YER GEAR.

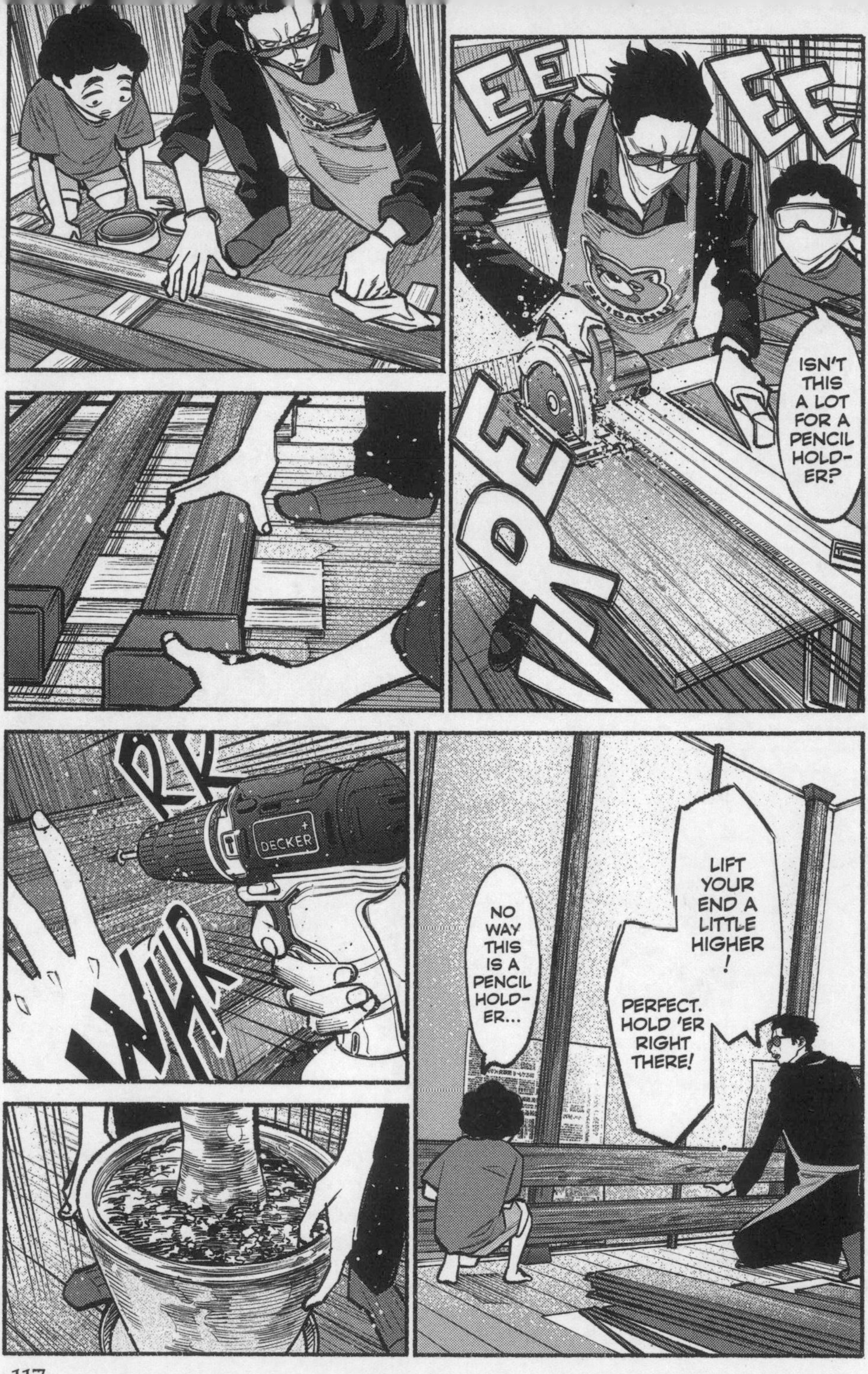
EE
EE
ISN'T THIS A LOT FOR A PENCIL HOLDER?
LIFT YOUR END A LITTLE HIGHER!
NO WAY THIS IS A PENCIL HOLDER...
PERFECT. HOLD 'ER RIGHT THERE!
DECKER

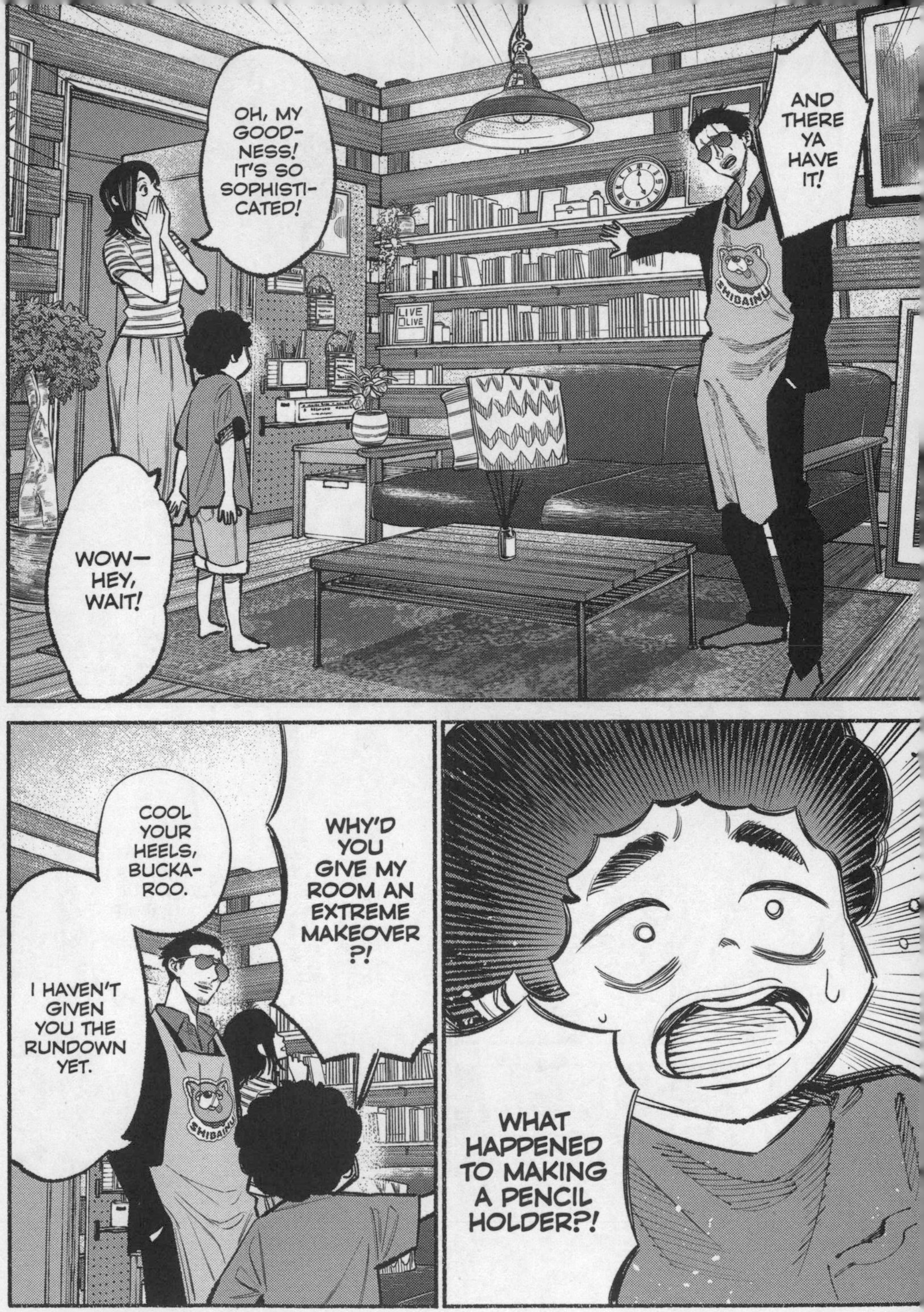
AND THERE YA HAVE IT!
OH, MY GOODNESS! IT'S SO SOPHISTICATED!
WOW— HEY, WAIT!
WHAT HAPPENED TO MAKING A PENCIL HOLDER?!
WHY'D YOU GIVE MY ROOM AN EXTREME MAKEOVER?!
COOL YOUR HEELS, BUCKAROO.
I HAVEN'T GIVEN YOU THE RUNDOWN YET.

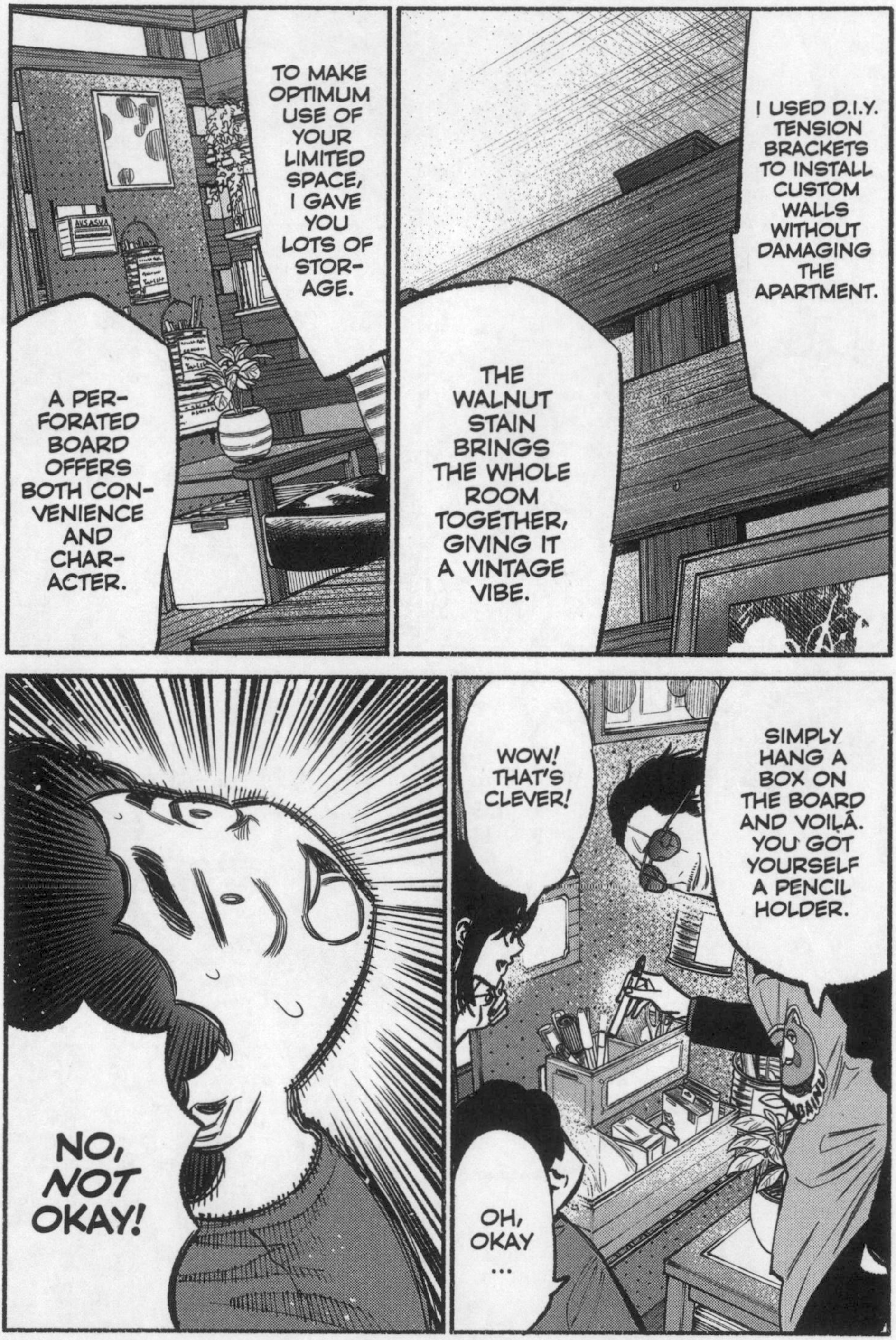
I USED D.I.Y. TENSION BRACKETS TO INSTALL CUSTOM WALLS WITHOUT DAMAGING THE APARTMENT.
THE WALNUT STAIN BRINGS THE WHOLE ROOM TOGETHER, GIVING IT A VINTAGE VIBE.
TO MAKE OPTIMUM USE OF YOUR LIMITED SPACE, I GAVE YOU LOTS OF STOR-AGE.
A PER-FORATED BOARD OFFERS BOTH CON-VENIENCE AND CHAR-ACTER.
SIMPLY HANG A BOX ON THE BOARD AND VOILÀ. YOU GOT YOURSELF A PENCIL HOLDER.
WOW! THAT'S CLEVER!
OH, OKAY ...
NO, NOT OKAY!

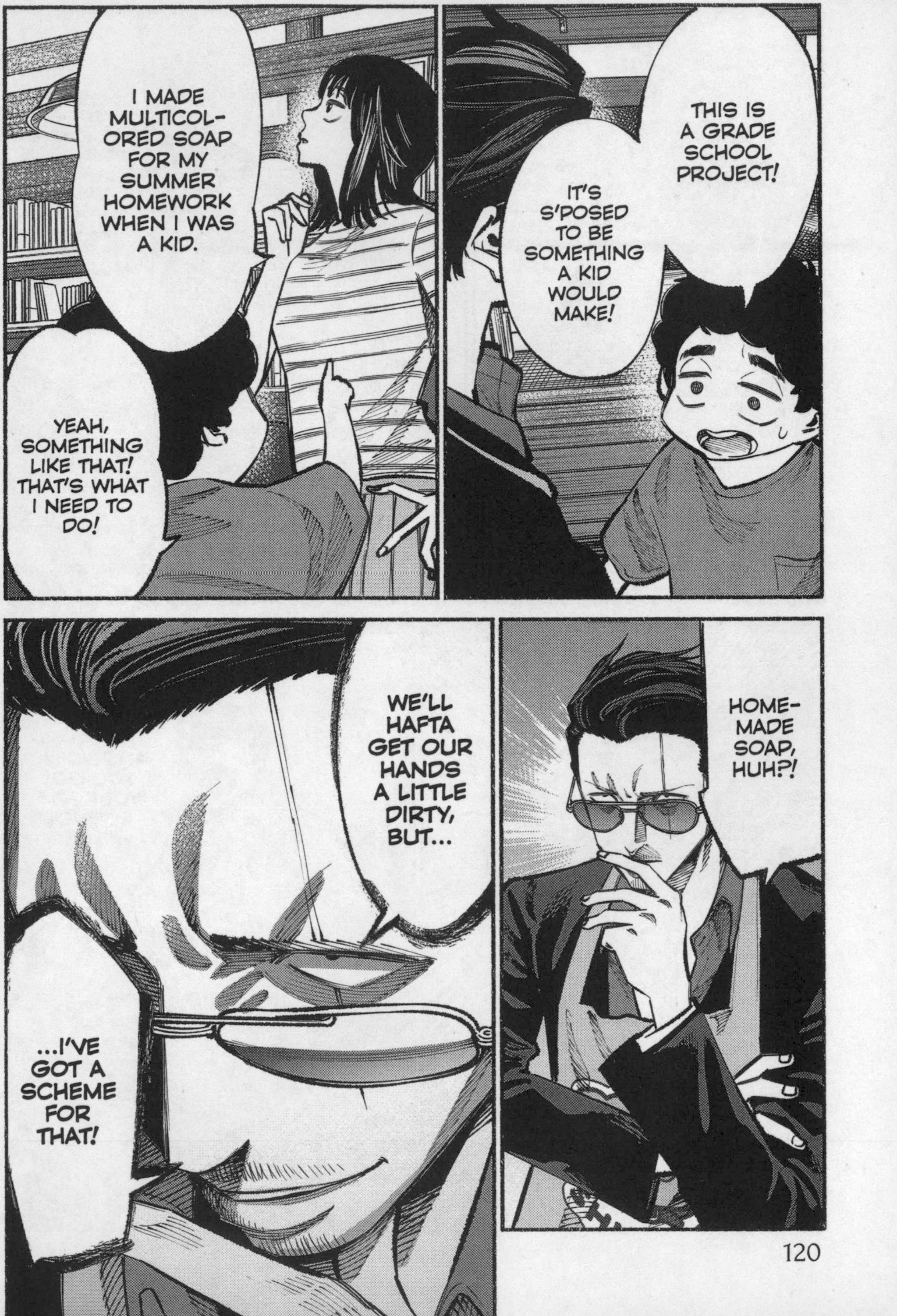
THIS IS A GRADE SCHOOL PROJECT!
IT'S S'POSED TO BE SOMETHING A KID WOULD MAKE!
I MADE MULTICOLORED SOAP FOR MY SUMMER HOMEWORK WHEN I WAS A KID.
YEAH, SOMETHING LIKE THAT! THAT'S WHAT I NEED TO DO!
HOME-MADE SOAP, HUH?!
WE'LL HAFTA GET OUR HANDS A LITTLE DIRTY, BUT...
...I'VE GOT A SCHEME FOR THAT!

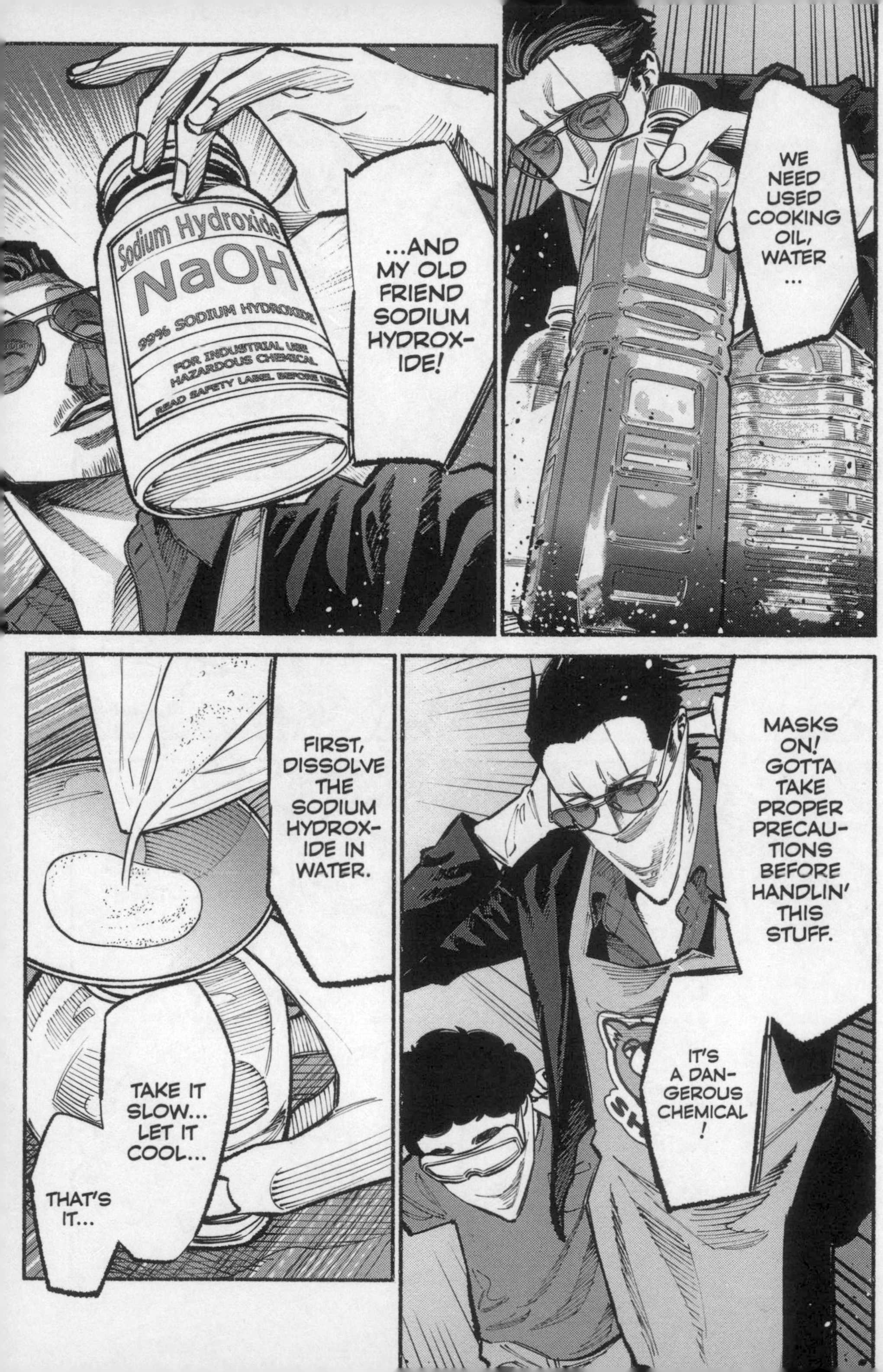
WE NEED USED COOKING OIL, WATER ...
...AND MY OLD FRIEND SODIUM HYDROX-IDE!
Sodium Hydroxide
NaOH
99% SODIUM HYDROXIDE
FOR INDUSTRIAL USE
HAZARDOUS CHEMICAL
READ SAFETY LABEL BEFORE USE
MASKS ON! GOTTA TAKE PROPER PRECAU-TIONS BEFORE HANDLIN' THIS STUFF.
IT'S A DAN-GEROUS CHEMICAL!
FIRST, DISSOLVE THE SODIUM HYDROX-IDE IN WATER.
TAKE IT SLOW... LET IT COOL...
THAT'S IT...

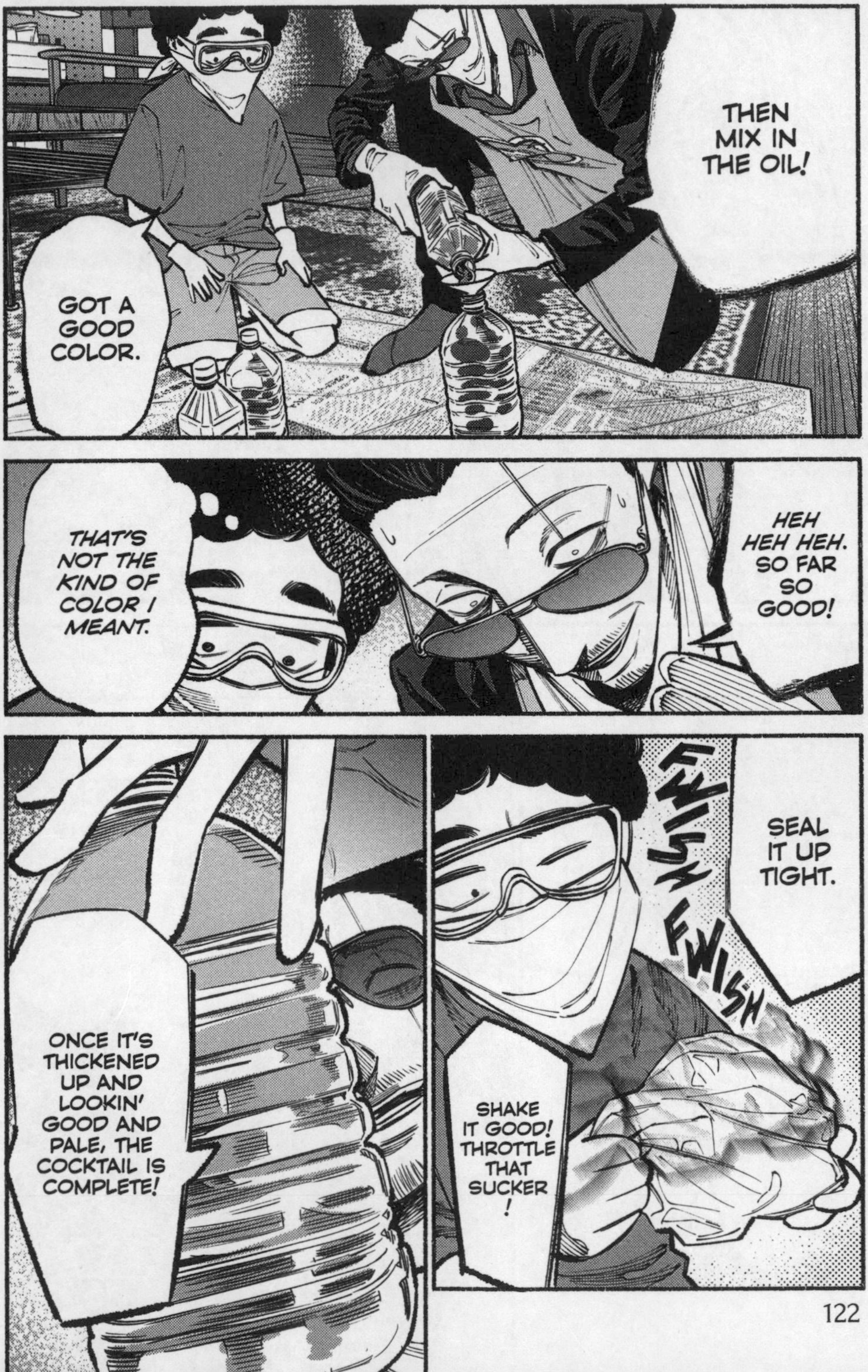
THEN MIX IN THE OIL!
GOT A GOOD COLOR.
HEH HEH HEH. SO FAR SO GOOD!
THAT'S NOT THE KIND OF COLOR I MEANT.
SEAL IT UP TIGHT.
FWISH FWISH
SHAKE IT GOOD! THROTTLE THAT SUCKER!
ONCE IT'S THICKENED UP AND LOOKIN' GOOD AND PALE, THE COCKTAIL IS COMPLETE!

ALMOST DONE. POUR THE MIXTURE INTO AN EMPTY MILK CARTON AND WAIT FOR IT TO HARDEN.

HOW LONG?

IN SUMMER, THREE DAYS.

OKAY!

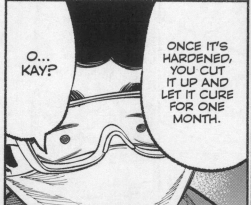

ONCE IT'S HARDENED, YOU CUT IT UP AND LET IT CURE FOR ONE MONTH.

O... KAY?

BUT IT'S THE LAST DAY OF SUMMER VACATION...

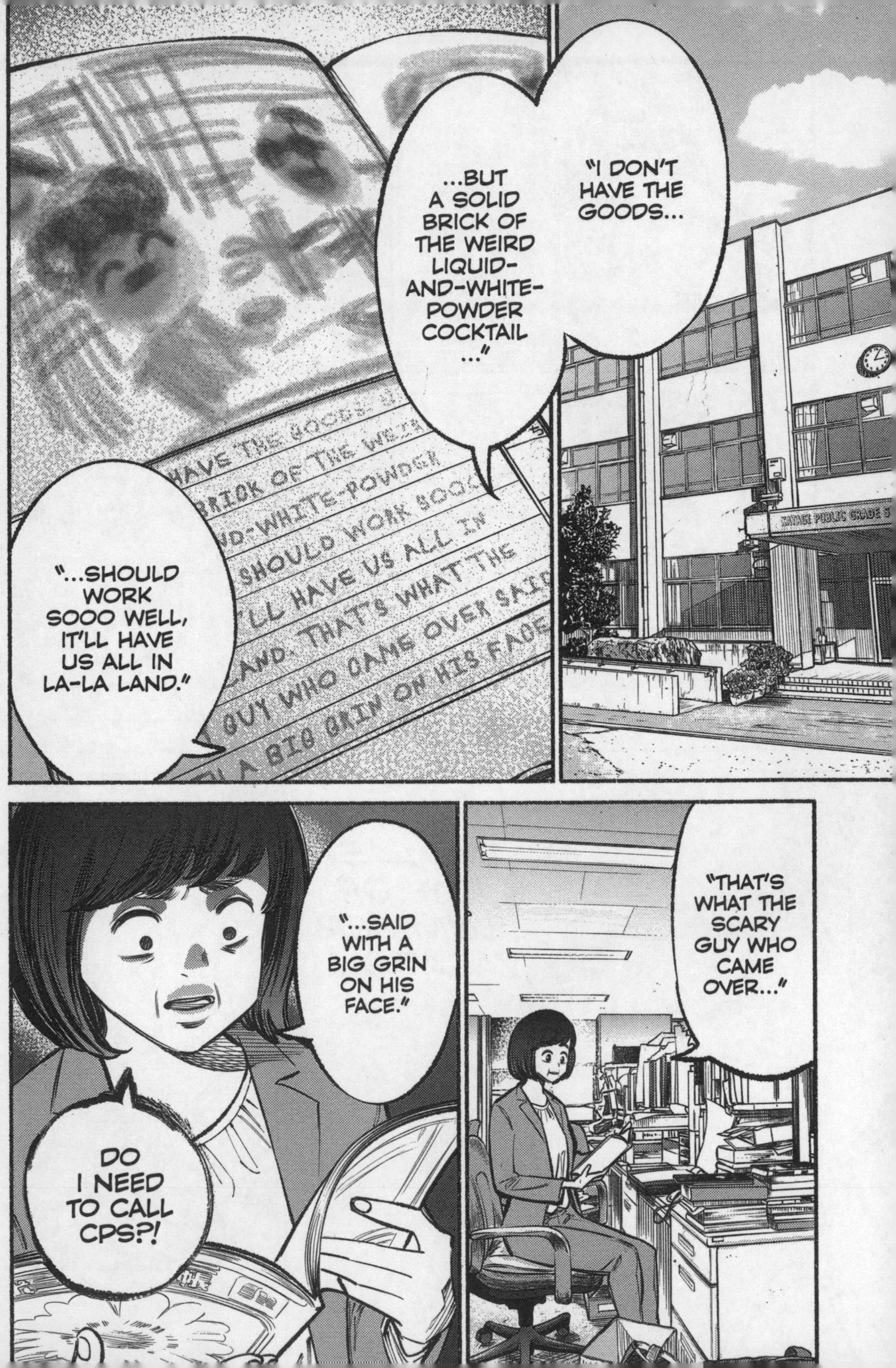
"I DON'T HAVE THE GOODS...
...BUT A SOLID BRICK OF THE WEIRD LIQUID-AND-WHITE-POWDER COCKTAIL ..."
"...SHOULD WORK SOOO WELL, IT'LL HAVE US ALL IN LA-LA LAND."
"THAT'S WHAT THE SCARY GUY WHO CAME OVER..."
"...SAID WITH A BIG GRIN ON HIS FACE."
DO I NEED TO CALL CPS?!

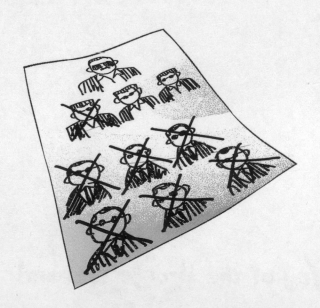

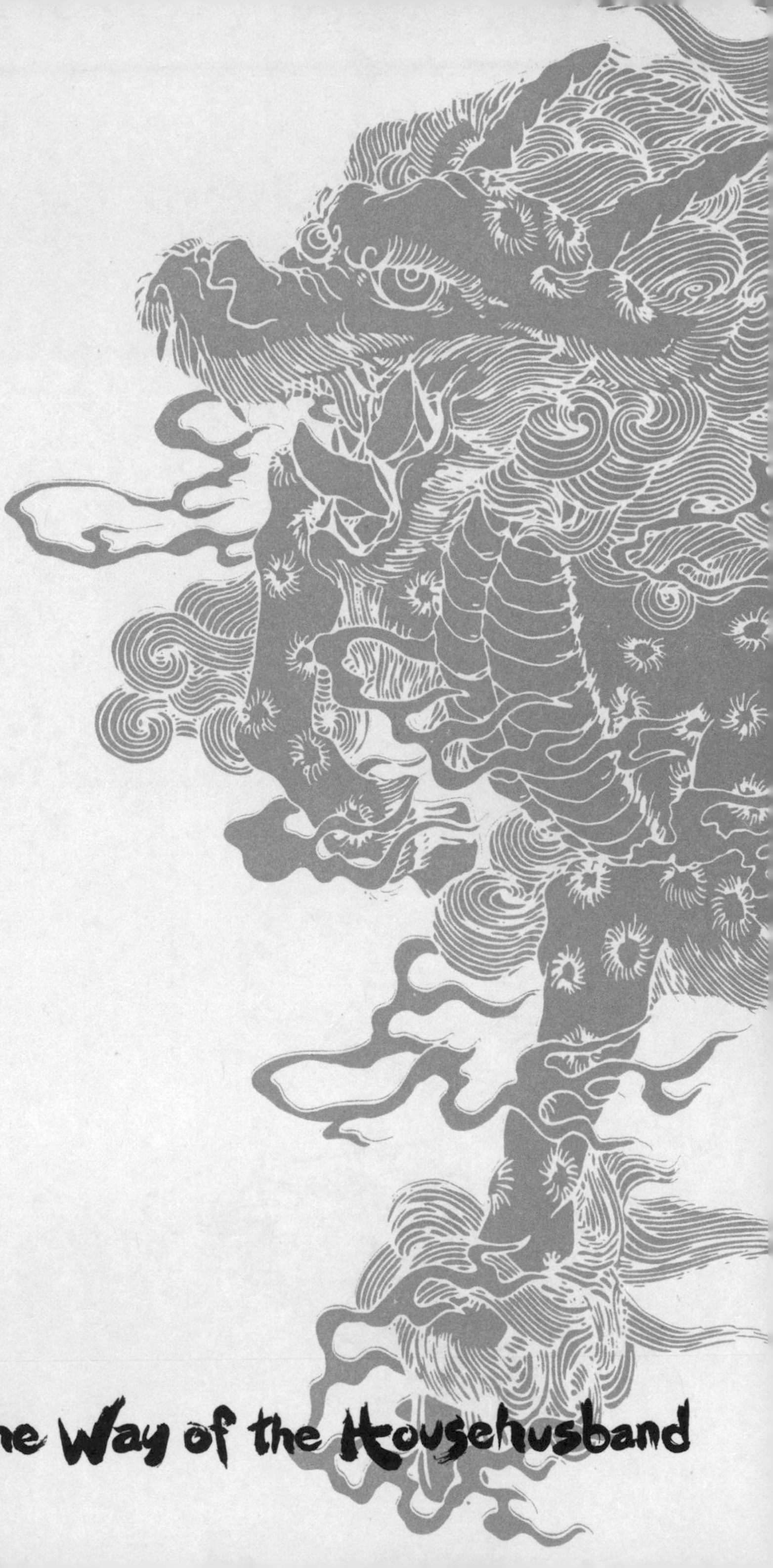

The Way of the Househusband

CHAPTER 36

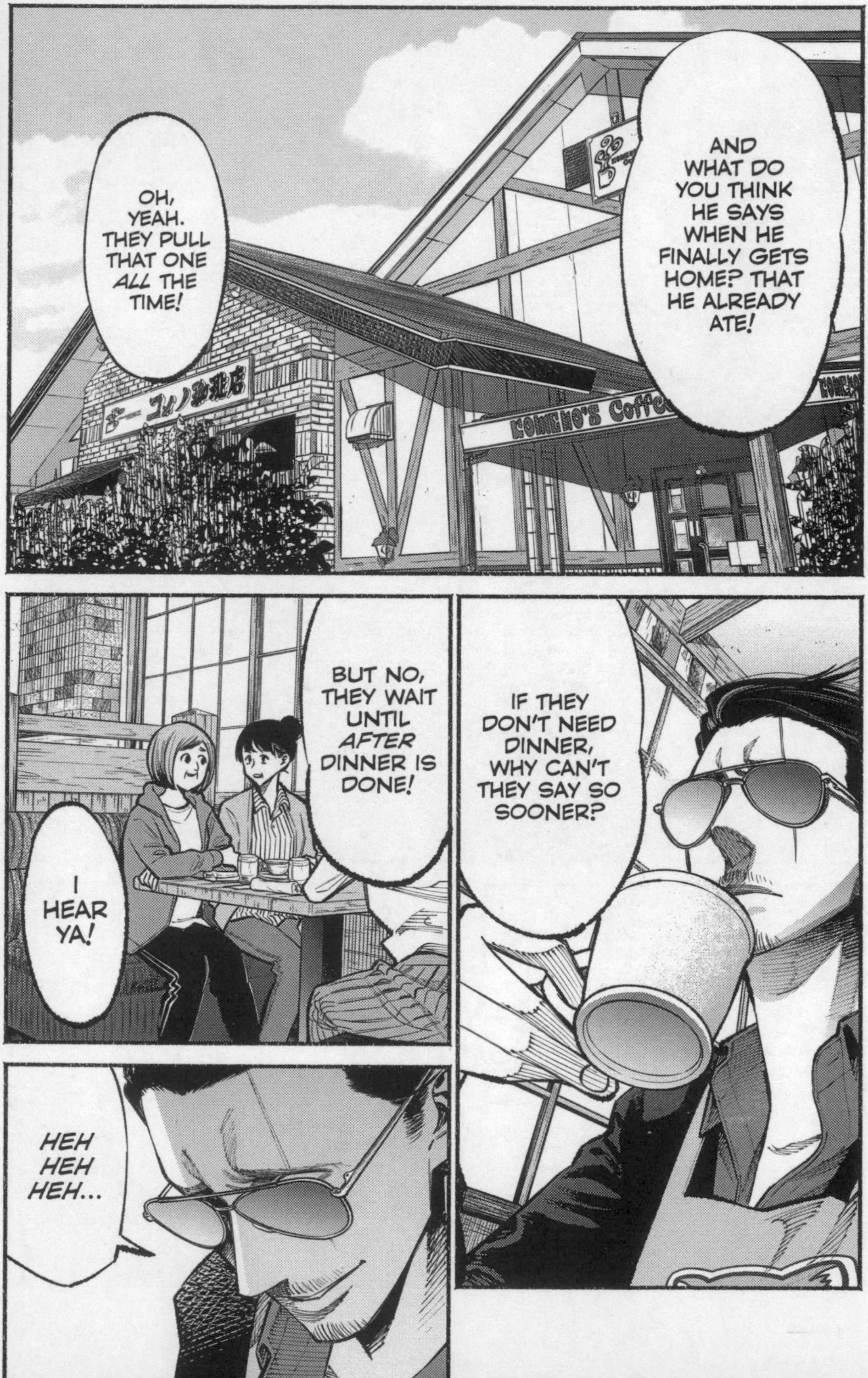
AND WHAT DO YOU THINK HE SAYS WHEN HE FINALLY GETS HOME? THAT HE ALREADY ATE!
OH, YEAH. THEY PULL THAT ONE *ALL* THE TIME!
IF THEY DON'T NEED DINNER, WHY CAN'T THEY SAY SO SOONER?
BUT NO, THEY WAIT UNTIL *AFTER* DINNER IS DONE!
I HEAR YA!
HEH HEH HEH...

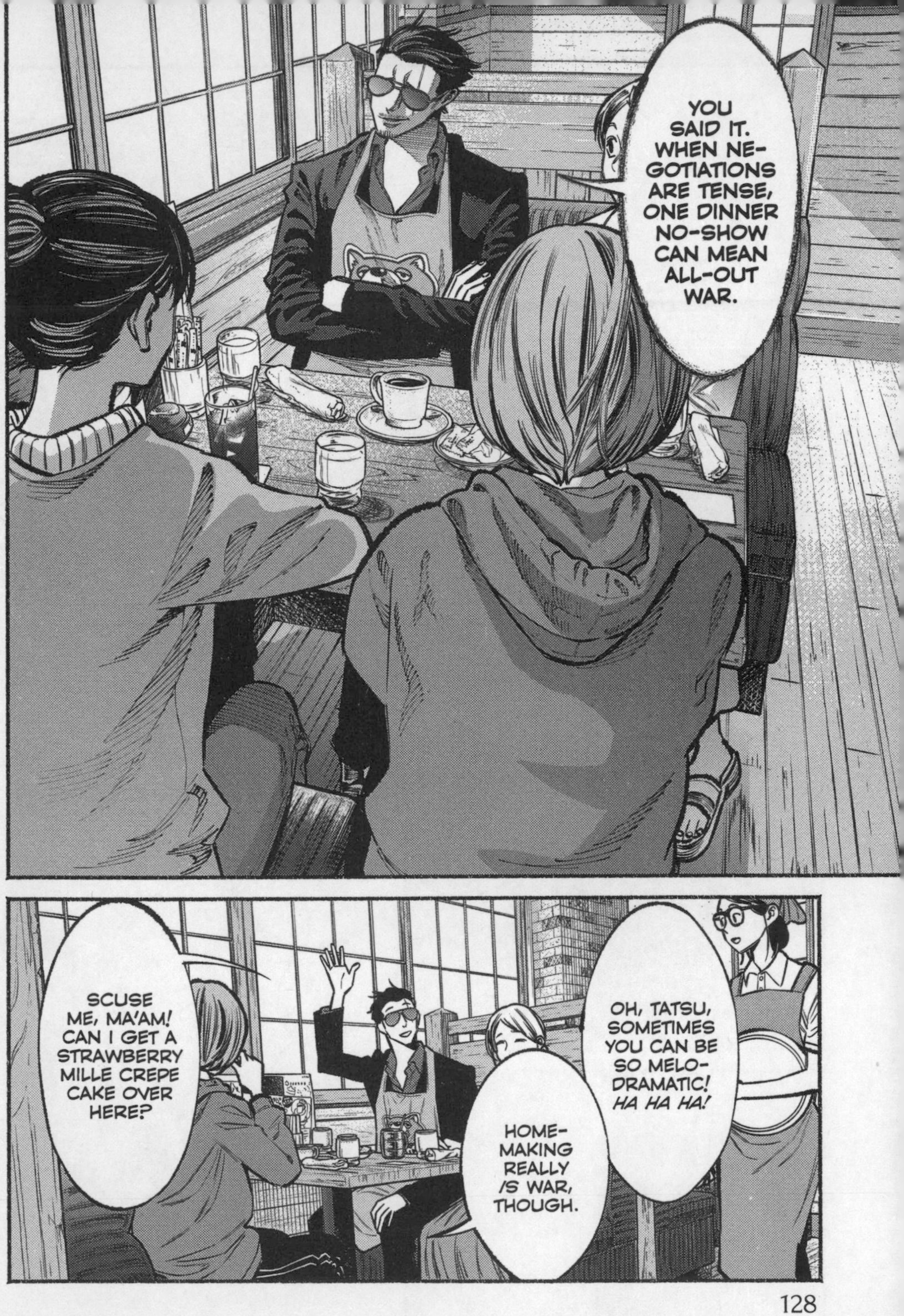
YOU SAID IT. WHEN NE-GOTIATIONS ARE TENSE, ONE DINNER NO-SHOW CAN MEAN ALL-OUT WAR.
OH, TATSU, SOMETIMES YOU CAN BE SO MELO-DRAMATIC! *HA HA HA!*
HOME-MAKING REALLY *IS* WAR, THOUGH.
SCUSE ME, MA'AM! CAN I GET A STRAWBERRY MILLE CREPE CAKE OVER HERE?

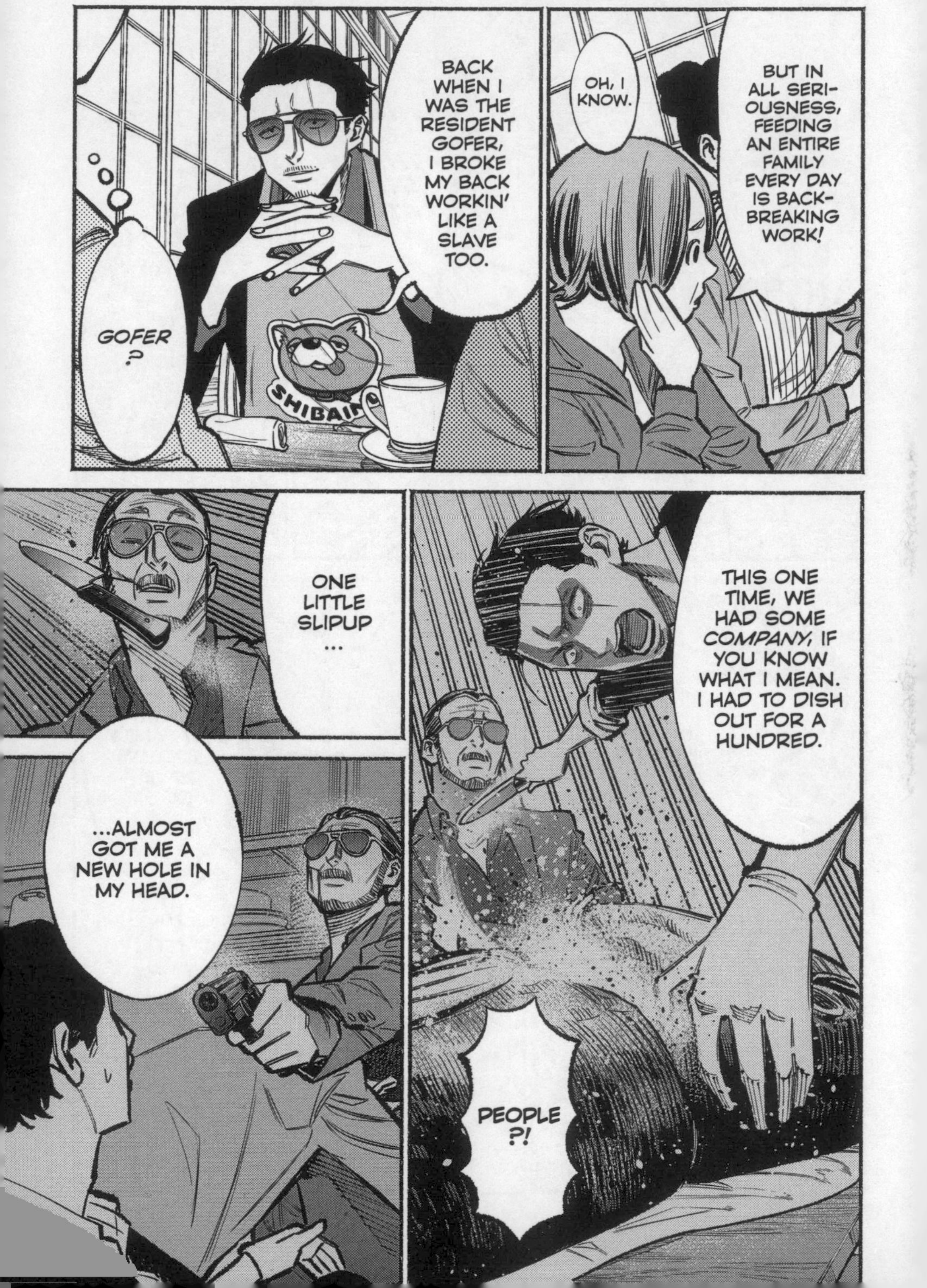
OH, I KNOW.
BUT IN ALL SERI-OUSNESS, FEEDING AN ENTIRE FAMILY EVERY DAY IS BACK-BREAKING WORK!
BACK WHEN I WAS THE RESIDENT GOFER, I BROKE MY BACK WORKIN' LIKE A SLAVE TOO.
GOFER?
SHIBAINU
THIS ONE TIME, WE HAD SOME *COMPANY*, IF YOU KNOW WHAT I MEAN. I HAD TO DISH OUT FOR A HUNDRED.
PEOPLE?!
ONE LITTLE SLIPUP...
...ALMOST GOT ME A NEW HOLE IN MY HEAD.

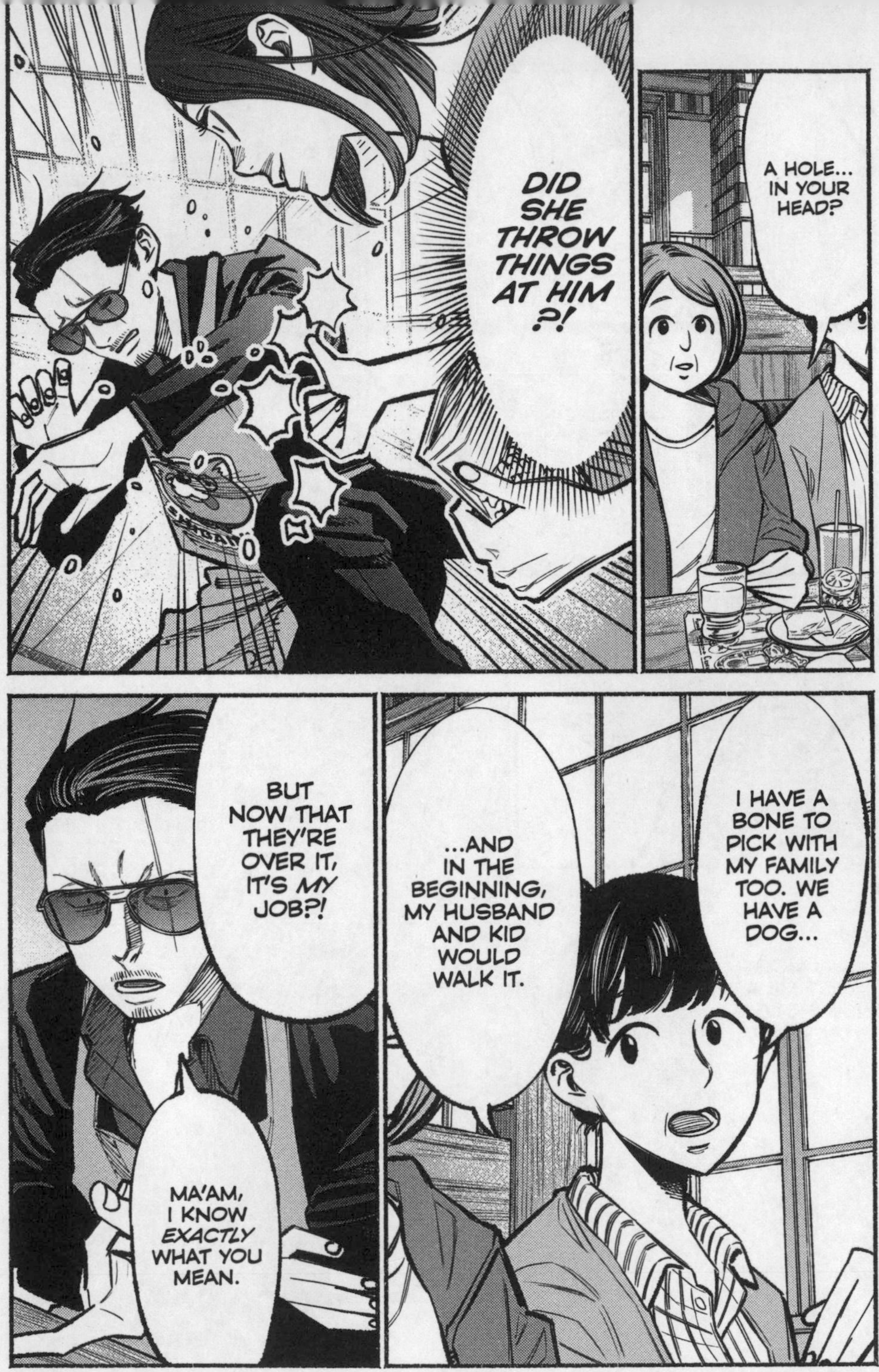
A HOLE... IN YOUR HEAD?
DID SHE THROW THINGS AT HIM?!
I HAVE A BONE TO PICK WITH MY FAMILY TOO. WE HAVE A DOG...
...AND IN THE BEGINNING, MY HUSBAND AND KID WOULD WALK IT.
BUT NOW THAT THEY'RE OVER IT, IT'S *MY* JOB?!
MA'AM, I KNOW *EXACTLY* WHAT YOU MEAN.

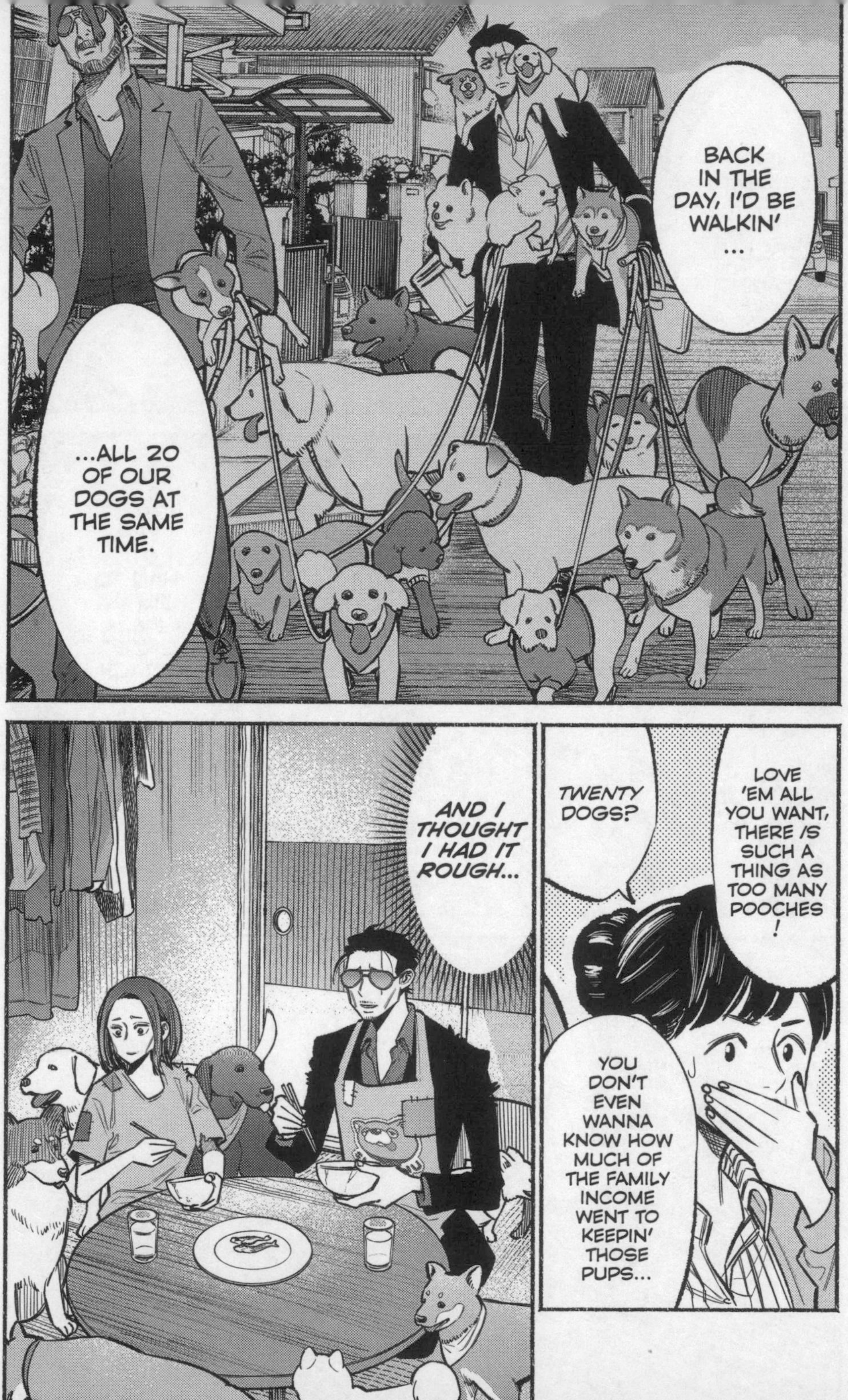
BACK IN THE DAY, I'D BE WALKIN' ...
...ALL 20 OF OUR DOGS AT THE SAME TIME.
LOVE 'EM ALL YOU WANT, THERE *IS* SUCH A THING AS TOO MANY POOCHES!
TWENTY DOGS?
YOU DON'T EVEN WANNA KNOW HOW MUCH OF THE FAMILY INCOME WENT TO KEEPIN' THOSE PUPS...
AND I THOUGHT I HAD IT ROUGH...

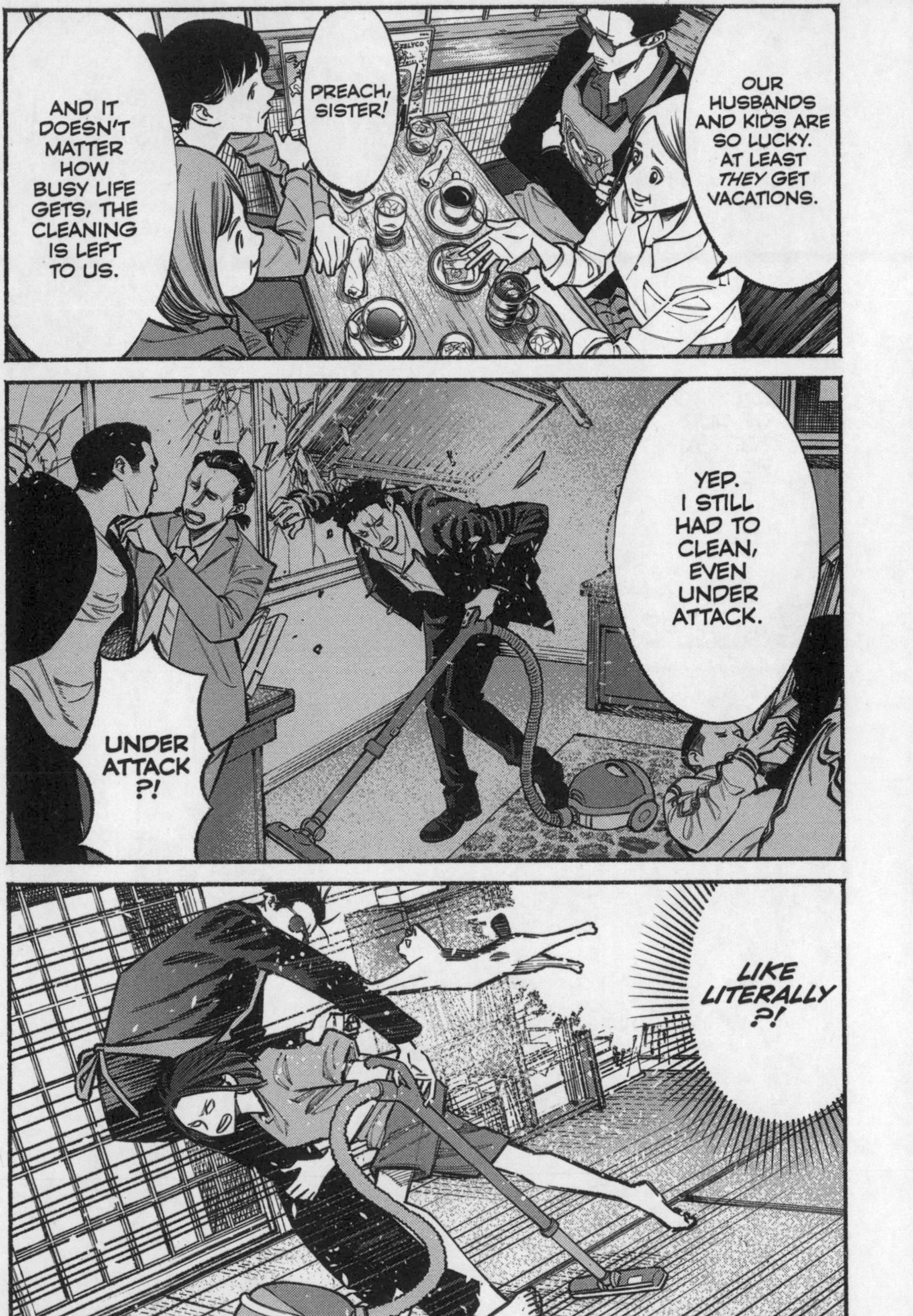
OUR HUSBANDS AND KIDS ARE SO LUCKY. AT LEAST *THEY* GET VACATIONS.
PREACH, SISTER!
AND IT DOESN'T MATTER HOW BUSY LIFE GETS, THE CLEANING IS LEFT TO US.
YEP. I STILL HAD TO CLEAN, EVEN UNDER ATTACK.
UNDER ATTACK ?!
LIKE LITERALLY ?!

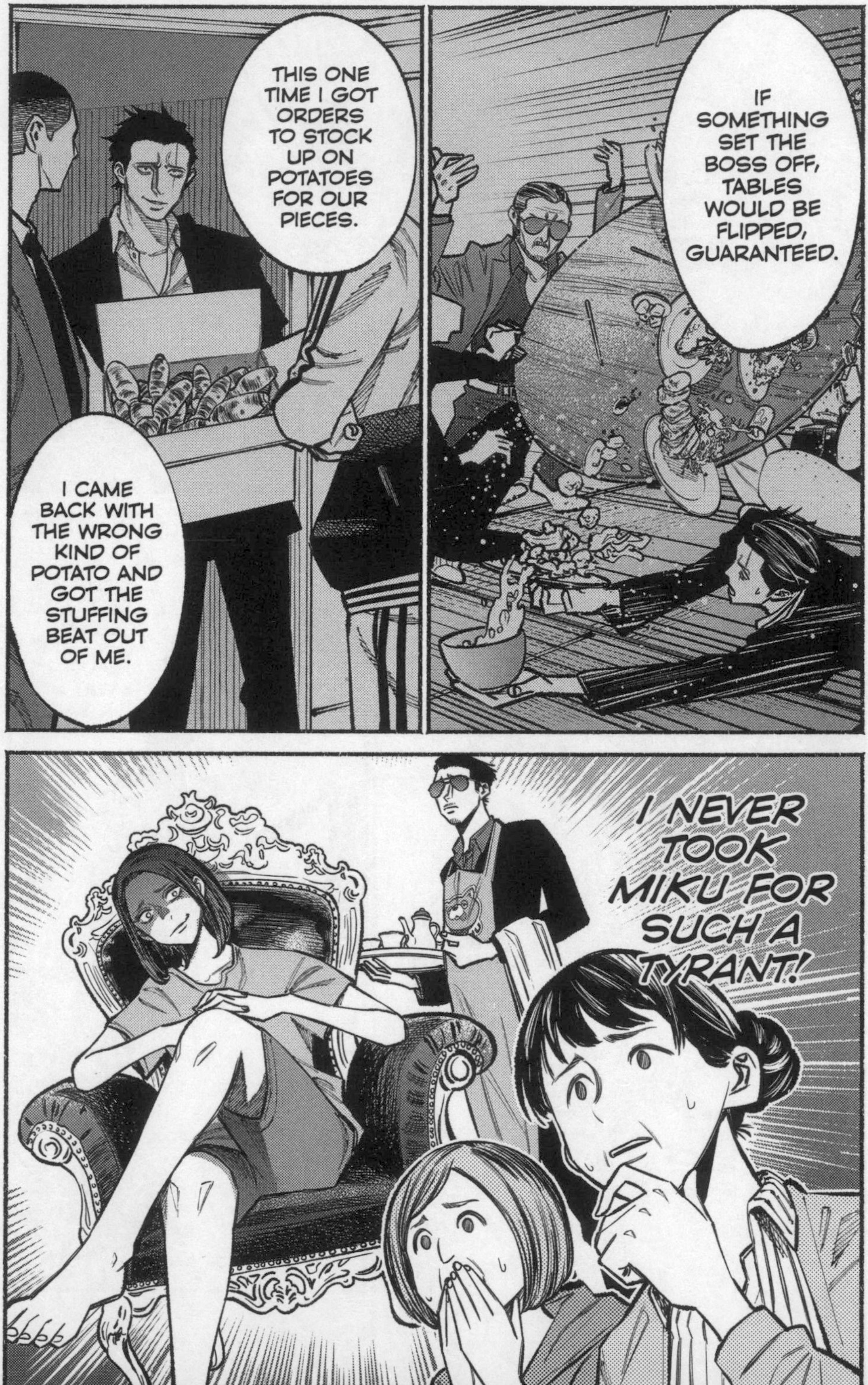
IF SOMETHING SET THE BOSS OFF, TABLES WOULD BE FLIPPED, GUARANTEED.
THIS ONE TIME I GOT ORDERS TO STOCK UP ON POTATOES FOR OUR PIECES.
I CAME BACK WITH THE WRONG KIND OF POTATO AND GOT THE STUFFING BEAT OUT OF ME.
I NEVER TOOK MIKU FOR SUCH A TYRANT!

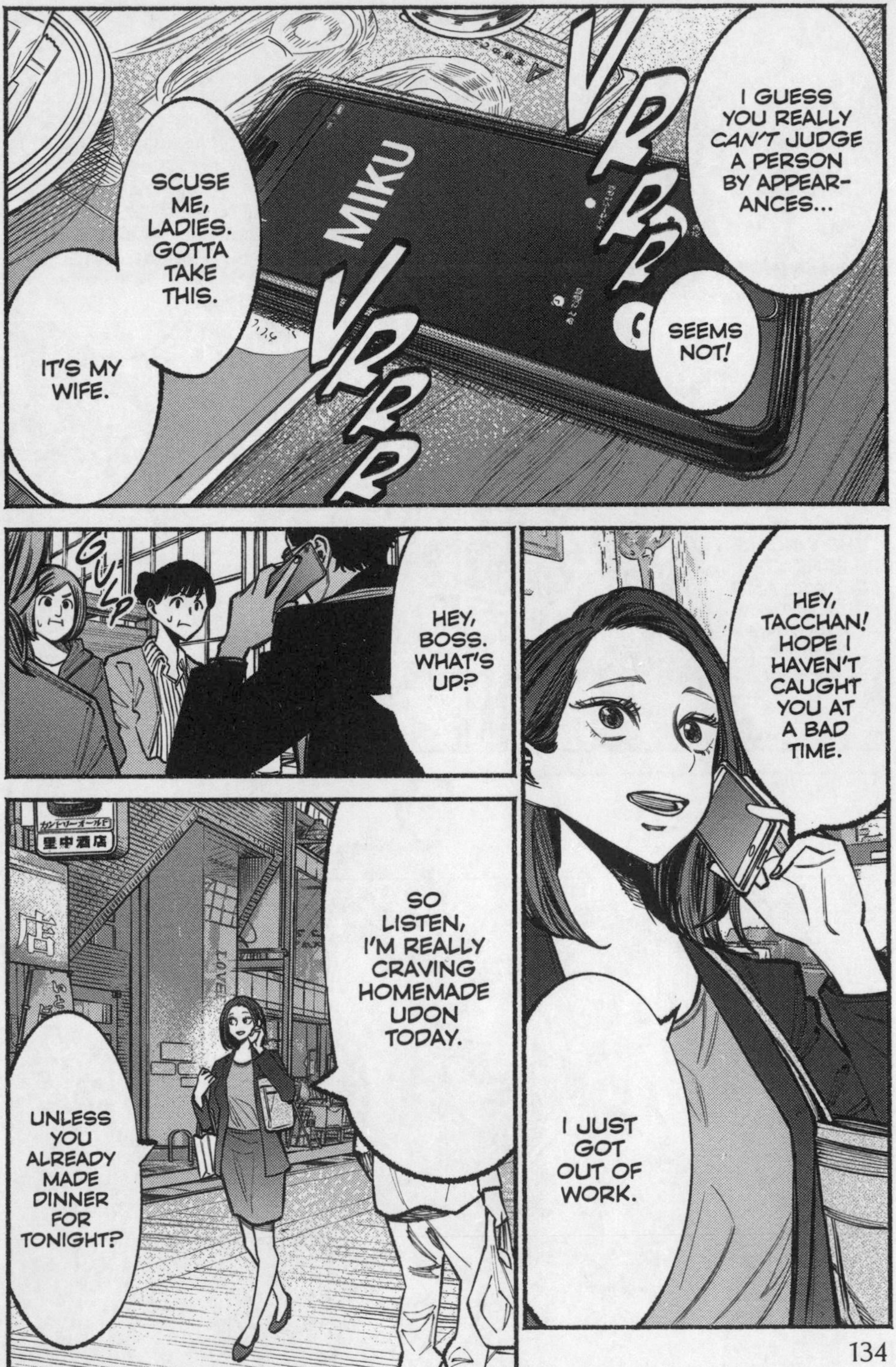
I GUESS YOU REALLY *CAN'T* JUDGE A PERSON BY APPEARANCES...
SEEMS NOT!
VRRR
MIKU
VRRR
SCUSE ME, LADIES. GOTTA TAKE THIS.
IT'S MY WIFE.
GULP
HEY, BOSS. WHAT'S UP?
HEY, TACCHAN! HOPE I HAVEN'T CAUGHT YOU AT A BAD TIME.
I JUST GOT OUT OF WORK.
SO LISTEN, I'M REALLY CRAVING HOMEMADE UDON TODAY.
UNLESS YOU ALREADY MADE DINNER FOR TONIGHT?

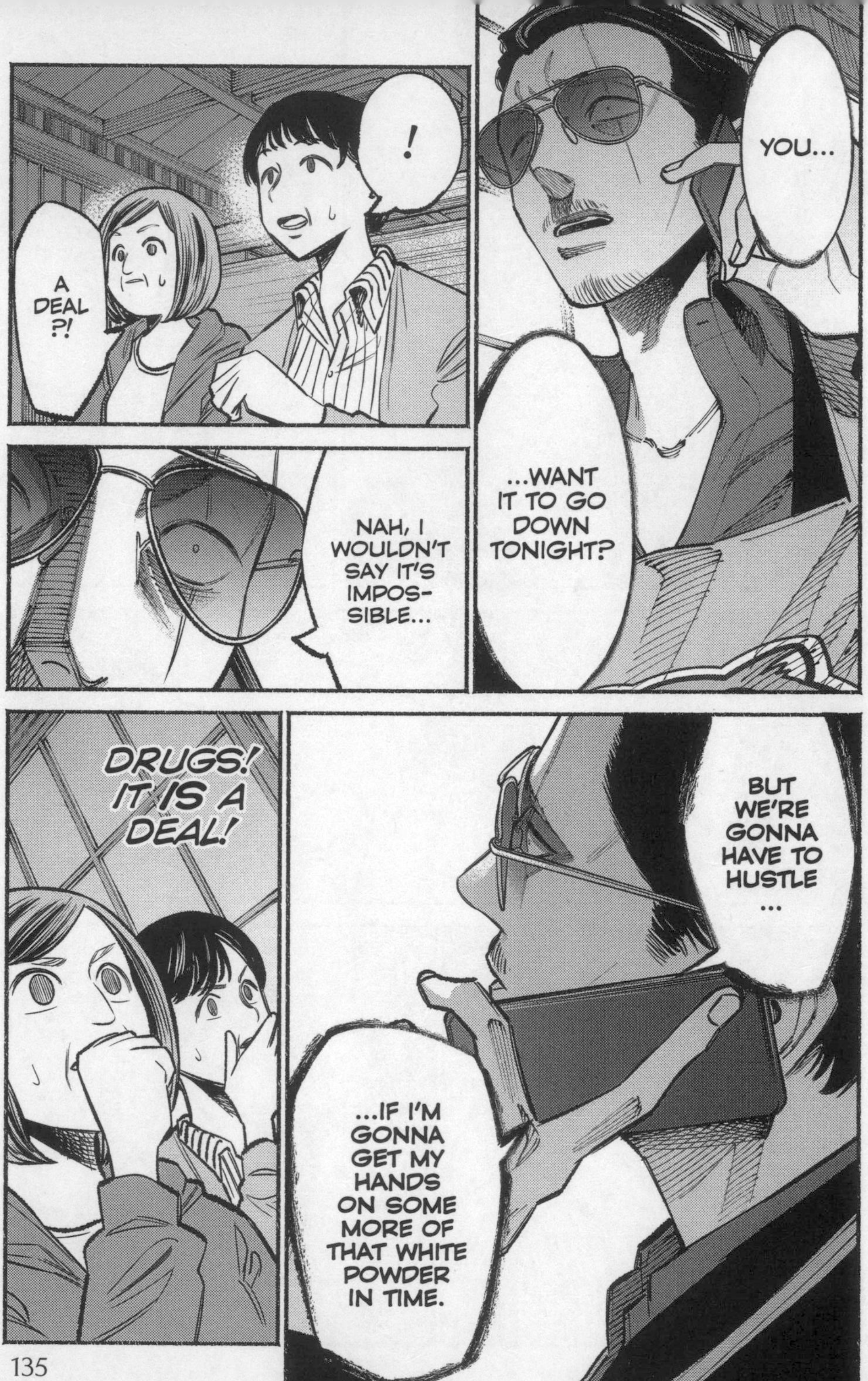
YOU...
...WANT IT TO GO DOWN TONIGHT?
!
A DEAL ?!
NAH, I WOULDN'T SAY IT'S IMPOSSIBLE...
BUT WE'RE GONNA HAVE TO HUSTLE ...
...IF I'M GONNA GET MY HANDS ON SOME MORE OF THAT WHITE POWDER IN TIME.
DRUGS! IT IS A DEAL!

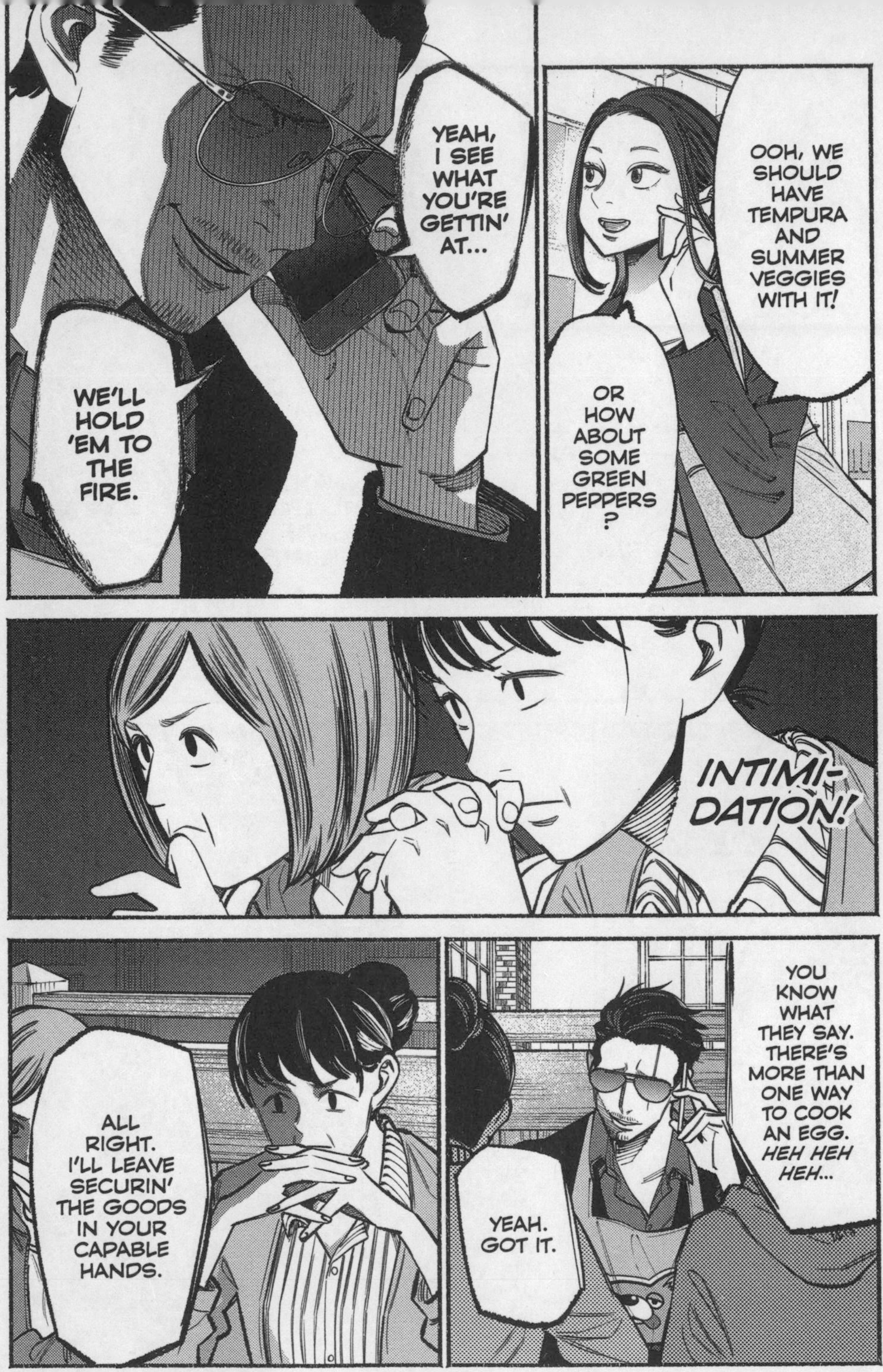
OOH, WE SHOULD HAVE TEMPURA AND SUMMER VEGGIES WITH IT!
OR HOW ABOUT SOME GREEN PEPPERS?
YEAH, I SEE WHAT YOU'RE GETTIN' AT...
WE'LL HOLD 'EM TO THE FIRE.
INTIMI-DATION!
YOU KNOW WHAT THEY SAY. THERE'S MORE THAN ONE WAY TO COOK AN EGG. *HEH HEH HEH...*
YEAH. GOT IT.
ALL RIGHT. I'LL LEAVE SECURIN' THE GOODS IN YOUR CAPABLE HANDS.

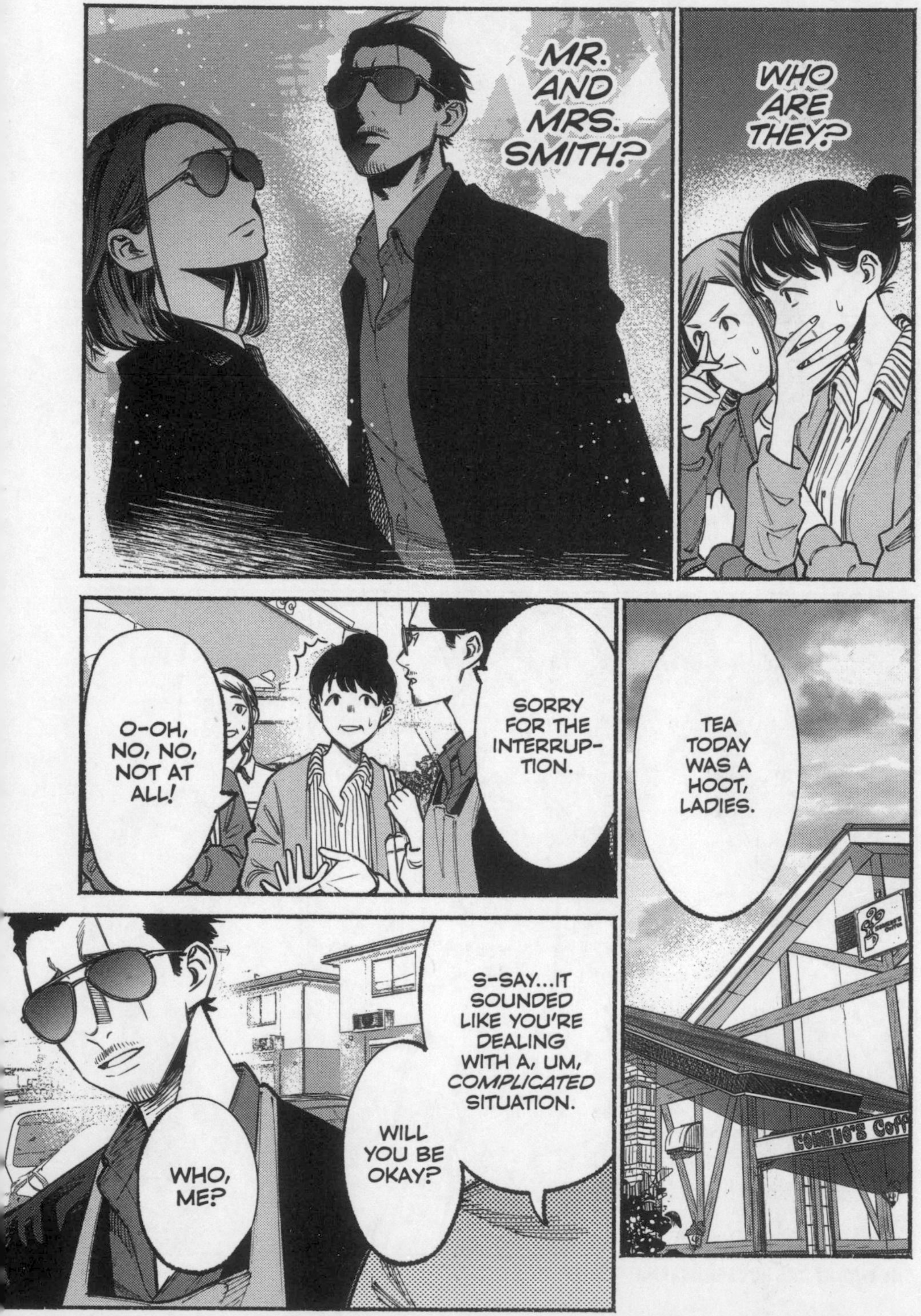
WHO ARE THEY?
MR. AND MRS. SMITH?
TEA TODAY WAS A HOOT, LADIES.
SORRY FOR THE INTERRUPTION.
O-OH, NO, NO, NOT AT ALL!
S-SAY...IT SOUNDED LIKE YOU'RE DEALING WITH A, UM, *COMPLICATED* SITUATION.
WILL YOU BE OKAY?
WHO, ME?

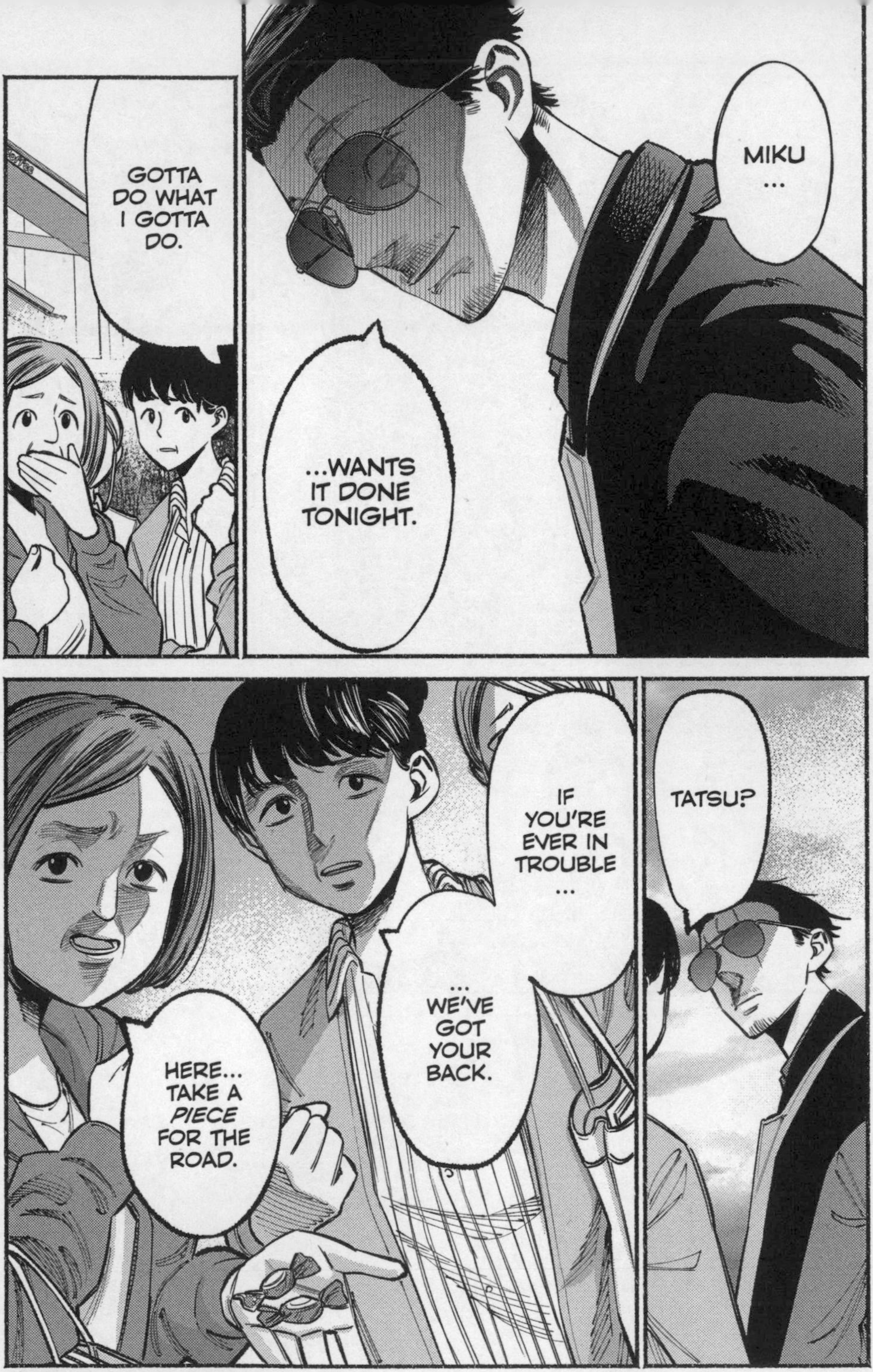
MIKU ...
...WANTS IT DONE TONIGHT.
GOTTA DO WHAT I GOTTA DO.
TATSU?
IF YOU'RE EVER IN TROUBLE ...
... WE'VE GOT YOUR BACK.
HERE... TAKE A *PIECE* FOR THE ROAD.

THE WAY OF THE HOUSEHUSBAND ④ END

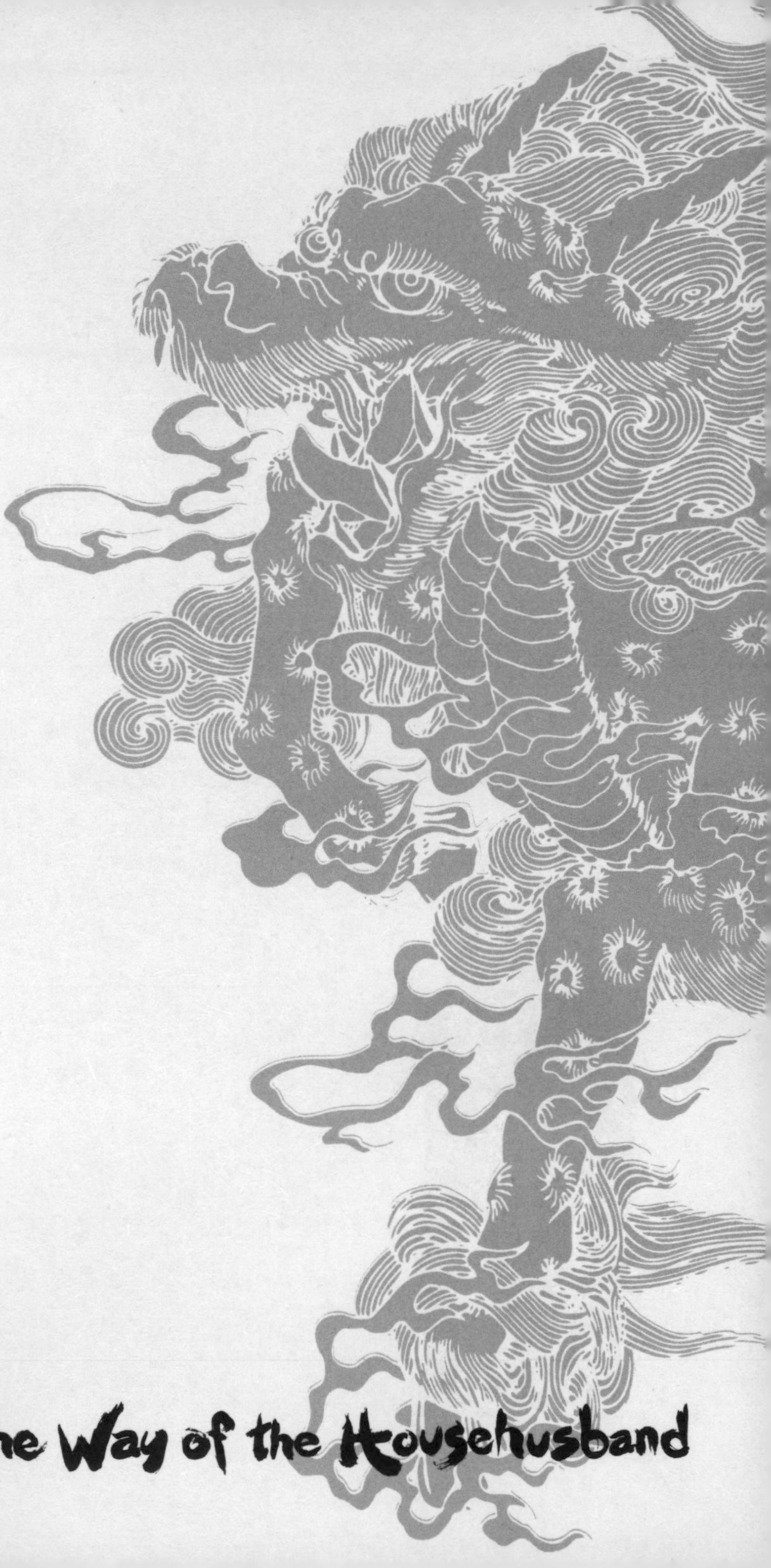

The Way of the Househusband

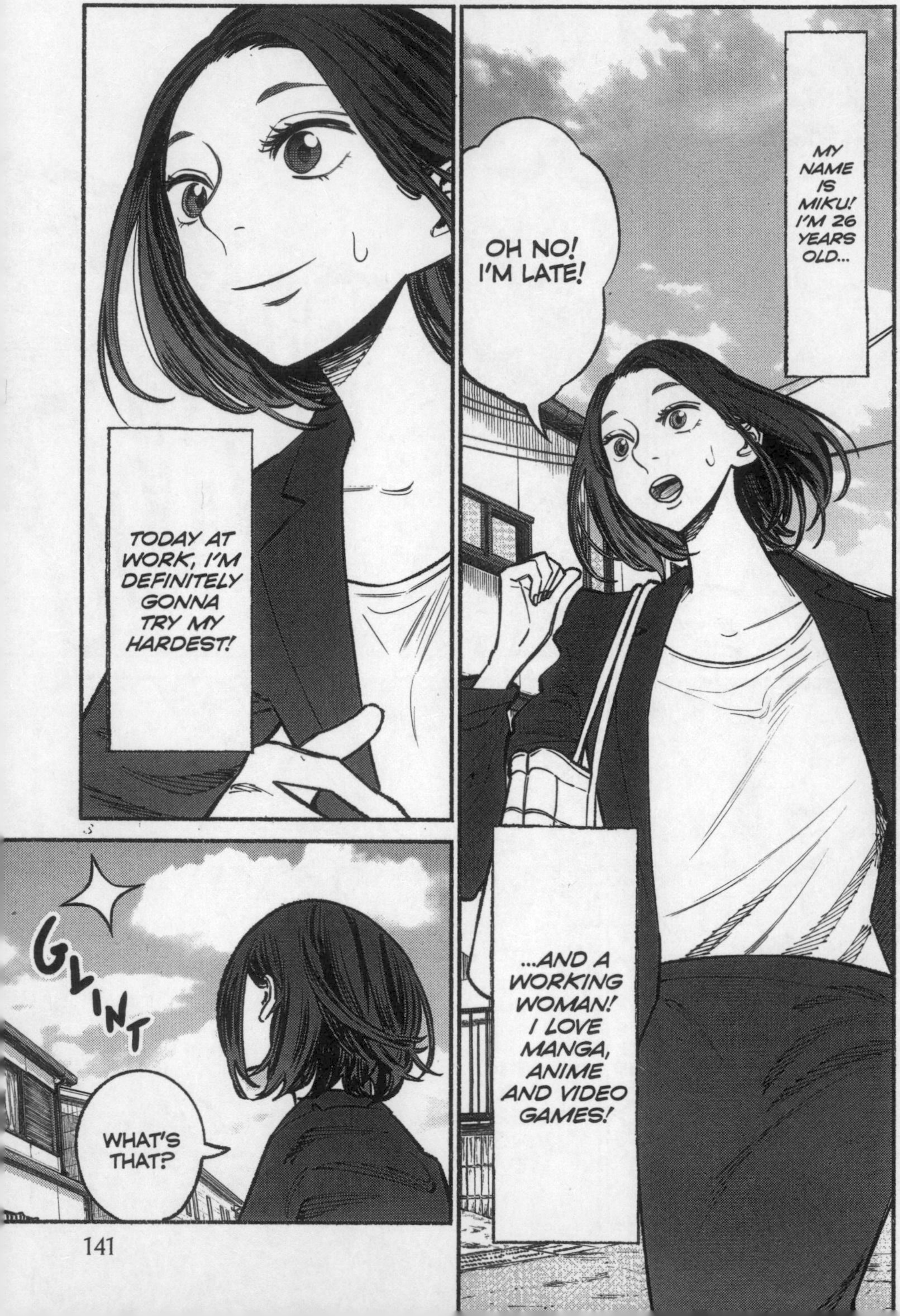
MY NAME IS MIKU! I'M 26 YEARS OLD...
OH NO! I'M LATE!
...AND A WORKING WOMAN! I LOVE MANGA, ANIME AND VIDEO GAMES!
TODAY AT WORK, I'M DEFINITELY GONNA TRY MY HARDEST!
GLINT
WHAT'S THAT?

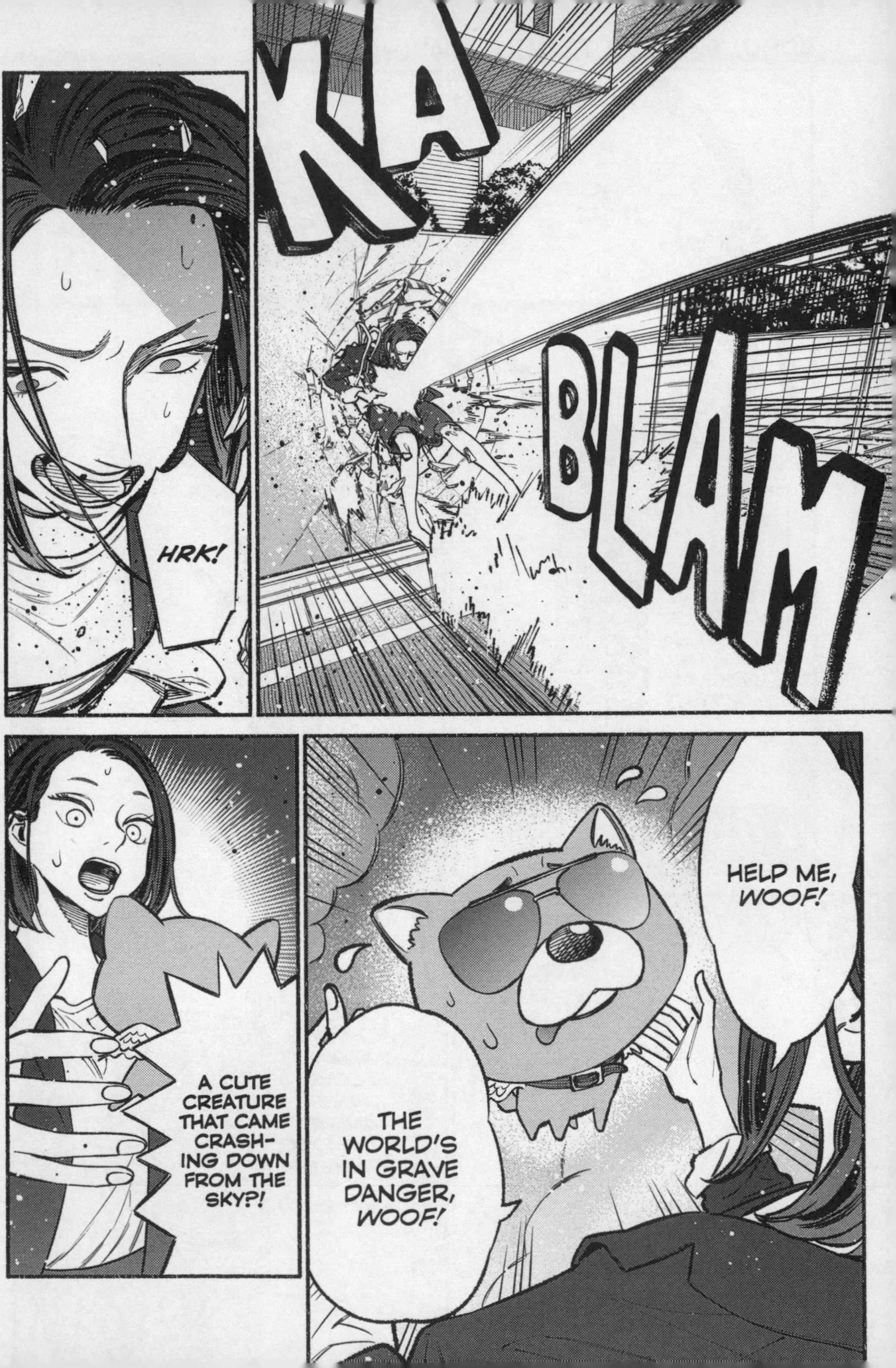
KA
BLAM
HRK!
HELP ME, WOOF!
THE WORLD'S IN GRAVE DANGER, WOOF!
A CUTE CREATURE THAT CAME CRASHING DOWN FROM THE SKY?!

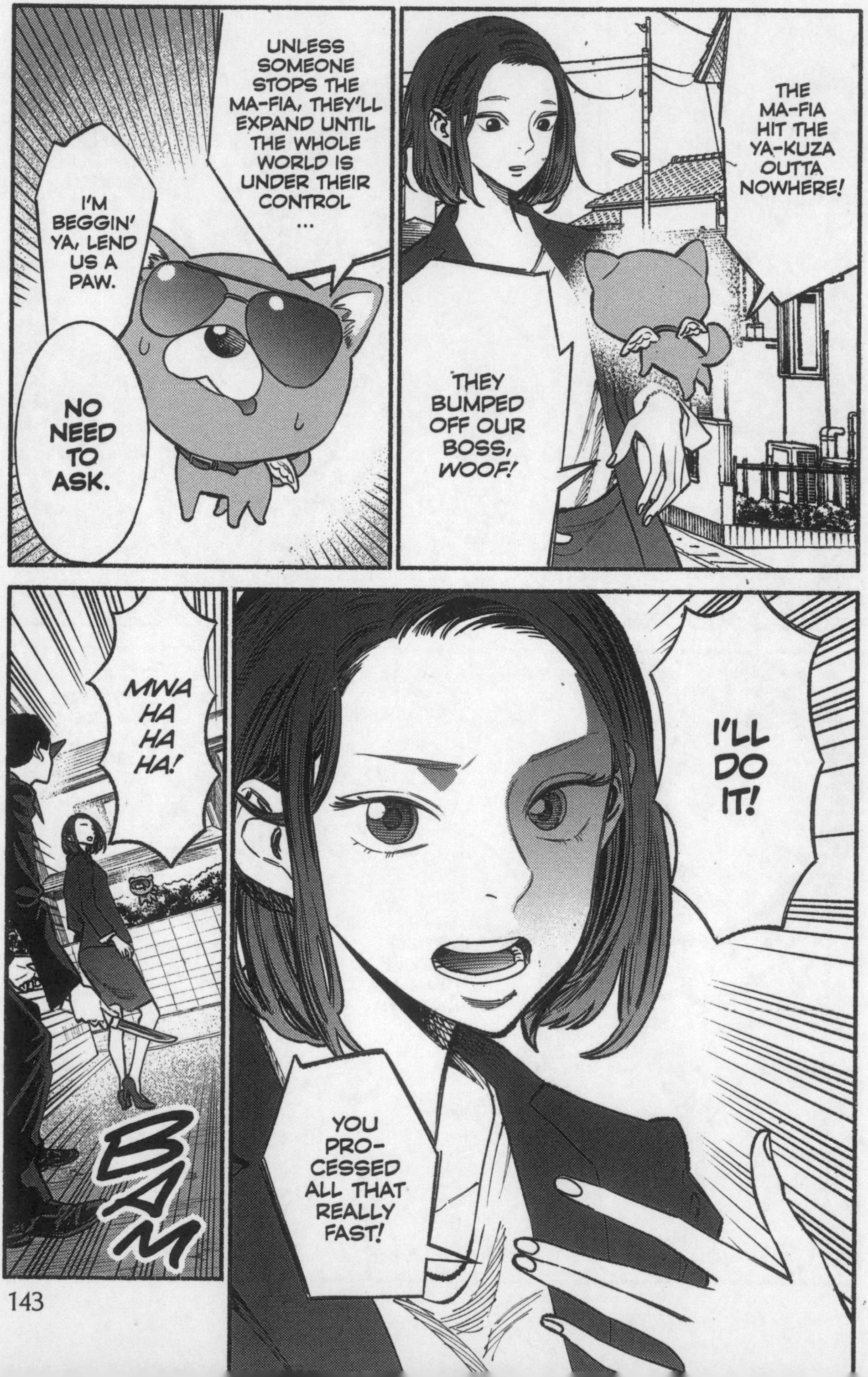
THE MA-FIA HIT THE YA-KUZA OUTTA NOWHERE!
THEY BUMPED OFF OUR BOSS, WOOF!
UNLESS SOMEONE STOPS THE MA-FIA, THEY'LL EXPAND UNTIL THE WHOLE WORLD IS UNDER THEIR CONTROL ...
I'M BEGGIN' YA, LEND US A PAW.
NO NEED TO ASK.
I'LL DO IT!
YOU PRO-CESSED ALL THAT REALLY FAST!
MWA HA HA HA!
BAM

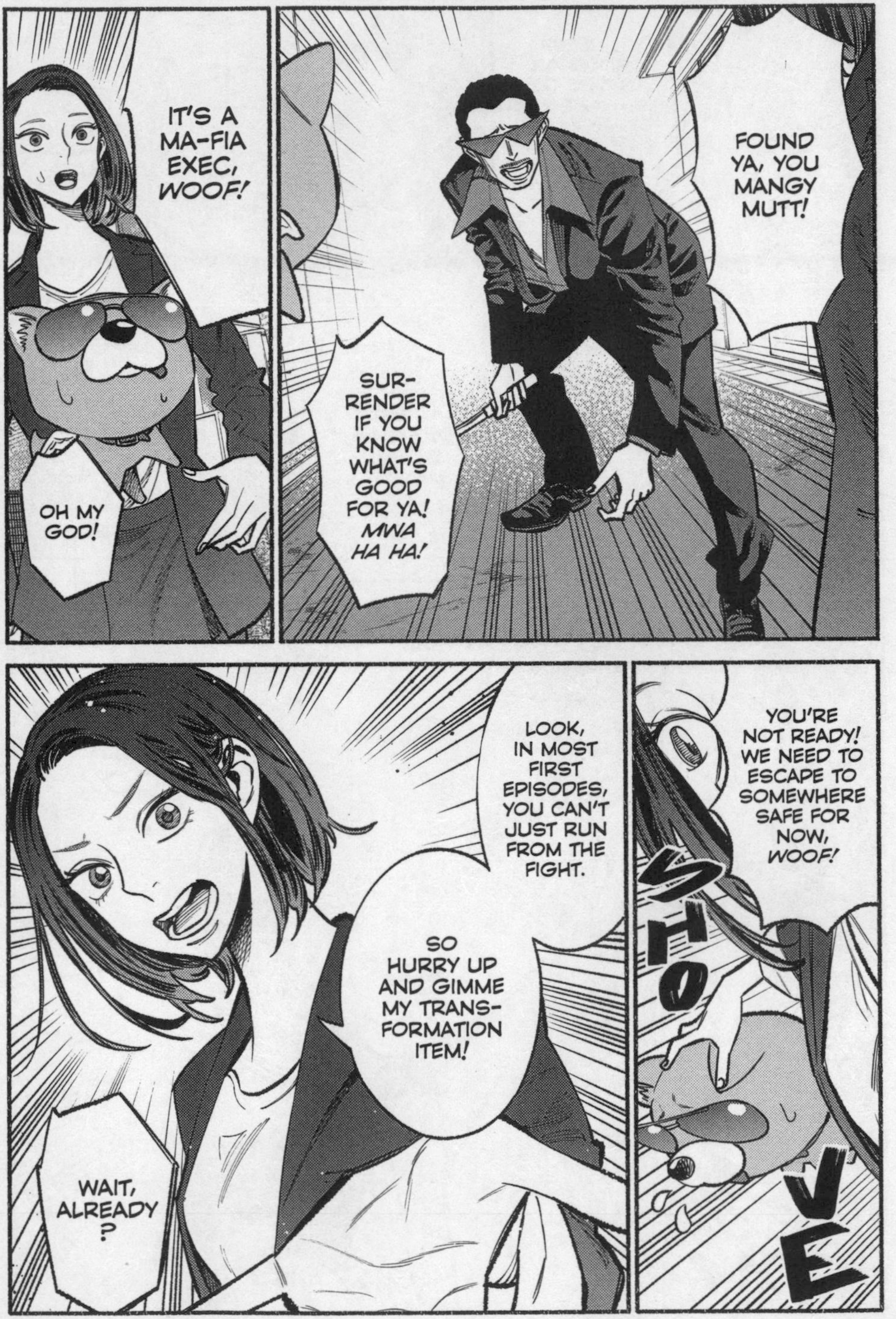
FOUND YA, YOU MANGY MUTT!
SUR-RENDER IF YOU KNOW WHAT'S GOOD FOR YA! *MWA HA HA!*
IT'S A MA-FIA EXEC, *WOOF!*
OH MY GOD!
YOU'RE NOT READY! WE NEED TO ESCAPE TO SOMEWHERE SAFE FOR NOW, *WOOF!*
SHOVE
LOOK, IN MOST FIRST EPISODES, YOU CAN'T JUST RUN FROM THE FIGHT.
SO HURRY UP AND GIMME MY TRANS-FORMATION ITEM!
WAIT, ALREADY?

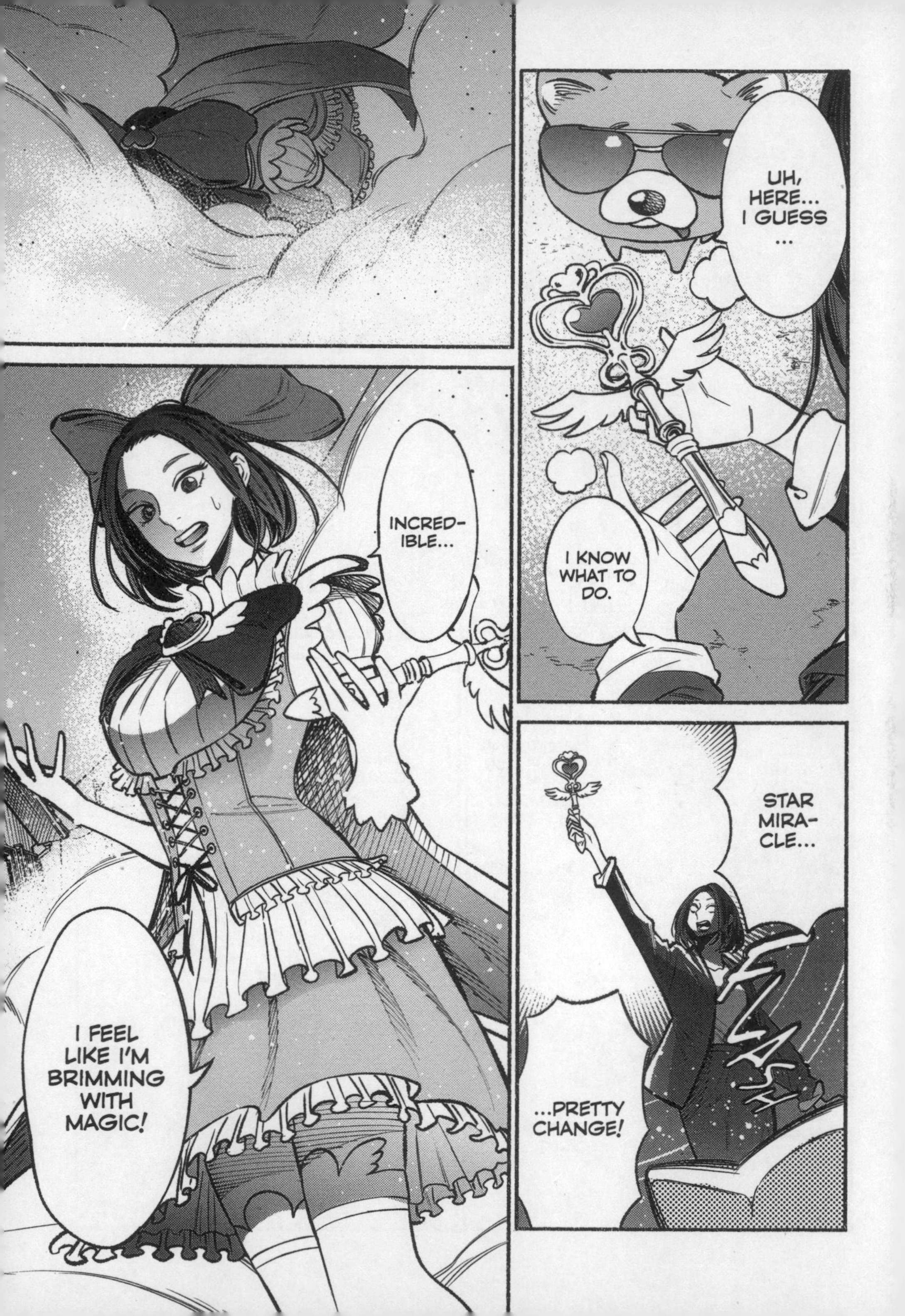
UH, HERE... I GUESS ...
I KNOW WHAT TO DO.
STAR MIRACLE...
...PRETTY CHANGE!
FLASH
INCREDIBLE...
I FEEL LIKE I'M BRIMMING WITH MAGIC!

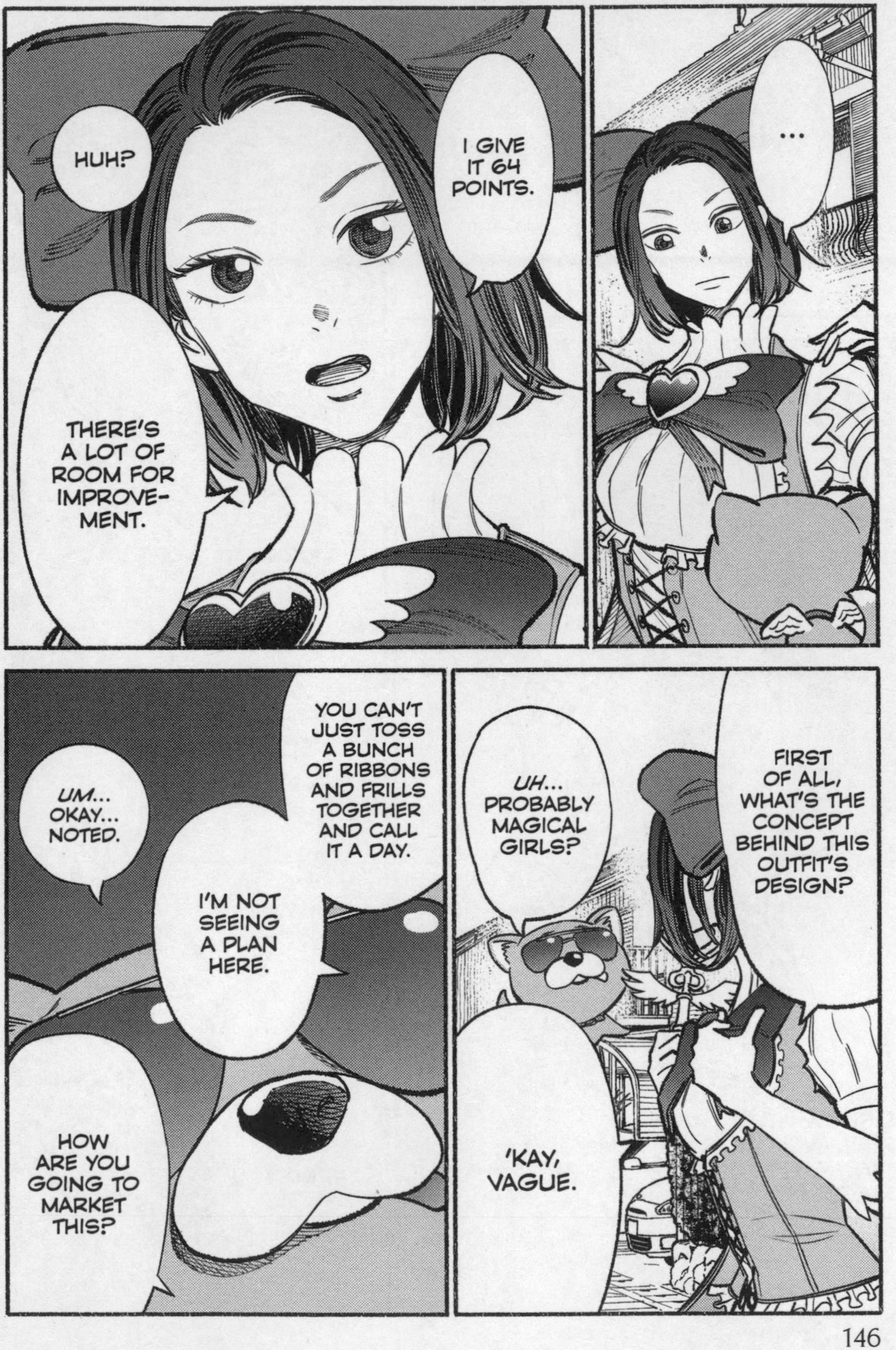
...
I GIVE IT 64 POINTS.
HUH?
THERE'S A LOT OF ROOM FOR IMPROVE-MENT.
FIRST OF ALL, WHAT'S THE CONCEPT BEHIND THIS OUTFIT'S DESIGN?
UH... PROBABLY MAGICAL GIRLS?
'KAY, VAGUE.
YOU CAN'T JUST TOSS A BUNCH OF RIBBONS AND FRILLS TOGETHER AND CALL IT A DAY.
UM... OKAY... NOTED.
I'M NOT SEEING A PLAN HERE.
HOW ARE YOU GOING TO MARKET THIS?

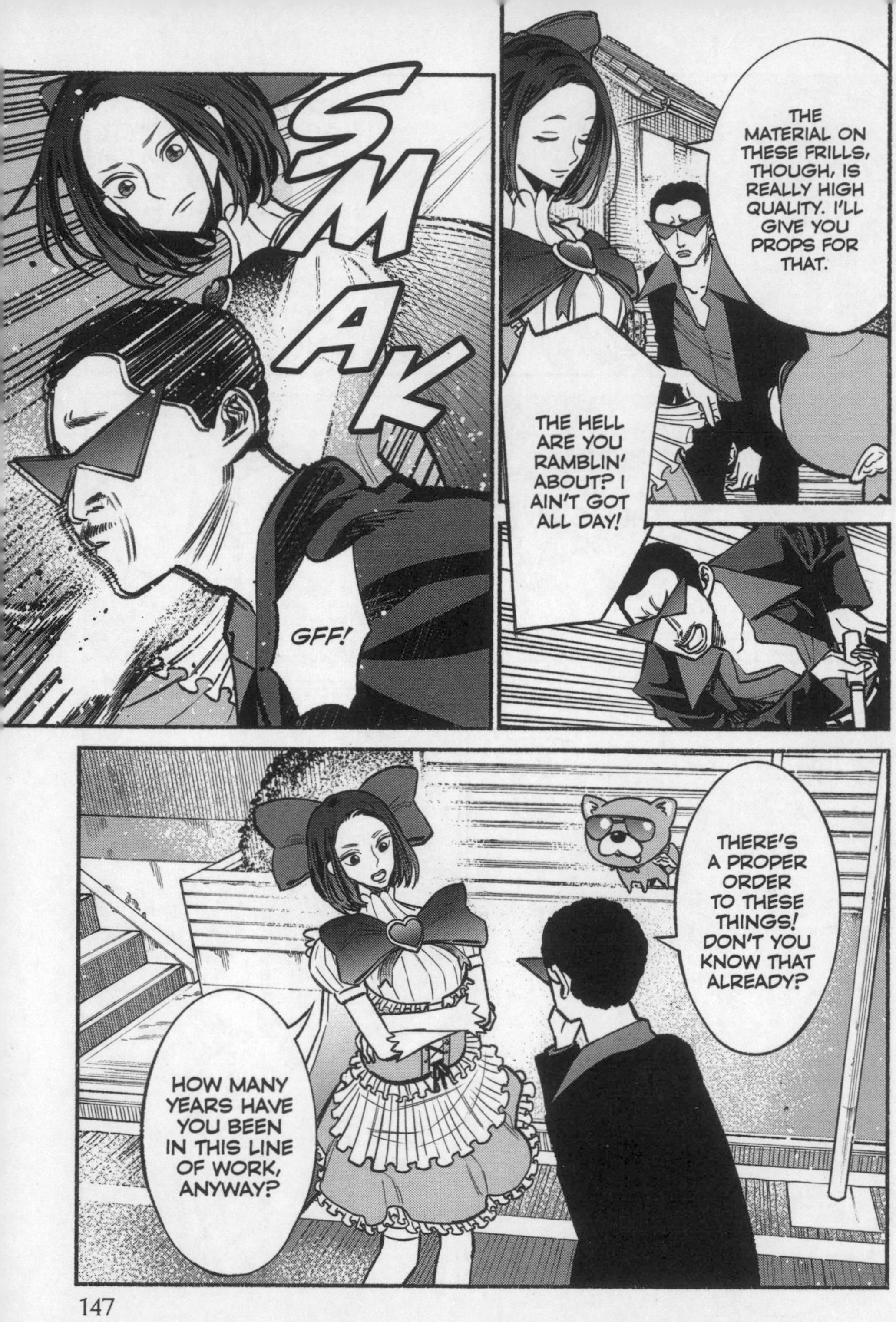
THE MATERIAL ON THESE FRILLS, THOUGH, IS REALLY HIGH QUALITY. I'LL GIVE YOU PROPS FOR THAT.
THE HELL ARE YOU RAMBLIN' ABOUT? I AIN'T GOT ALL DAY!
SMAK
GFF!
THERE'S A PROPER ORDER TO THESE THINGS! DON'T YOU KNOW THAT ALREADY?
HOW MANY YEARS HAVE YOU BEEN IN THIS LINE OF WORK, ANYWAY?

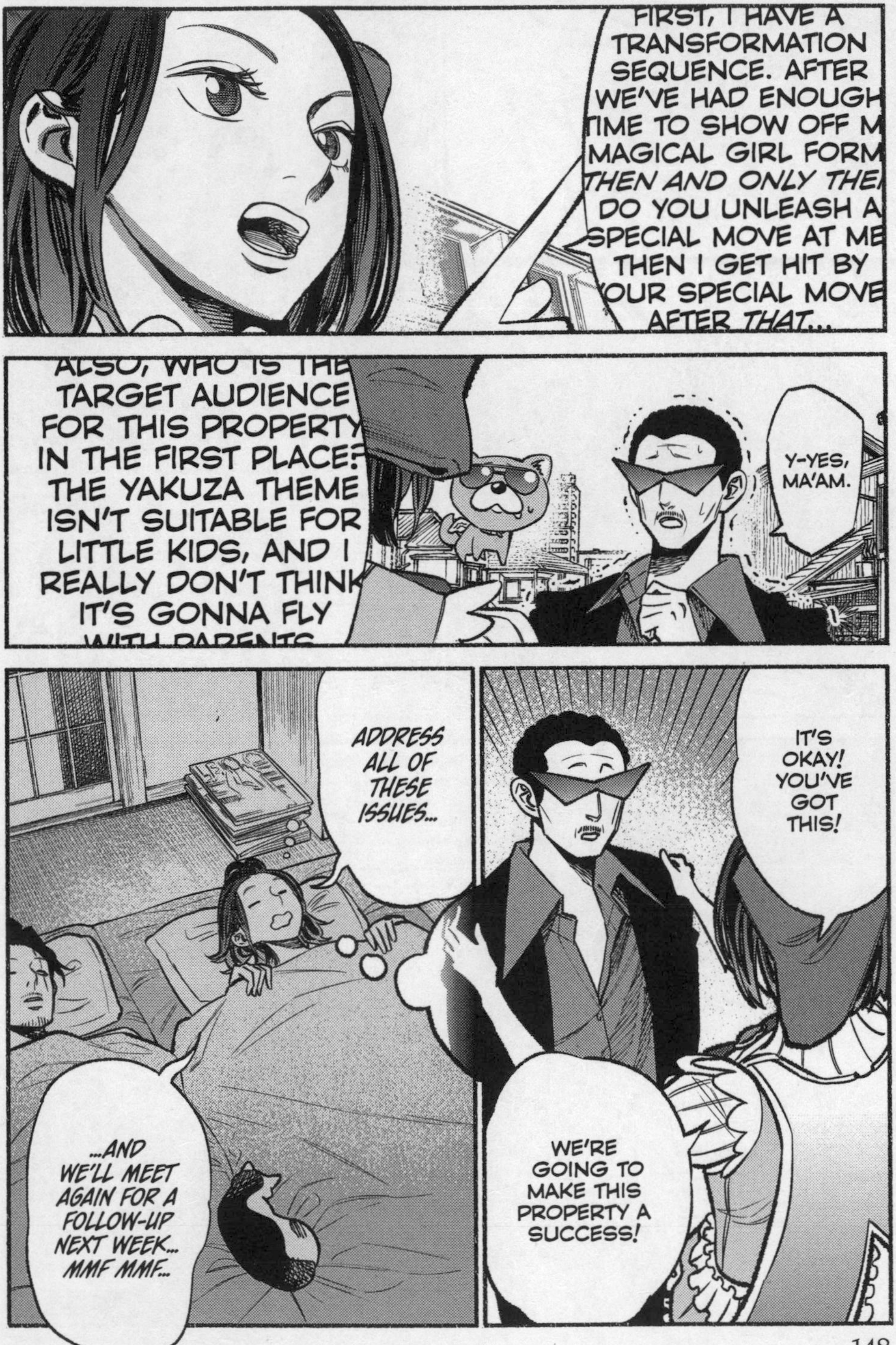
FIRST, I HAVE A TRANSFORMATION SEQUENCE. AFTER WE'VE HAD ENOUGH TIME TO SHOW OFF MY MAGICAL GIRL FORM *THEN AND ONLY THEN* DO YOU UNLEASH A SPECIAL MOVE AT ME. THEN I GET HIT BY YOUR SPECIAL MOVE AFTER *THAT*...
ALSO, WHO IS THE TARGET AUDIENCE FOR THIS PROPERTY IN THE FIRST PLACE? THE YAKUZA THEME ISN'T SUITABLE FOR LITTLE KIDS, AND I REALLY DON'T THINK IT'S GONNA FLY WITH PARENTS...
Y-YES, MA'AM.
IT'S OKAY! YOU'VE GOT THIS!
WE'RE GOING TO MAKE THIS PROPERTY A SUCCESS!
ADDRESS ALL OF THESE ISSUES...
...AND WE'LL MEET AGAIN FOR A FOLLOW-UP NEXT WEEK... MMF MMF...

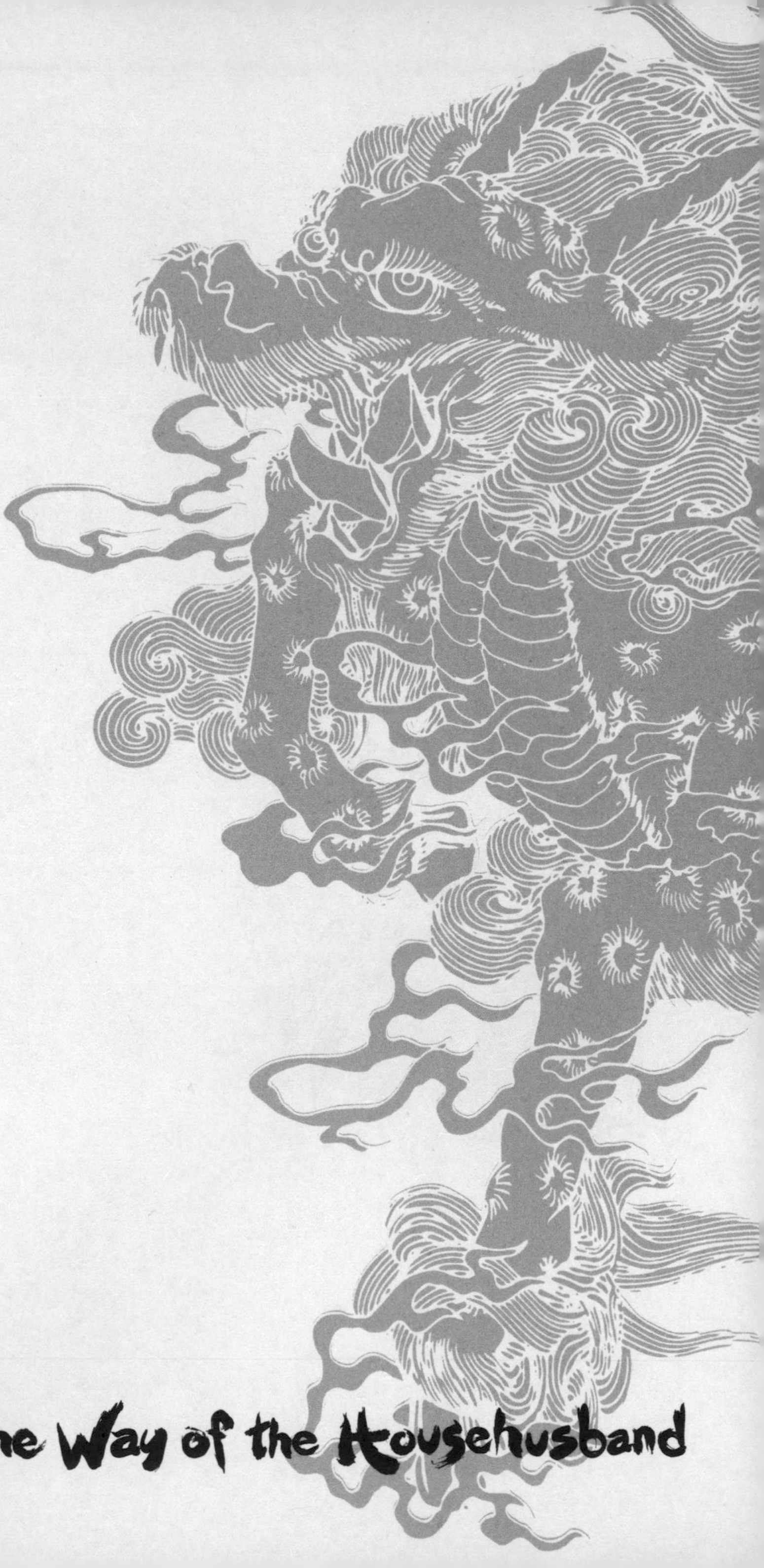

The Way of the Househusband

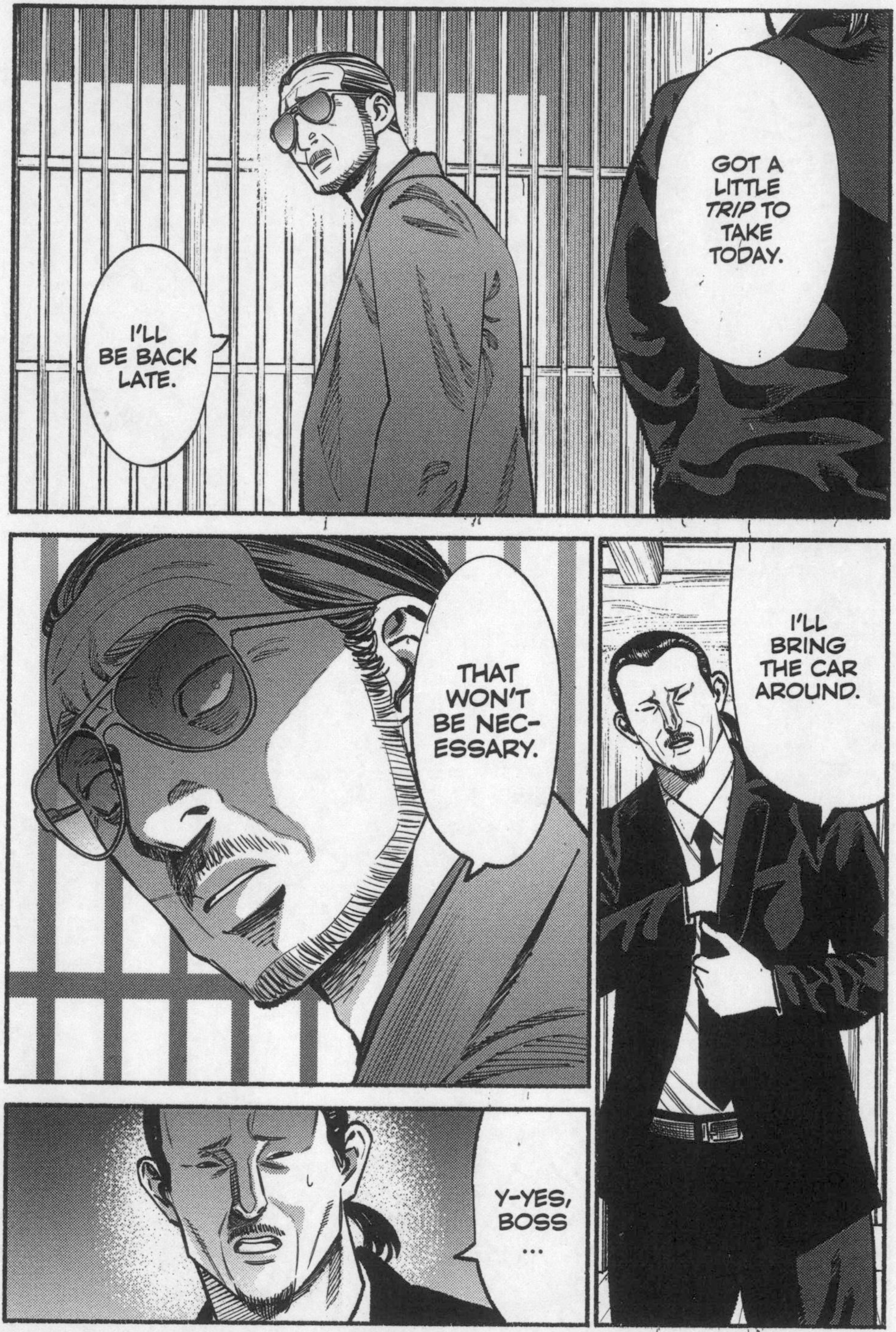
GOT A LITTLE *TRIP* TO TAKE TODAY.
I'LL BE BACK LATE.
I'LL BRING THE CAR AROUND.
THAT WON'T BE NEC-ESSARY.
Y-YES, BOSS ...

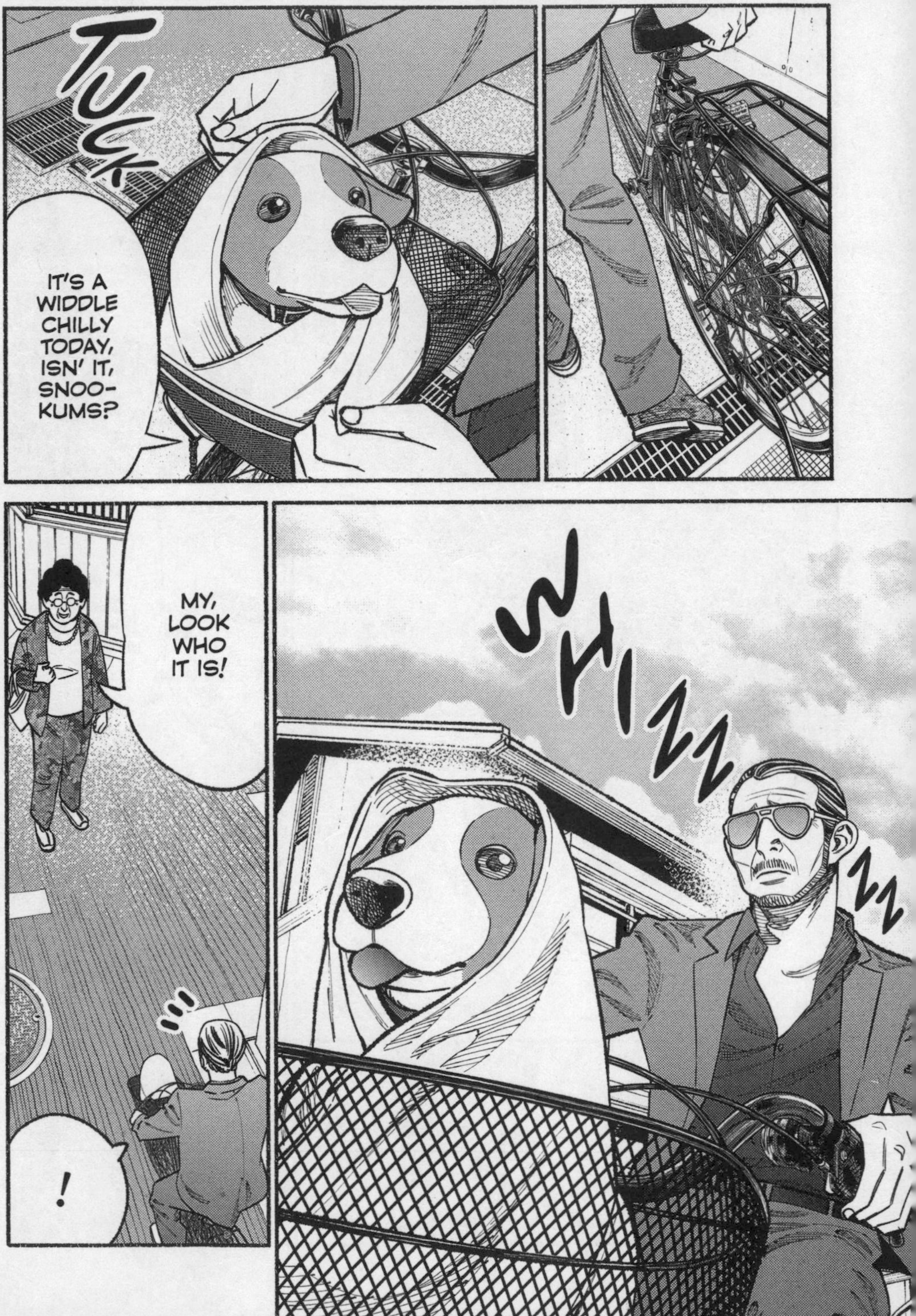
TUCK
IT'S A WIDDLE CHILLY TODAY, ISN' IT, SNOOKUMS?
WHIZZZZ
MY, LOOK WHO IT IS!
!

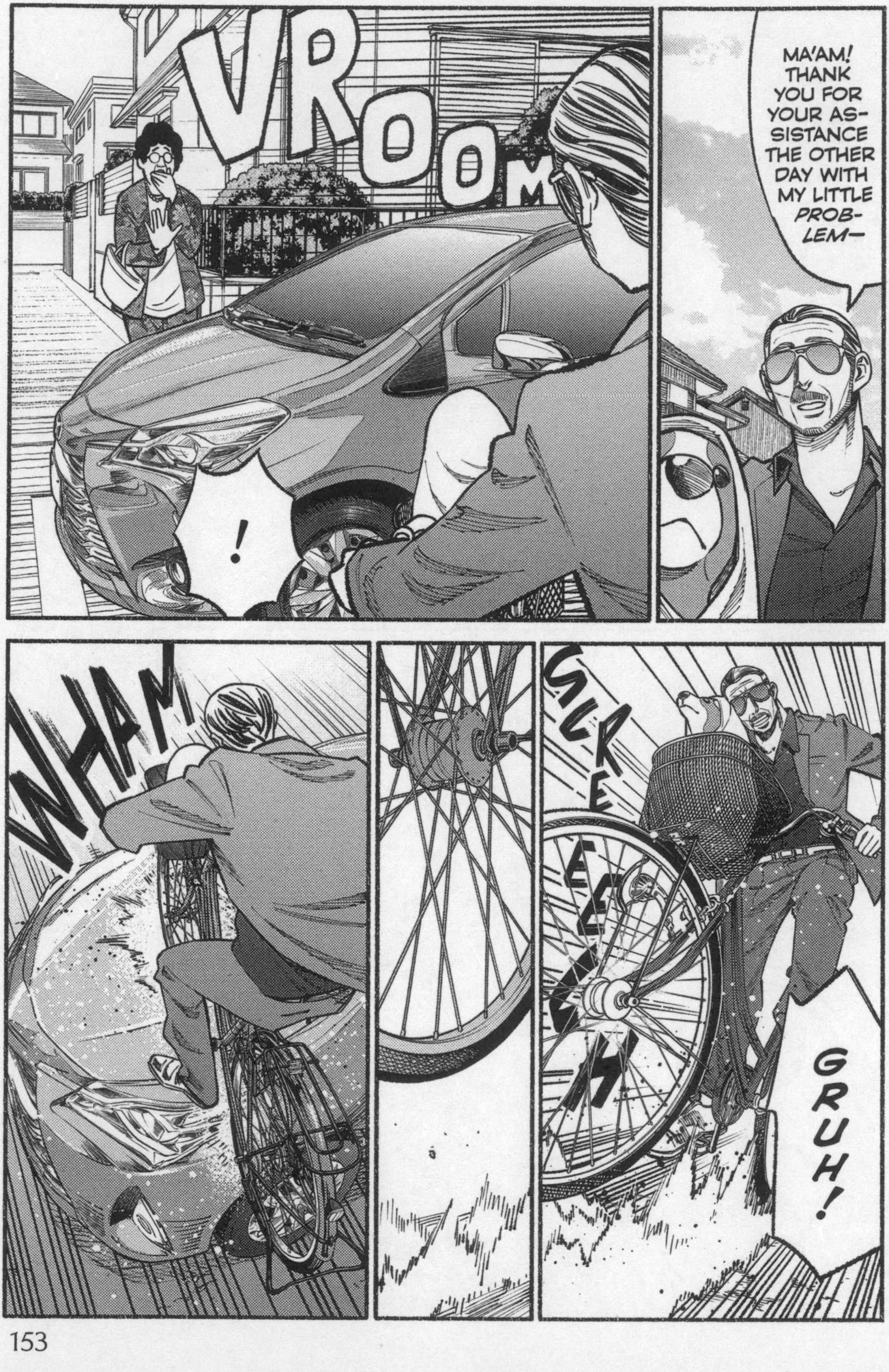
MA'AM! THANK YOU FOR YOUR ASSISTANCE THE OTHER DAY WITH MY LITTLE *PROBLEM*—
VROOOM
!
SCREEECH
GRUH!
WHAM

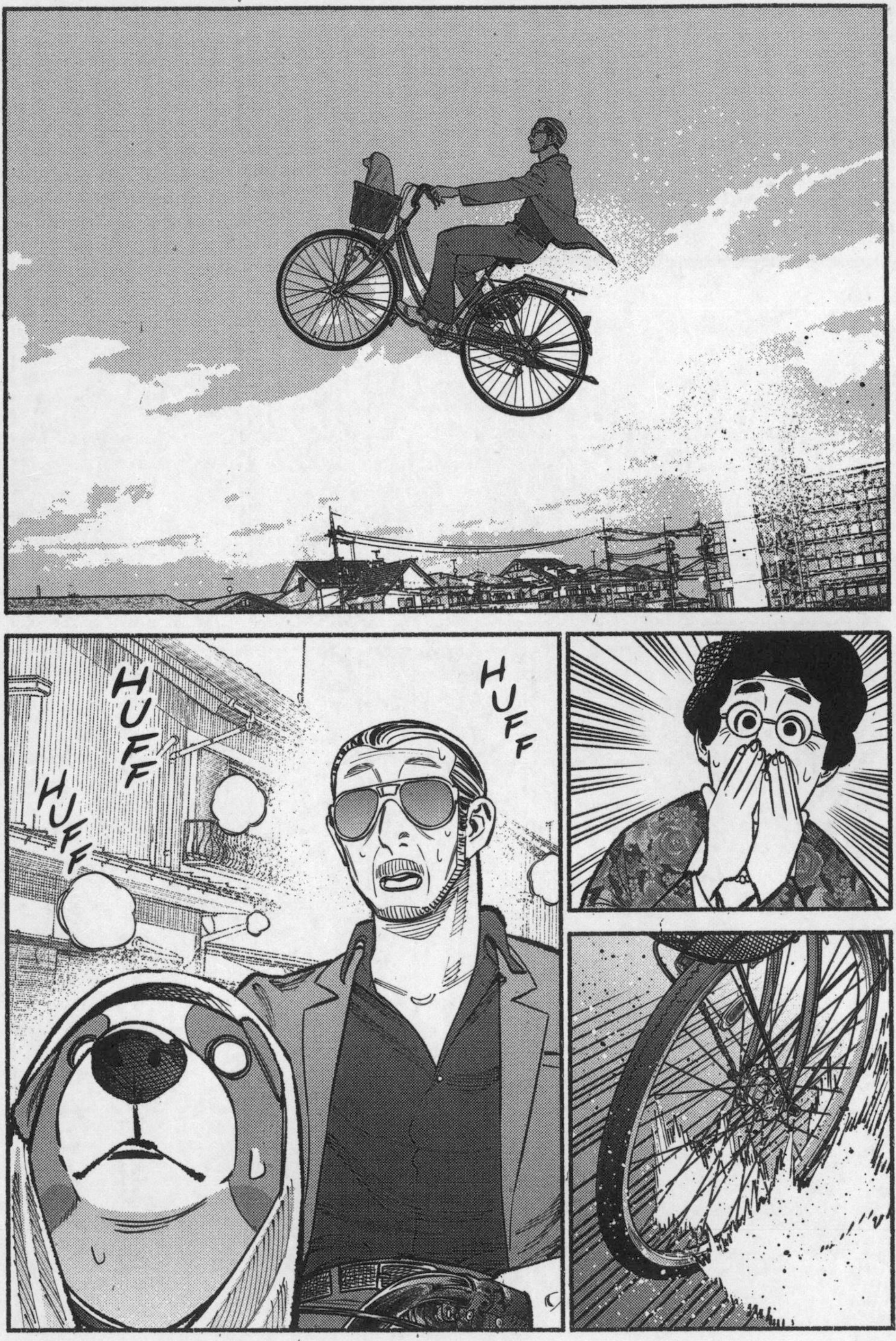
HUFF
HUFF
HUFF

PINKY (2)

BONUS MANGA ③ GIN'S WALK ③

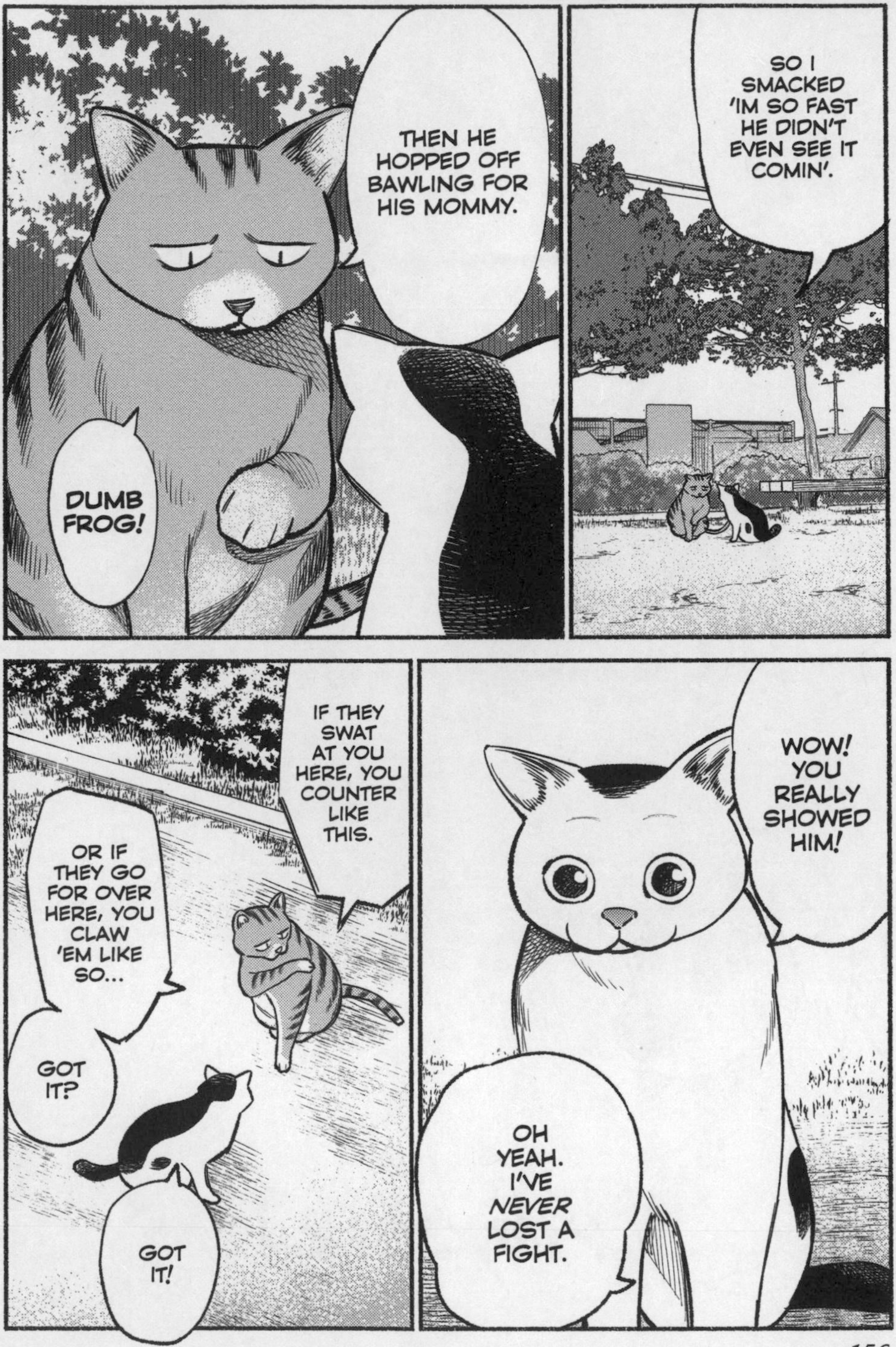
SO I SMACKED 'IM SO FAST HE DIDN'T EVEN SEE IT COMIN'.
THEN HE HOPPED OFF BAWLING FOR HIS MOMMY.
DUMB FROG!
WOW! YOU REALLY SHOWED HIM!
OH YEAH. I'VE *NEVER* LOST A FIGHT.
IF THEY SWAT AT YOU HERE, YOU COUNTER LIKE THIS.
OR IF THEY GO FOR OVER HERE, YOU CLAW 'EM LIKE SO...
GOT IT?
GOT IT!

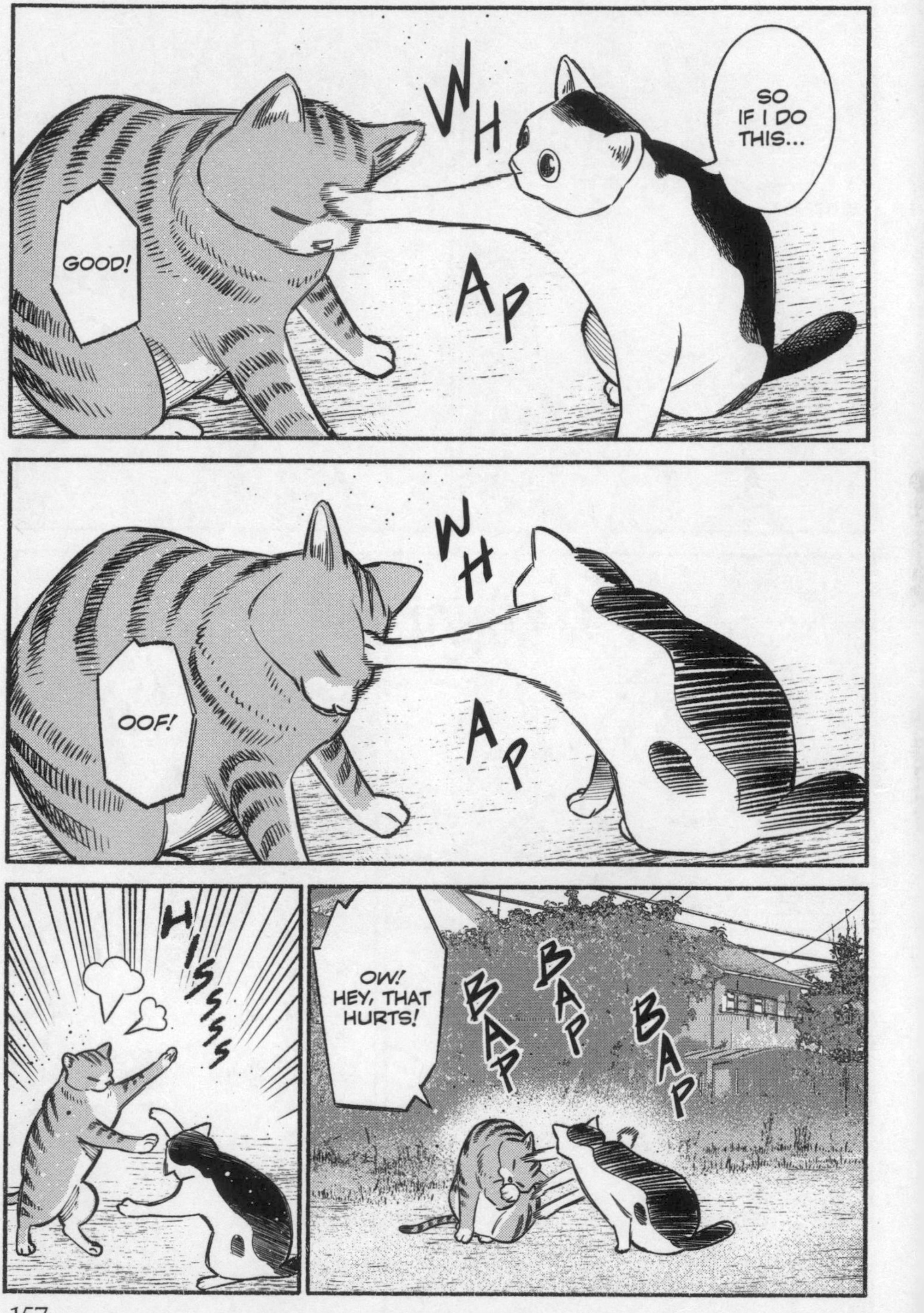
SO IF I DO THIS...
WHAP
GOOD!
WHAP
OOF!
OW! HEY, THAT HURTS!
BAP
BAP
BAP
BAP
HISSSS

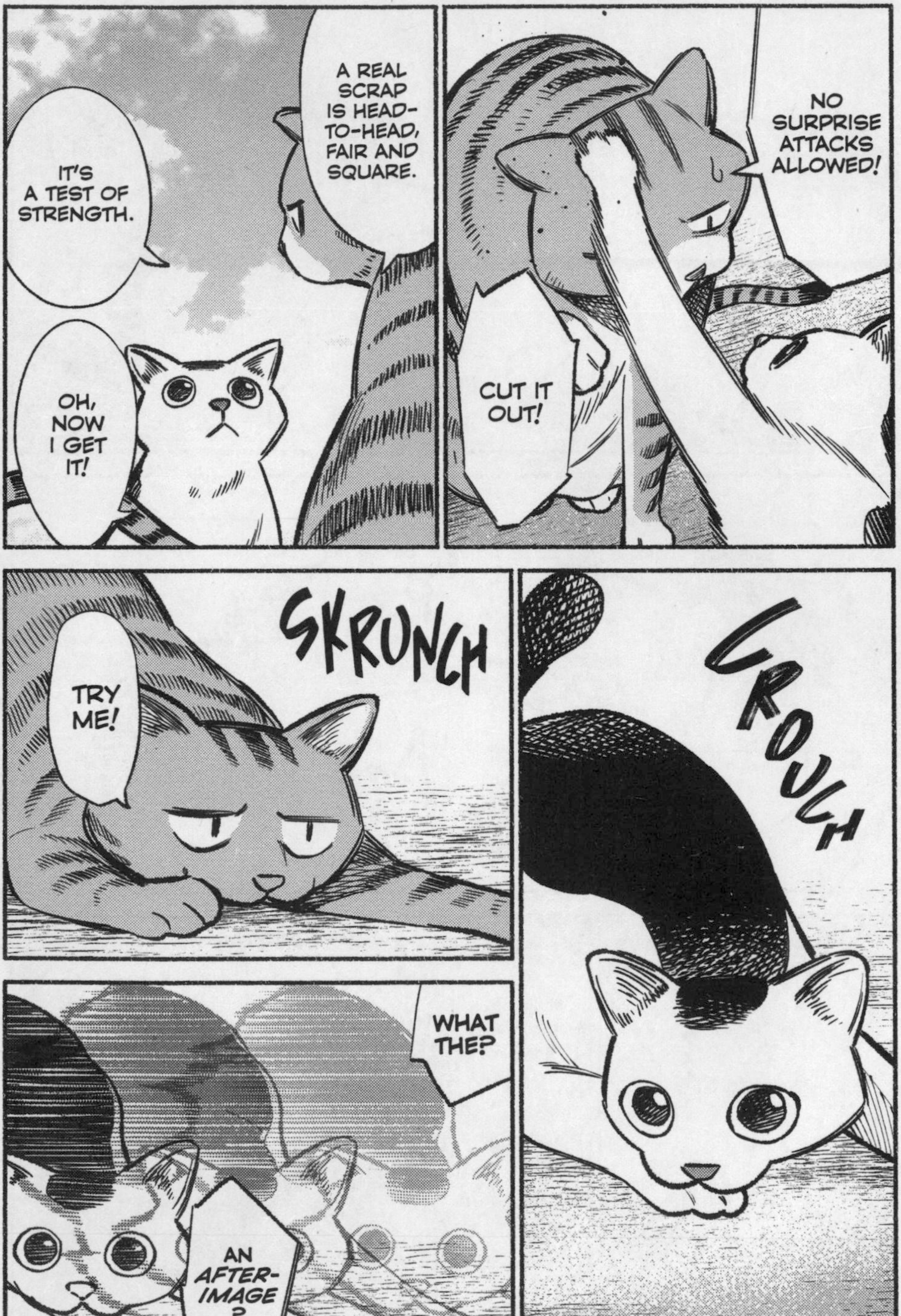
NO SURPRISE ATTACKS ALLOWED!
CUT IT OUT!
A REAL SCRAP IS HEAD-TO-HEAD, FAIR AND SQUARE.
IT'S A TEST OF STRENGTH.
OH, NOW I GET IT!
CROUCH
SKRUNCH
TRY ME!
WHAT THE?
AN AFTER-IMAGE?

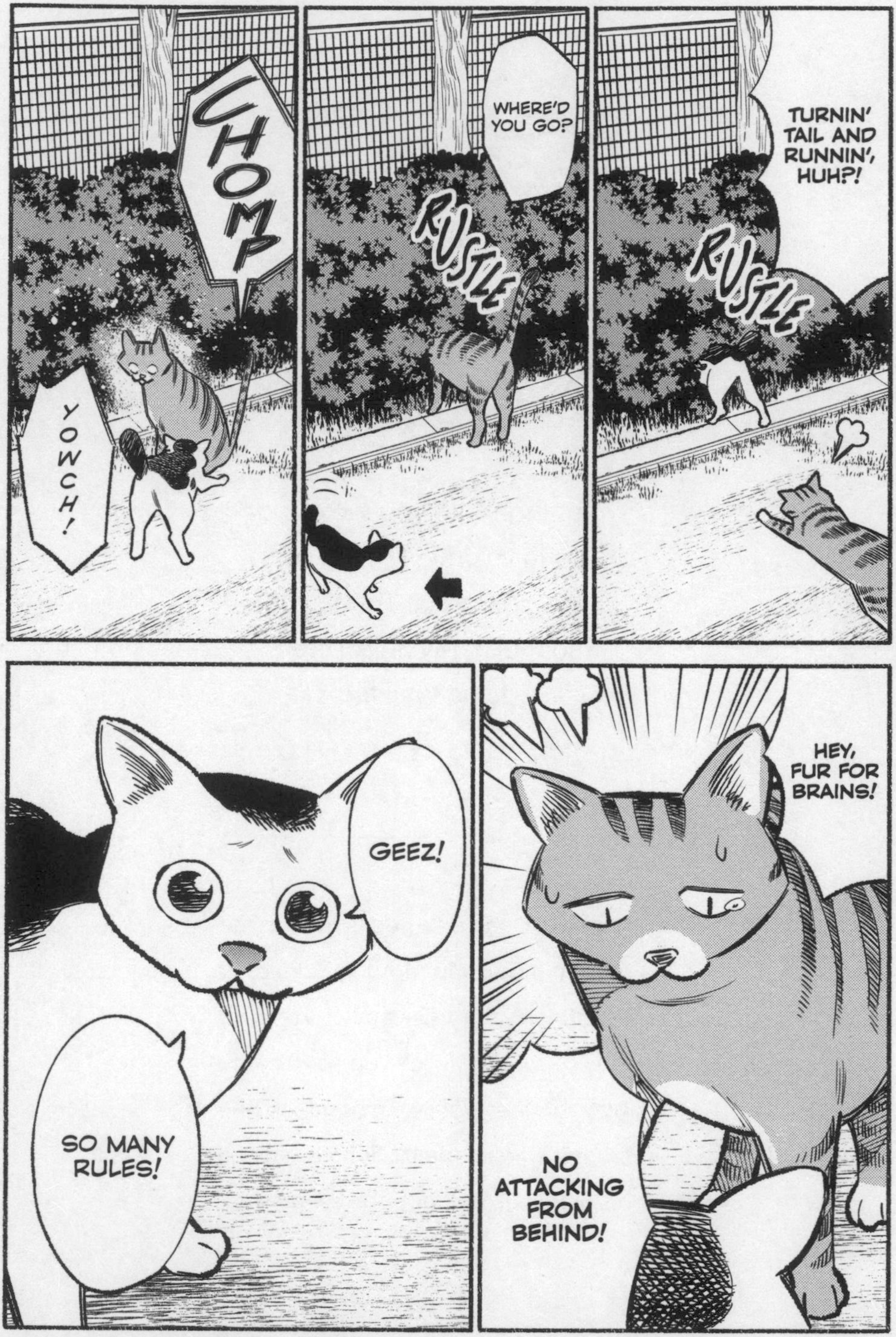
TURNIN' TAIL AND RUNNIN', HUH?!
RUSTLE
WHERE'D YOU GO?
RUSTLE
CHOMP
YOWCH!
HEY, FUR FOR BRAINS!
NO ATTACKING FROM BEHIND!
GEEZ!
SO MANY RULES!

HOW'D YOU LIKE THE BOOK? IT'S LOOKING LIKE VOLUME 5 WILL BE OUT IN JUNE.

SPECIAL THANKS - MIDORINO, HIROE, BOSS KIMU

It's thanks to you we got a fourth volume. I'm not even exaggerating. Thank you so much. My Shiba Inu is doing well too.

KOUSUKE OONO

Kousuke Oono debuted in 2016 in the manga magazine *Monthly Comics @ Bunch* with the one-shot "Legend of Music." Oono's follow-up series, *The Way of the Househusband*, is the creator's first serialization as well as his first English-language release.

The Way of the House Husband

VOLUME 4

VIZ SIGNATURE EDITION

STORY AND ART BY
KOUSUKE OONO

TRANSLATION: **Amanda Haley**
ENGLISH ADAPTATION: **Jennifer LeBlanc**
TOUCH-UP ART & LETTERING: **Bianca Pistillo**
DESIGN: **Francesca Truman**
EDITOR: **Jennifer LeBlanc**

GOKUSHUFUDO volume 4
© Kousuke Oono 2019
All Rights Reserved
English translation rights arranged
with SHINCHOSHA PUBLISHING CO.
through Tuttle-Mori Agency, Inc, Tokyo

Printed in the U.S.A.

Published by VIZ Media, LLC
P.O. Box 77010
San Francisco, CA 94107

10 9 8 7 6 5 4 3 2 1
First printing, September 2020

VIZ MEDIA   *VIZ SIGNATURE*

viz.com   vizsignature.com

SPECIALLY MADE
BUBBLE TEA

380 YEN

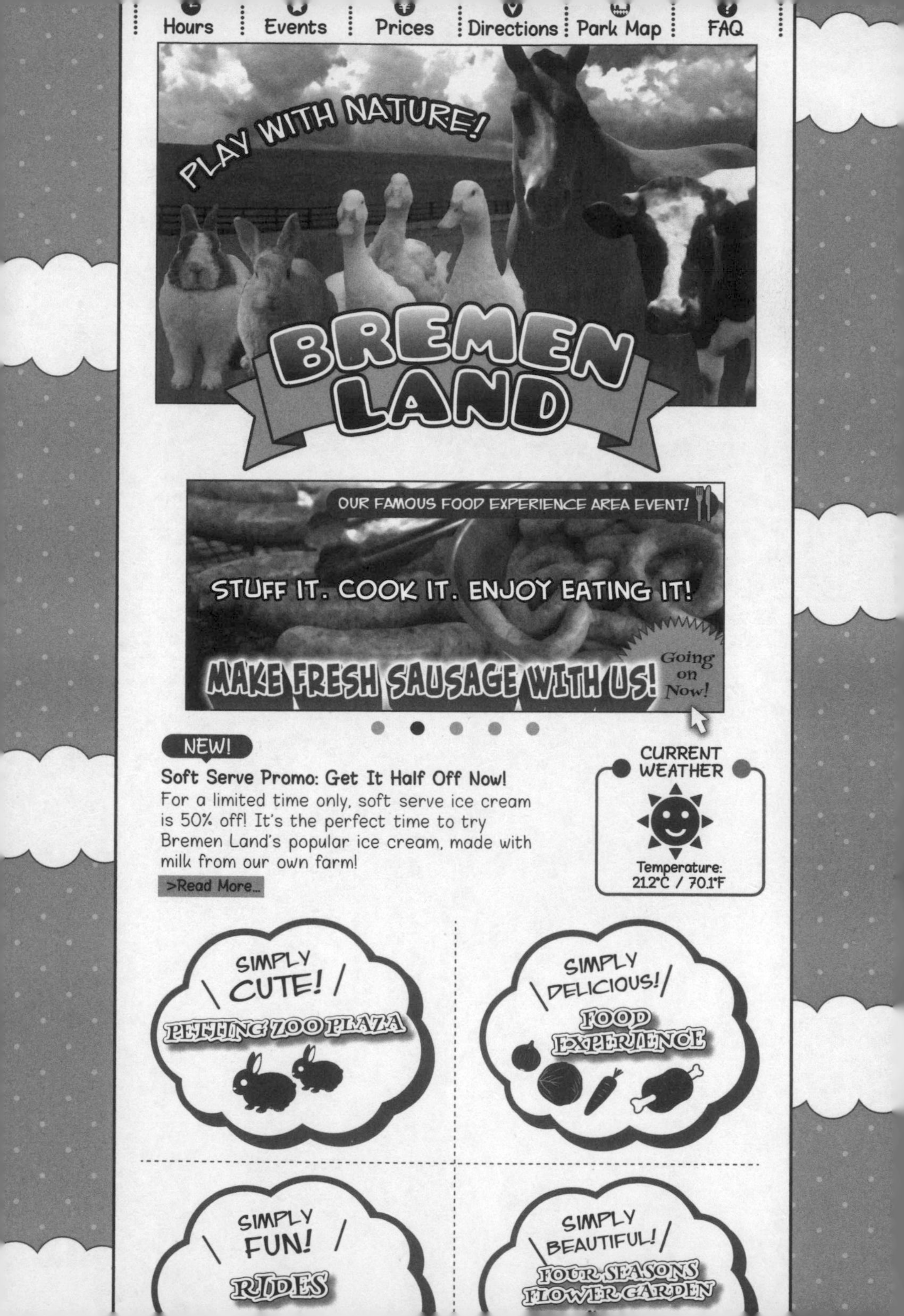
Hours
Events
Prices
Directions
Park Map
FAQ
PLAY WITH NATURE!
BREMEN LAND
OUR FAMOUS FOOD EXPERIENCE AREA EVENT!
STUFF IT. COOK IT. ENJOY EATING IT!
MAKE FRESH SAUSAGE WITH US!
Going on Now!
NEW!
Soft Serve Promo: Get It Half Off Now!
For a limited time only, soft serve ice cream is 50% off! It's the perfect time to try Bremen Land's popular ice cream, made with milk from our own farm!
>Read More...
CURRENT WEATHER
Temperature: 21.2°C / 70.1°F
SIMPLY CUTE!
PETTING ZOO PLAZA
SIMPLY DELICIOUS!
FOOD EXPERIENCE
SIMPLY FUN!
RIDES
SIMPLY BEAUTIFUL!
FOUR SEASONS FLOWER GARDEN

Cats of the Louvre

by TAIYO MATSUMOTO

A surreal tale of the secret world of the cats of the Louvre, told by Eisner Award winner Taiyo Matsumoto.

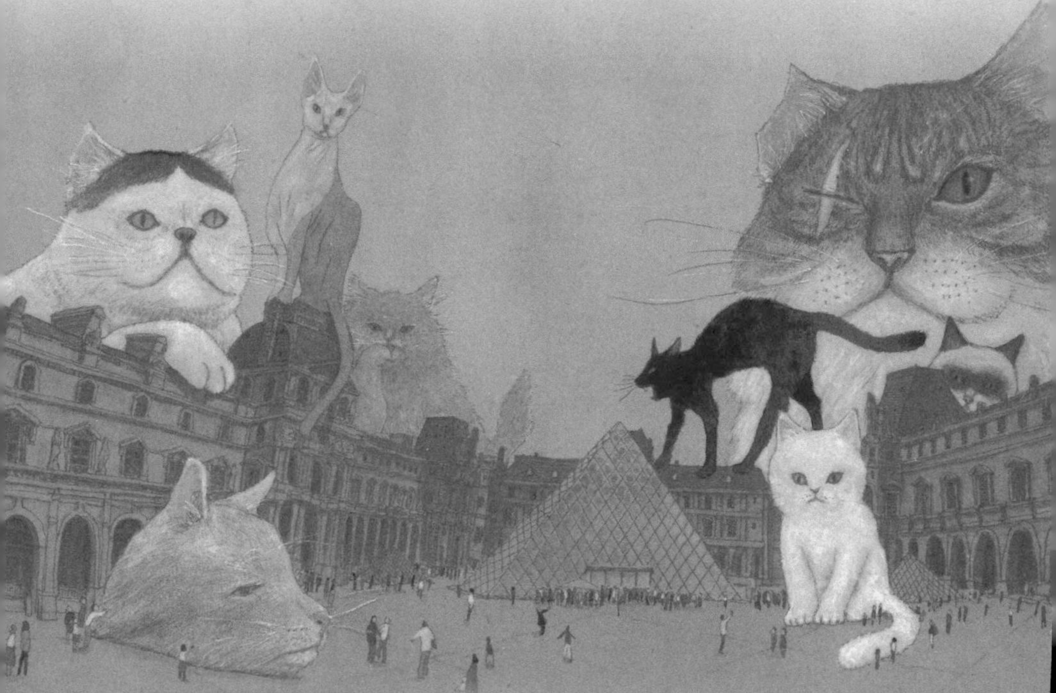

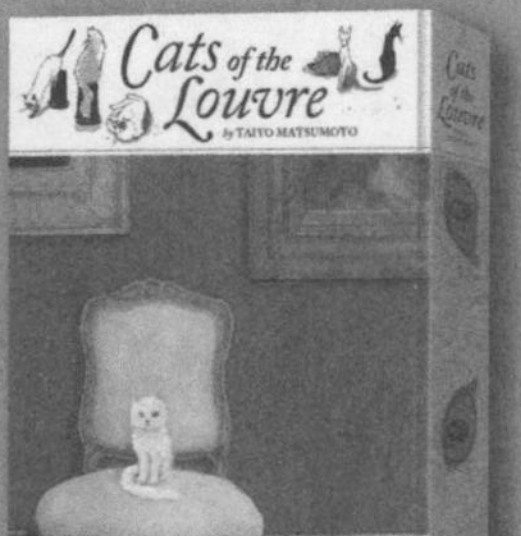
Cats of the Louvre
by TAIYO MATSUMOTO

The world-renowned Louvre museum in Paris contains more than just the most famous works of art in history. At night, within its darkened galleries, an unseen and surreal world comes alive—a world witnessed only by the small family of cats that lives in the attic. Until now…

Translated by *Tekkonkinkreet* film director Michael Arias.

BEASTARS

Story & Art by Paru Itagaki

At this high school, instead of jocks and nerds, the students are divided into carnivores and herbivores.

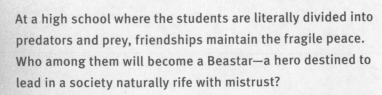

At a high school where the students are literally divided into predators and prey, friendships maintain the fragile peace. Who among them will become a Beastar—a hero destined to lead in a society naturally rife with mistrust?

CHILDREN OF THE WHALES

In this postapocalyptic fantasy, a sea of sand
swallows everything but the past.

In an endless sea of sand drifts the
Mud Whale, a floating island city
of clay and magic. In its chambers a
small community clings to survival,
cut off from its own history by the
shadows of the past.

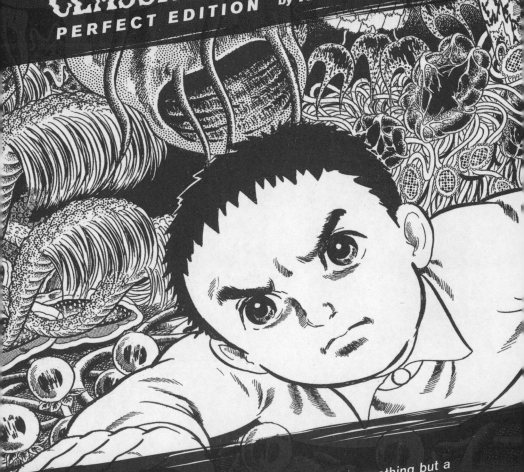

THE DRIFTING CLASSROOM
PERFECT EDITION
by KAZUO UMEZZ

Out of nowhere, an entire school vanishes, leaving nothing but a hole in the ground. While parents mourn and authorities investigate, the students and teachers find themselves not dead but stranded in a terrifying wasteland where they must fight to survive.

COMPLETE IN 3 VOLUMES

UMEZZ PERFECTION! 8 HYORYU KYOSHITSU © 2007 Kazuo UMEZZ/SHOGAKUKAN